Beyond Food Production

Beyond Food Production

The Role of Agriculture in Poverty Reduction

Edited by

Fabrizio Bresciani

Economist, Food and Agriculture Organization of the United Nations, Rome, Italy

and

Alberto Valdés

Research Associate, Catholic University, Santiago, Chile

Published by the

Food and Agriculture Organization of the United Nations

and

Edward Elgar
Cheltenham, UK • Northampton, MA, USA

Published by
Edward Elgar Publishing Limited
Glensanda House
Montpellier Parade
Cheltenham
Glos GL50 1UA
UK

Edward Elgar Publishing, Inc.
William Pratt House
9 Dewey Court
Northampton
Massachusetts 01060
USA

A catalogue record for this book
is available from the British Library

Library of Congress Control Number: 2006047230

ISBN: 978 1 84720 075 4
FAO ISBN: 978 92 5 105534 3 (Hardback)
FAO ISBN: 978 92 5 105535 1 (Paperback)

Printed and bound in Great Britain by MPG Books Ltd, Bodmin, Cornwall

Contents

Contributors

Ramatu M. Al-Hassan Senior Lecturer, Department of Agricultural Economics and Agribusiness, University of Ghana, Legon, Ghana

Gustavo Anríquez Economist, Food and Agriculture Organization of the United Nations, Rome, Italy and University of Maryland, College Park, USA.

Fabrizio Bresciani Economist, Food and Agriculture Organization of the United Nations, Rome, Italy

Sheryl Hendriks Associate Professor, School of Agricultural Sciences and Agribusiness, University of KwaZulu-Natal, Pietermaritzburg, South Africa

John Baptist D. Jatoe Department of Food, Agricultural and Resource Economics, University of Guelph, Guelph, Canada

Johann Kirsten Professor and Chair of the Department of Agricultural Economics, Extension and Rural Development at the University of Pretoria, Pretoria, South Africa

Ramón López Professor, Department of Agricultural and Resource Economics, University of Maryland, College Park, USA

Mike Lyne Professor, School of Agricultural Sciences and Agribusiness, University of KwaZulu-Natal, Pietermaritzburg, South Africa

Charles L. Machethe Professor, Department of Agricultural Economics, Extension and Rural Development, University of Pretoria, Pretoria, South Africa

Julian May Associate Professor, School of Development Studies, University of KwaZulu-Natal, Durban, South Africa

Manoj Panda Professor, Indira Gandhi Institute of Development Research, Mumbai, India

Cecilia Punt Manager: Macro-economics, Department of Agriculture, Western Cape, South Africa

Isidro Soloaga Professor, Universidad de las Américas, Puebla, Mexico and Director of the Center for Research in Economics and Public Policy (CIEPP-UDLAP)

Sudarno Sumarto Director, SMERU Research Institute, Jakarta, Indonesia

Asep Suryahadi Senior Researcher, SMERU Research Institute, Jakarta, Indonesia

Mario Torres Analyst, Santander Asset Management, Grupo Santander, Madrid, Spain

Alberto Valdés Research Associate, Catholic University, Santiago, Chile

PART I

Synthesis and theoretical background

1. The role of agriculture in poverty reduction: a synthesis of the country case studies

Fabrizio Bresciani and Alberto Valdés

1.1 INTRODUCTION

This chapter discusses the main findings of the study on the role of agriculture in poverty alleviation, one of the seven modules included in the Food and Agriculture Organization (FAO) study on the role of agriculture (RoA). The analysis builds on that literature and examines four main channels through which agricultural growth may reduce poverty. Six country case studies investigate the importance of rural labor markets, farm incomes, food prices, and linkages with the rest of the economy in connecting agricultural growth with poverty reduction. By comparing the experience of these six countries at different stages of development, the RoA Project contributes to the understanding and documentation of how the role of agriculture evolves along the development path. The RoA case studies suggest that governments should look at agriculture in an extended way, including the influence of forward and backward linkages with the rest of the economy, and the critical role that the often weak degree of labor market integration between economic sectors plays in reducing the potential impact of agricultural growth in raising the income of rural households. An effective rural poverty alleviation strategy calls for a broad economy-wide perspective on the role of agriculture in the overall growth process.

1.2   POVERTY REDUCTION AND THE ROLE OF AGRICULTURE

1.2.1   The Role of Agriculture in Poverty Reduction: The RoA Project's Contribution

Poverty reduction has become a major policy goal for developing-country governments and the international community. During the last decade, research on the measures of poverty, its determinants, and on the role of growth in reducing poverty has been substantial. There is now a large amount of evidence showing that growth and poverty reduction are positively correlated (Danielson, 2001; Dollar and Kraay, 2002; Bigsten and Levine, 2004).[1] Yet, as Timmer (2002: 1524) eloquently puts it:

> [A] statistical result that reports a strong linkage between economic growth and poverty alleviation under nearly all circumstances seems somehow to miss the growing numbers of poor, as well as the anecdotal stories about widening income gaps and the poor left behind, stories with powerful political resonance. It would be useful to know if it is possible to improve the connection between growth and poverty alleviation, especially through the sectoral composition of growth.

In examining the sectoral contribution to poverty reduction, agricultural growth has traditionally been regarded as instrumental for a number of reasons (for example, Schultz, 1993). Rural poverty represents the major share of total poverty in most developing countries[2] and agriculture is a major source of income for poor rural households. Through its multiple consumption and production linkages and externalities with the rest of the economy, agriculture in low-income economies has been considered an engine of growth for the rural and overall economy (for example, Johnston and Mellor, 1961; Hazell and Haggblade, 1989). Since the importance of agricultural growth in poverty reduction has increasingly been regarded as transcending its share of total GDP, the policy bias against agriculture has come under severe scrutiny (for example, Krueger et al., 1988).

Cross-country evidence comparing the impact on poverty of agricultural and non-agricultural growth has begun to emerge only recently. Using a unique dataset from India, Ravallion and Datt (1996) and Datt and Ravallion (1998) showed that rural growth – dominated and spurred on in that country by agricultural growth – was not only effective for poverty reduction *per se*, but had a stronger effect on poverty reduction than other sectors of the economy such as manufacturing and services. Importantly, the contribution of rural growth to poverty reduction was not limited to rural areas. At least in India, it has also had a significant impact on poverty reduction in urban areas. In addition, agricultural growth can contribute to reducing income inequality in both urban and rural areas.

Timmer's (2002) econometric analysis estimates an elasticity of connection representing the marginal impact of a sector's growth on the mean income of the poorest. He finds that the degree to which the poor share in growth varies from country to country and is especially sensitive to the degree of income inequality. For countries where the disparity (or income gap) between the richest and poorest is relatively small, growth in agricultural labor productivity is slightly but consistently more important in generating per capita income in every quintile of the income distribution. For countries where the income gap is large, the elasticities of connection of both sectors for the poorest quintile are small, but rise sharply with income levels. This leads Timmer to conclude that for high income gap countries, the poorest quintile could run the risk of being left out of the growth process and the rich benefit considerably from income growth.

More recently, the relative sectoral contribution to poverty reduction has been re-examined. For example, econometric analysis by Warr (2002), pooling data from Indonesia, Thailand, Malaysia and the Philippines, finds that growth in the services sector has had the strongest poverty-reduction effect. Using time-series data from Taiwan, Warr and Wang (1999) find that industrial growth has had the strongest impact on poverty reduction.

More recent quantitative analysis by Bravo-Ortega and Lederman (2005) takes a similar look at per capita income by quintiles, but uses more countries (84), updated to 2002 (de Ferranti et al., 2005, Chapter 3). In comparing the sectoral growth contribution to improving the income of the poor in Latin American (LA) countries, non-LA countries, and high-income (HI) countries, they conclude that in terms of absolute impact, the direct effect of growth in non-agriculture is more important than the one deriving from agricultural growth. However, agriculture has a relatively greater impact on poverty than its observed share in the economy as a whole. This is largely the result of indirect effects of agricultural growth on non-agricultural growth which stimulates poverty reduction as well. For example, for LA countries, the elasticity of the income of the poor to agricultural growth is 0.28, while the elasticity to non-agricultural growth is 0.77. In non-LA countries, the elasticities are 0.46 and 0.58, respectively. In HI countries, agricultural growth has increased poverty (elasticity equal to –0.08), contrary to non-agricultural growth (elasticity equal to 0.90). A 1 percent growth in agriculture is found to increase non-agricultural GDP by 0.12 percent in LA countries, while the reverse effect – non-agricultural growth on agriculture's GDP – is smaller. In non-LA countries, a 1 percent increase in agricultural GDP leads to an increase of non-agricultural GDP by 0.15 percent, while a 1 percent increase in non-agricultural GDP has a negative impact on agricultural GDP (–0.17 percent). The conclusion is that while agricultural growth is good for the poor and contributes positively to overall growth beyond its *accounting* share in GDP, in absolute terms it is its growth in the non-agricultural sector that matters the most for the poor. But, critical for this discussion, the work by Timmer (2002) and Bravo-Ortega and Lederman (2005) shows that for developing countries, agricultural growth has a relatively greater impact on poverty than its observed share in the economy, largely the result of the spillover of agricultural to non-agricultural growth.[3] Of course these results from cross-section analysis are averages for many countries and miss some important deviant cases.[4]

While these findings suggest that the role of agricultural growth in improving the 'quality' of growth is at best mixed, they raise two important issues. First, estimates of growth multipliers and of the impact of growth composition do not allow for inferences on which channels are important in translating agricultural growth into reduced poverty. The growth composition literature provides little systematic information to guide policy makers, except the finding that agriculture should receive particular attention beyond its size in the economy.[5] Second, it is not clear whether agricultural growth has relevance in poverty reduction in lower-middle- and middle-income countries, where agriculture's share in total GDP is lower than in the rest of the developing world. Related to this point is the issue of whether the relative importance of the various channels through which agricultural growth affects the poor changes as development occurs.

The RoA project addresses these two concerns by adopting a comparative approach, which identifies the various channels through which agricultural growth 'connects' overall growth to the poor in countries at different stages of development. This means moving from a 'reduced' form to a 'structural' approach in identifying the constraints to the poverty-reduction role of agricultural growth. In addition, it allows us to compare the elasticity of poverty to agricultural and non-agricultural growth among countries, by regions, and by level of development.

1.2.2   Channels Linking Agricultural Growth to Poverty Reduction

Agriculture's role in poverty reduction can be looked at in two ways. If growth trickles down to the poor (Dollar and Kraay, 2002), agricultural growth will, at a minimum, indirectly benefit the poor, even if the share of first-round benefits of that growth are largely captured by the non-poor. Following a different approach, Bravo-Ortega and Lederman (2005) compare a 1 percent growth in agriculture and non-agriculture and find that the latter contributes more to poverty reduction. This is of course a reflection of agriculture's smaller share in total GDP. An alternative way to assess agriculture's contribution that controls for its smaller size is to set the overall growth rate (at 0 percent or at a historically determined level) and to let agricultural growth compensate for the reduced non-agriculture growth. This is the route followed by the Chile case study. The Indonesia case study, on the other hand, uses the historical growth performance of the two sectors and their respective poverty elasticities to estimate agriculture's share in total poverty reduction. As we shall see, both studies point to agriculture's relevant contribution. Such conclusions are based on evidence obtained from aggregate data. As discussed above, it is important to assess the *channels* through which agricultural growth manifests its comparative advantage in poverty reduction. Analyzing these channels allows analysts to provide policy makers with insights beyond the importance of agriculture as a sector.

The RoA project focused on three key channels that link agricultural growth to poverty trends in rural and urban areas:[6]

- the labor market channel, through employment and wage effects;
- the direct smallholder income effect coupled with the growth multipliers effects; and
- the food-price effect.

Labor market channel

Agriculture is intensive in its use of unskilled labor relative to other sectors of the economy, perhaps with the exception of the informal sector. One would therefore expect that agricultural growth would raise the employment of unskilled labor relative to skilled labor. An increase in employment will translate into an increase in wages, the magnitude of which depends on the supply elasticity of the two types of labor. This is the local (that is, rural) first-round impact. Yet, the increase in real rural wages could have benefits that go beyond the rural sector. In countries where the agricultural sector employs a substantial share of unskilled labor, and rural and urban labor markets are integrated, the unskilled wage in agriculture may in fact become the reservation wage for the marginal unskilled urban laborer. Thus, under appropriate conditions, agriculture's growth will lead to higher wages in both rural and urban areas, providing a strong impetus towards the reduction of poverty.

A key question is, which pattern of agricultural growth yields a larger impact on rural labor markets? Growth based on high value-added crops with robust forward linkages with agro-industry may enhance the connection between agricultural growth and the labor market. On the other hand, agricultural growth tilted towards crops with little processing and/or transformation before consumption or export may weaken the connection. While the pattern (or composition) of agricultural growth may depend to a large extent on prevailing agro-ecological conditions, economic policies may play an influential role by altering production incentives.

The direct and indirect income effect

Growth in small-farm income is a powerful factor in reducing poverty in societies where a large share of the population is still self-employed in the agricultural sector. In addition to its direct effect on poverty, raising farm incomes generates indirect effects through growth multipliers, benefiting poor households engaged in the production of non-farm commodities consumed by agriculture. The approach followed by the RoA case studies addresses two related questions. First, would an increase in farm income have enough potential to pull the smallholder sector out of poverty?[7] Second, to what extent will an increase in farm income translate into higher regional income through consumption and production multipliers and how would that increase be distributed among different types of households?

The food-price channel

Food prices are important to the poor, especially for low-income urban consumers and poor farmers that are net buyers of food. The RoA case studies look at the link between agricultural growth and food prices by employing a time-series analysis so as to separate long- and short-term effects. The relevant question from a policy point of view is the extent to which agricultural growth translates into *permanent* effects on food prices at the national level.[8] Where aggregate food price indices are dominated by movements in the price of tradables, one would expect that growth in agricultural output would lead to a short-term decline in the general price of food and non-tradable food crops, but in the long run much of this variation would be reabsorbed. If this is the case, food prices would mostly be affected by movements in the real exchange rate.

1.2.3   The Structure of the Book

The next section of this chapter will explain how the countries participating in the RoA project were selected and will review their main characteristics in terms of socio-economic indicators. Section 1.4 will then provide a cross-country synthesis comparing the main results of the six case studies selected for this book. The discussion is organized around the channels that link agricultural growth with poverty and the estimation of the reduced-form elasticities of poverty to sectoral growth. In the final section we draw conclusions from this comparative exercise and discuss future avenues of research.

In Chapter 2, Ramón López discusses the nature and importance of the channels examined in this book. This is followed by the six RoA project case studies on the comparative analysis of the role of agriculture in poverty reduction. In alphabetical order, the case studies are from Chile, Ghana, India, Indonesia, Mexico and South Africa.

1.3 COMPARING THE RoA COUNTRIES: RELEVANT TRENDS AND CHARACTERISTICS

1.3.1 RoA Country Selection

As part of the RoA project research on agricultural growth and poverty, case studies were carried out in six developing countries from three regions: Africa, Asia and Latin America. The country selection was based on several criteria. First, variation in terms of the level of development as measured by income per capita in year 2000, based on the World Bank's Atlas method. Second, differences in per capita calorie intake – closely correlated with per capita income. Third, variation in terms of the major farming systems that characterize agricultural sector and land use. Fourth, availability and quality of data in agricultural census and household surveys. Finally, countries would also differ in terms of their net trade position for food and agricultural products. The combination of these criteria was intended to lead to a selection of countries that would cover a range of characteristics representative of most developing countries and with enough contrasts in terms of development paths.

Table 1.1 classifies the six countries included in the study on the basis of a subset of the above-mentioned criteria. Three countries (Indonesia, India and Ghana) are low and three are upper middle income (Chile, Mexico and South Africa). The six countries are quite different in terms of the farming systems that characterize their use of land and the structure of agricultural production. Finally, there is also some variation among selected countries in terms of their net agricultural and food trade positions. During the 1990s, Mexico has been a net food and agricultural importer; India has been a net food and agricultural exporter; and Indonesia, Ghana, South Africa and Chile have all been both net food importers and net agricultural exporters.

1.3.2 Main Socio-economic Characteristics of the Selected Countries

The role that agriculture plays in connecting the poor to overall growth will depend on several factors, including the sector's size, its production structure, its relative labor, capital and land endowments, and the extent of

Table 1.1 Country-selection criteria

Subregion	Country	Income per capita level		Calorie intake per capita	Major farming systems studied	Ag. and food trade position	
		Low	Upper middle			NFI or NFX	NAI or NAX
E. Asia	Indonesia	*		2880	Terraced paddy, lowland rice, tree crop mixed, sparse	NFI	NAX
S. Asia	India	*		2470	Rice, rice/wheat, rainfed mixed, irrigated areas in rainfed farming systems	NFX	NAX
W. Africa	Ghana	*		2670	Tree crop based	NFI	NAX
S. Africa	S. Africa		*	na	Maize mixed, large commercial and smallholder, sparse	NFI	NAX
S. America	Chile		*	2820	Irrigated, moist temperate mixed-forest, sparse	NFI	NAX
N. America	Mexico		*	3130	Beans maize, irrigated, coastal plantation and mixed, dryland mixed	NFI	NAI

Note: Definition of food used for the food trade position: cereals + oilseeds + meat total + diary products and eggs + oils and fats. All data of household surveys are of national coverage unless specified otherwise.
NFI: net food importers; NFX: net food exporters; NAI: net agricultural importers; NAX: net agricultural exporters.

Sources: Income per capita level: economies are divided according to 2000 GNI per capita, calculated using the World Bank Atlas method. The groups are: low income, $755 or less; lower-middle income, $756–$2995; upper-middle income, $2996–$9265; and high income, $9266 or more; Calorie intake per capita (kcal/person/day): SOFI (2000). Major farming systems: FAO–World Bank (2001). Agricultural and food trade position: RoA project computations.

integration between agriculture and the rest of the economy, including foreign trade. Presumably, the elasticity of poverty with respect to agricultural growth will also depend on the initial level and depth of poverty. To better appreciate the diversity of the six RoA countries with respect to these conditions, Table 1.2 highlights some significant indicators of their agricultural structure and performance during the 1990s, the decade covered by the RoA case studies.

In terms of structural transformation, the 1990s saw the share of agriculture in total GDP decrease by more than 10 percent in all these countries. Agricultural value added per worker, a measure of labor productivity, increased for all the RoA countries but at different rates. Chile and South Africa had the highest increase in labor productivity in agriculture, while Ghana and Indonesia had the lowest. With the exception of South Africa, where GDP declined in real terms between 1990 and 2000, the favorable agricultural value-added trend took place in a broader context of economy-wide growth.

The six countries differ in several aspects in terms of growth patterns in the 1990s. Chile saw a slight reduction in the amount of arable and permanent crop land[9] and a slight increase in the ratio of land to agricultural labor force.[10] This, in conjunction with a high increase in labor productivity, suggests that Chile's agriculture has undergone a process of capital deepening, an aspect that recent literature focusing on the surge in the production of fruits and vegetables has investigated (Foster and Valdés, 2006).

Ghana could be classified as abundant in agricultural labor, with more than 50 percent of its labor force employed in agriculture with low productivity.[11] Yet, its land to labor ratio has increased over the 1990s, mainly due to an expanding agricultural frontier. The expansion into marginal areas has kept the growth of labor productivity rather low. As the expansion of the agricultural frontier comes to an end, Ghana will face increasing pressure towards low labor productivity in agriculture, unless more farm workers find their way into non-farm activities. During the 1990s, the gap between agricultural and non-agricultural labor productivity remained relatively stable.

India could also be classified as an agricultural labor-abundant country. In contrast with Indonesia it has witnessed a decline in its land to labor ratio. This is the result of a relatively stable arable and permanent crop area and an increase in the agricultural labor force. The low pace in the growth of agricultural labor productivity can be ascribed in part to the evolution of the land/labor ratio as suggested by a relatively high growth in the agricultural labor force during the 1990s.

Although in Indonesia the share of agricultural labor in the total labor force has declined and is currently below 50 percent, the land to labor ratio

Table 1.2   Rural and agricultural characteristics of selected RoA countries

	Chile			Ghana			India		
	1990	2000	%Δ	1990	2000	%Δ	1990	2000	%Δ
GDP per capita, PPP (constant 1995 US$)	3,283	5,305	61.6	343	407	18.8	324	463	42.7
Agriculture value added per worker (constant 1995 US$)	5,155	6,039	17.1	529	568	7.2	350	391	11.9
Agriculture, value added (% of GDP, constant local currency)	9.25	6.03	−34.8	44.63	40.56	−9.1	28.93	21.78	−24.7
Labor force in agriculture (000)	938	980	4.5	4,208	5,471	30.0	229,417	263,369	14.8
Total labor force (000)	4,993	6,212	24.4	7,095	9,621	35.6	358,344	441,618	23.2
Share of labor force in agriculture (%)	18.79	15.78	−16.0	59	57	−4.1	64	60	−6.8
Agriculture value added per worker (constant local currency)	–	–	17.0	–	–	6.5	–	–	11.9
Value added per worker (constant local currency)	–	–	50.8	–	–	12.4	–	–	38.5
Ratio of non-agriculture to agriculture labor productivity	2.0	2.6	28.9	1.3	1.4	5.5	2.2	2.7	23.7
Rural population	2,191	2,140	−2.3	9,707	10,987	13.2	630,285	735,684	16.7
Total population (000)	13,100	15,224	16.2	15,277	19,593	28.3	846,418	1,016,938	20.1
Share of rural population in total population	0.17	0.14	−16.0	0.64	0.56	−11.7	0.74	0.72	−2.8
Arable land (000 ha)	2,802	1,979	−29.4	2,700	3,950	46.3	163,138	161,785	−0.8
Arable land per ag laborer	3.0	2.0	−32.4	0.6	0.7	12.5	0.7	0.6	−13.6
Arable land and permanent crops per (000 ha)	3,049	2,297	−24.7	4,200	6,100	45.2	169,438	169,755	0.2
Arable land and permanent crops per ag laborer	3.3	2.3	−27.9	1.0	1.1	11.7	0.7	0.6	−12.7

	Indonesia			Mexico			South Africa		
	1990	2000	%Δ	1990	2000	%Δ	1990	2000	%Δ
GDP per capita, PPP (constant 1995 US$)	777	1,015	30.6	3,187	3,803	19.3	4,113	3,912	-4.9
Agriculture value added per worker (constant 1995 US$)	688	747	8.5	1,575	1,781	13.1	3,417	4,061	18.8
Agriculture, value added (% of GDP, constant local currency)	20.66	16.63	-19.5	6.10	5.03	-17.5	4.52	4.08	-9.8
Labor force in agriculture (000)	44,086	49,309	11.8	8,531	8,551	0.2	1,931	1,742	-9.8
Total labor force (000)	79,905	101,953	27.6	30,671	40,047	30.6	14,301	18,210	27.3
Share of labor force in agriculture (%)	55	48	-12.3	28	21	-23.2	14	10	-29.2
Agriculture value added per worker (constant local currency)	–	–	8.8	–	–	15.6	–	–	18.9
Value added per worker (constant local currency)	–	–	18.5	–	–	7.6	–	–	-6.6
Ratio of non-agriculture to agriculture labor productivity	2.7	2.9	8.9	4.6	4.2	-6.9	3.0	2.3	-21.4
Rural population	126,419	122,696	-2.9	22,921	25,034	9.2	18,854	19,584	3.9
Total population (000)	182,117	211,559	16.2	83,225	98,933	18.9	36,848	44,000	19.4
Share of rural population in total population	0.69	0.58	-16.5	0.28	0.25	-8.1	0.51	0.45	-13.0
Arable land (000 ha)	20,253	20,500	1.2	24,000	24,800	3.3	13,440	14,753	9.8
Arable land per ag laborer	0.5	0.4	-9.5	2.8	2.9	3.1	7.0	8.5	21.7
Arable land and permanent crops per (000 ha)	31,973	33,600	5.1	25,900	27,300	5.4	14,300	15,712	9.9
Arable land and permanent crops per ag laborer	0.7	0.7	-6.0	3.0	3.2	5.2	7.4	9.0	21.8

Source: World Bank (2004) and FAOSTAT (2005).

has declined as the expansion of its agricultural frontier did not keep up with the growth of its agricultural labor force. During the 1990s, labor productivity growth in agriculture has been sluggish and below that of the rest of the economy.

In Mexico and South Africa, agriculture has been characterized by higher rates of labor productivity growth in agriculture compared to the agricultural sectors in the other countries (except Chile) and to their own non-agricultural sectors, which results in a narrowing gap in inter-sectoral labor productivity. In both countries the land to labor ratio is increasing due to a modest expansion of the agricultural frontier and stagnating (Mexico) or declining (South Africa) growth in their agricultural labor force.

In terms of poverty, as shown in Table 1.3 the six countries have performed differently, and to some extent countered what their labor productivity growth would suggest. Paradoxically, in South Africa and Mexico, where agricultural labor productivity growth has been strongest, the incidence of poverty (at the national as well as the rural levels) has not gone down during the decade under observation, and in South Africa it appears that it even increased. Ghana, India and Indonesia, the RoA countries in which growth in labor productivity has been the least, have managed to reduce the incidence of poverty at the rural and national levels. Chile, where the growth in labor productivity was highest among the RoA countries, was also able to substantially reduce its national and urban poverty.

The present discussion does not attempt to explain the observed trends and poverty outcomes. For this, the reader is referred to the case studies. The next section does, however, synthesize the results of the case studies and present themes and ideas around which the results of the case studies can be organized in order to better understand the nexus between poverty and agricultural growth.

1.4   LINKING AGRICULTURAL GROWTH TO POVERTY REDUCTION: A SYNTHESIS OF THE EMPIRICAL EVIDENCE FROM THE RoA CASE STUDIES

1.4.1   Labor Employment and Wage Effects

Real wage increases in agriculture are an important sign of improved living standards in rural areas, since it is expected that remuneration of unskilled labor in rural industries, including agriculture, would tend to equalize at the margin, adjusted for the cost of mobility. What might not be evident is the

Table 1.3   Trends in poverty rates (based on national poverty lines)

	1990	1991	1992	1993	1994	1995	1996	1997	1998	1999	2000	Per capita GDP, PPP (constant 2000 US$)	
												1990	2004
National													
Chile	38.5	–	32.4	–	27.4	–	23.1	–	21.6	–	20.6	5,817	10,631
Ghana	–	–	51.7	–	–	–	–	–	–	39.5	–	1,611	2,143
India	36.4	37.4	–	–	35.0	–	–	–	–	–	–	1,702	2,883
Indonesia	32.7	–	–	25.3	–	–	17.4	–	–	27.0	–	2,268	3,316
Mexico[1]	–	–	24.4	–	21.5	–	29.7	–	27.3	–	18.0	7,647	9,046
South Africa[2]	–	–	–	27.8	–	–	–	–	46.2	–	–	10,053	10,357
Rural													
Chile	39.4	–	33.4	–	30.8	–	30.6	–	27.6	–	23.8	–	–
Ghana	–	–	63.6	–	–	–	–	–	–	49.5	–	–	–
India	36.4	37.4	43.5	–	37.3	–	–	–	–	–	27.2	–	–
Indonesia	39.7	–	–	32.9	–	–	23.3	–	–	33.9	46.1	–	–
Mexico	–	–	44.7	–	49.8	–	60.5	–	57.1	–	–	–	–
South Africa	–	–	–	34.0	–	–	–	–	60.0	–	–	–	–

Notes:
1. Food poverty reported in the case of Mexico is the household budget which only covers food expenditures (extreme poverty line).
2. The poverty line is based on fixed household subsistence costs, food and basic clothing costs. See Chapter 8 for details.
   N.B. The above poverty rates are not strictly comparable across countries due to differences in the criteria for fixing the poverty line. With the exception of Mexico, the poverty line is defined as covering food and other fixed household subsistence costs (e.g., housing, clothing, etc.).

Sources: Data from respective country case studies in Part II, this volume.

fact that unskilled laborers employed in urban-based or non-agricultural industries may also benefit indirectly from an increase in agricultural productivity. To the extent that agriculture employs a substantial share of unskilled laborers, wages prevailing in the agricultural sector will influence the opportunity cost for urban (unskilled) laborers as well.[12] This economy-wide effect of agricultural growth on poverty at the national level has not received much attention in the literature. Four countries – Chile, India, Mexico and South Africa – provide evidence on how agricultural growth has an economy-wide effect on the wage of the unskilled, and thereby on poverty.

The Chile and Mexico case studies follow a common approach to the measurement of the impact of agricultural growth on poverty. First, based on the theory of duality, a model of demand for skilled and unskilled labor is estimated using the real wages of the skilled and unskilled labor, the cost of capital, and agricultural and non-agricultural GDP as explanatory variables. The derived labor demand estimates are then used to obtain the demand elasticities for both unskilled and skilled labor with respect to agricultural and non-agricultural GDP and wages.[13] Table 1.4 reports the derived demand elasticities for skilled and unskilled labor obtained by these two studies, where unskilled workers are defined as having fewer than eight years of schooling. A key difference in the two studies is the definition of agricultural output. In the Mexico study agricultural output refers to primary production of agriculture, while in the Chile study agricultural output includes both the primary and the agro-industrial sectors.

Table 1.4   Derived demand elasticities for skilled and unskilled labor, Chile and Mexico

	Price elasticities			Growth elasticities	
	Unskilled labor	Skilled labor	Capital	Agricultural output[1]	Non-agricultural output
Chile					
Unskilled labor	−0.28*	0.63***	−0.35	0.66***	0.37***
Skilled labor	0.21***	−0.28**	0.07	0.43***	0.67***
Mexico					
Unskilled labor	−1.30***	0.28***	1.05***	0.22*	0.57***
Skilled labor	0.42***	−0.55***	0.27**	0.06	0.88***

Notes: *** Significant at the 1% level, ** Significant at the 5% level, *Significant at the 10% level.
1.   For Chile, agricultural output includes both primary sectoral production plus agro-industrial production. For Mexico, it is limited to primary sectoral production.

As expected, results in both countries show that agricultural growth has a significant impact on the demand for unskilled workers. There are, however, important differences between the two countries. In the case of Mexico, a 1 percent increase in agricultural output has a moderate impact (0.22 percent increase) on the demand for unskilled labor, while in the case of Chile, it is substantial (0.66 percent increase). On the other hand, a 1 percent increase in non-agricultural GDP has a much larger impact on the demand for unskilled workers in Mexico (0.57 percent increase) than in the case of Chile (0.37 percent increase). What explains this difference? One consideration is the difference in the product composition of agriculture in the two countries, which could influence the extent of agriculture's inter-industry linkages. Recent analysis quantifying the size of backward and forward intersectoral linkages for some countries shows that the inclusion of forward linkages to downstream industries in the computation of a consolidated (or extended) agricultural output makes a substantial difference in the measurement of the size of agriculture (de Ferranti et al., 2005). In Mexico, while the share of primary agriculture in total GDP stood at 5.26 percent, the 'extended' agricultural sector contributed 8 percent of total GDP (a 52 percent increase). Similarly, in the case of Chile, the figures are 4.92 and 9.32 percent, respectively (an 89 percent increase). Returning to Table 1.4, these figures suggest that the stronger impact of agricultural growth on the demand for unskilled workers in Chile as compared to Mexico is due in part to the definition of agricultural output – an extended version in the former case and in its primary version in the latter. In assessing the overall role of agricultural growth in poverty reduction, it is important to take into account both its direct and its indirect effects, via forward and backward linkages.

Building on the above results, the Chile case study uses the estimated output elasticity of the demand for skilled and unskilled workers to measure the final impact of agricultural growth on poverty. This is achieved by using alternative assumptions regarding the wage elasticity of skilled and unskilled labor supply to derive the impact of agricultural growth on the wage of the unskilled. Changes in the wage of the unskilled are then used to simulate the impact of agricultural growth on poverty. Two scenarios are contrasted. The first scenario assumes that agricultural growth is *uncompensated* by growth in the rest of the economy. In this case, a growth rate of 4.5 percent of agricultural GDP (an average for Chile's rate of agriculture growth over the past decade) translates into an economy-wide reduction of the head count index of poverty by a magnitude of between 7 and 10 percent. The second scenario assumes that agricultural growth is *compensated* by a reduction of non-agricultural GDP so as to keep total GDP fixed. In this case the elasticity of the head count ratio with respect to agricultural growth ranges from 5.5 to 8.6 percent, a lower yet significant figure.[14] In spite of the relatively small size of agriculture in Chile's economy, its rapid growth has been a significant determinant in the reduction of poverty rates in the overall economy. We shall return to these results in Section 1.4.4 on the issue of the pattern of growth and poverty reduction.

The South Africa study presents a simulation analysis comparing the impact of an increase in exports of unprocessed agricultural commodities compared to exports of processed agricultural commodities (produced in the Western Cape district) on the regional labor market. A SAM (Social Accounting Matrix) model is used to capture interactions across the various subsectors and household activities; the external sector and the government are treated as exogenous variables. The study concludes that (a) a 5 percent increase in agricultural exports (30 percent of which undergo some processing before being exported), in addition to second-round effects on agricultural production, generates significant spillovers into industries such as chemicals, transportation and manufacturing; and (b) that while the benefits of this export expansion are higher for rural than for urban households, skilled agricultural laborers benefit slightly more than unskilled laborers. This differs from the results for Chilean agriculture. At the country level, however, the expansion of agricultural exports does not affect wage levels for skilled laborers in the non-farm sector. In contrast to the results for Chilean agriculture, where labor markets appear to be more integrated at the national level, results for South Africa suggest the existence of highly segmented labor markets, at least across sectors. Interestingly, the impact of agricultural export on wages and income distribution growth is stronger when exports include agro-processed products. This is consistent with the results for Chile, in that the post-harvest employment multiplier of primary agriculture appears to be a major force behind the impact of agricultural growth on poverty reduction.

The importance of rural labor markets as channels for transmitting the benefits of agricultural growth to the poor is also underscored by the India case study. The study examines the role played by per capita agricultural income and agricultural wages in rural poverty reduction. In those states that historically have been more successful at reducing poverty, the study shows that while statistically significant in reducing poverty, a 1 percent growth in per capita agricultural income has a lower impact on poverty than a 1 percent growth in the agricultural wage. When agricultural income is broken down in yields and per capita sown land, the study finds the former to be insignificant in explaining poverty reduction. On the contrary, agricultural area expansion has a strong negative impact on poverty. These results are interpreted as reflecting the importance of the employment and wage effects. The direct income effect of agricultural growth, proxied by yields, has no effect on the incidence of overall poverty, but is significant at the 10 percent level in explaining the reduction in poverty indices which are more sensitive to extreme poverty.[15] Overall, the effects of these agricultural-growth-related variables are found to run across the poor as well as the very poor so that the benefits of agricultural growth have not been limited to those near the poverty line. These results are then contrasted to the case of the high poverty states. Agricultural income growth, both as a whole and when broken down in its yields and land–labor ratio components, is found to have had no impact on poverty. On the other hand, as in the case of low poverty states, growth in agricultural wages has a strong effect on poverty. Altogether, these results are taken to underscore the role played by agricultural growth, mainly driven by the green revolution, in determining the success in poverty reduction, particularly through the employment channel rather than through the direct farm income channel. Yet, farm income growth is important for the very poor, suggesting that investment in irrigation would have an important impact on poverty reduction in those rural areas that could not share in the benefits of the green revolution.

What lessons can be drawn from these results? First, the wage and employment channel is extremely important in connecting agricultural growth to poverty reduction. This holds in the case of India as well as in the cases of Chile, Mexico and South Africa, countries at very different stages of development. Thus, a closer focus on the institutions that shape this channel's contribution to the poverty-reduction role of agriculture is warranted.

Second, the likelihood of the wage and employment channel leading agricultural growth to reduce both rural and urban poverty hinges on some important factors. First, there must be a reasonable degree of labor mobility between urban and rural areas. When labor mobility is low, a substantial differential between urban and rural wages may prevail, thus the transmission of higher wages in agriculture to urban areas would be quite limited. Besides geographic causes, convergence in real wages across sectors might not be observed for a variety of reasons relating to household characteristics (age, education), infrastructure, the cost of migration, cultural barriers to mobility, wage policy and the labor code. As a consequence, imbalances between the supply and demand of labor are discharged on the informal sector. Where rural labor markets are weakly integrated with the rest of the economy, the impact of agricultural growth on wages and poverty reduction through the labor linkages beyond the sector is likely to be quite limited.

The second conclusion we can draw from these case studies is that the pattern of agricultural growth matters, in particular the *output mix*. We come back to this point in Section 1.4.4, below. The results from Chile and South Africa suggest that integration of agriculture into international markets, particularly through an expansion of exports requiring labor-intensive activities, implies important consequences in terms of increasing labor productivity, employment and wages. The kind of agricultural-based expansion of non-traditional high-value exports (fruits, wine and vegetables) seen in Chile and South Africa has caused significant positive spillover effects on the non-farm sector primarily through the labor market This is particularly due to the employment effect in downstream industries (food processing, selection, packing and transportation and so on).

1.4.2 Direct and Indirect Income Effects through Small-farm Income Growth

Direct income effects through farm income

Rural areas are home to the majority of the poor and poverty is highly prevalent in small-farm households. Improving the farming income of these households is therefore considered key to eradicating rural poverty. The Chile and South Africa case studies assess the strength of this direct channel.

The report from Chile shows that the elasticity of poor farmers' income with respect to farm income growth is very small, about 0.1. This is due in part to the low participation of low-income, small farmers in Chile's agro-export boom over the past two decades. Moreover, one should consider that in Chile, agriculture represents a relatively small fraction of national GDP (about 5 percent), thus, unlike in the case of very poor economies, one would not expect significant farm household consumption multipliers to the rest of the economy. A third consideration, true of several Latin American countries, is that rural household income is becoming increasingly more diversified. The evidence, based on rural household analysis, shows that rural non-farm income represents more than 40 percent of total household income in nine out of 12 countries, and more than 50 percent for six countries (Reardon et al., 2001). Other factors besides income composition may limit the ability of farm income to reduce poverty among smallholders (see López and Valdés, 2000 for the role of agriculture in affecting rural poverty in Latin America). Market and policy failures are pervasive in rural factor and output markets and may hinder the ability of small farmers to fully exploit the revenues that could be generated by their assets.

More generally, the term 'smallholder' covers a range of situations which are quite heterogeneous. Within the small-farm sector there is a segment of farmers for whom possibilities of escaping poverty exclusively through farming appear to be very limited. The recent study by Jayne (2005: 118) on Eastern Africa concludes

> [T]he evidence suggests that farm size within the small farm sector is continuing to gradually decline . . . The bottom 25% of rural agricultural households are virtually landless, having access to 0.10 hectares per capita or less in each country examined. Under existing conditions, the ability of this bottom land quartile to escape poverty directly through agricultural productivity growth is limited . . .

The RoA study on South Africa comes to a similar conclusion with respect to the limited role agriculture can play in improving the conditions of subsistence farmers. A minimum level of commercialization is needed to move subsistence farmers out of poverty. This does not mean that subsistence farming does not have a positive role in buffering poor households, especially those previously engaged in informal jobs, from economic shocks. The basic message is that agriculture can be the basis for wealth accumulation only when it becomes a stable and relevant source of income growth, something achieved only by the relatively wealthier smallholder households. Given the polarization of access to farm land in South Africa, a major land redistribution program would be required in order to allow a substantial number of small farms to reach a viable size. Whether this is a realistic possibility or advisable recommendation, is a question that transcends the scope of the present analysis.[16]

The two case studies, together with the results from the India case study reviewed in the previous section, suggest that while agricultural productivity growth is important in lifting the poorest segment of smallholders out of poverty, it may not be all that is needed to reach this goal. This conclusion is very much related to the importance of non-farm activities in improving the income of poor farm households in developing countries. Although the nature of non-farm employment is dependent on how developed agriculture is in a given geographical context and on its linkages with non-agricultural activities, it is now well recognized that it contributes to a substantial share of household income. Provided that off-farm job opportunities are available, the share of labor that farm households allocate to non-farm activities increases as the ratio of labor endowment to land become larger *ceteris paribus*. As a result, one would expect that where opportunities for non-farm employment exist, the income structure of small farmers would be tilted towards a higher share of non-farm income. An increase in farm income will therefore have a reduced impact on overall household income. For given land and labor endowments, an increase in farm income will be associated with a fall in non-farm income, albeit less in absolute terms, so that the overall net gain might therefore be quite small after all.

The role of growth multipliers

There is a growing amount of literature on the 'multipliers' effects that agricultural growth has on other economic sectors (Adelman and Morris, 1973; Mellor, 1976; Bell and Hazell, 1980; Delgado et al., 1997). The findings concerned primarily the importance of linkages through farm-producer-generated household consumption rather than through inter-industry production linkages, in part because most of the above research focused on near-subsistence agriculture (primarily in South Asia). The RoA project examined growth multipliers by contrasting Ghana, a lower-income country characterized by a relatively equitable distribution of land access and a high share of income derived from agriculture, with South Africa, a middle-income country with a marked inequality in land access. Although extensively explored in the literature (for example, Delgado et al., 1997), growth multipliers have been included in the present study as a complement to the analysis of the other poverty-reduction channels.

Growth multipliers are higher when households spend a substantial portion of their money income on non-tradables (farm and non-farm products and services).[17] Analysis in Ghana shows that the poorest farm households have considerably higher marginal budget shares for farm non-tradables than richer farm households (0.62 of the poorest third versus 0.23 of the richest third). As result of the consumption multipliers, this implies that income growth among poor farm households would have positive spillovers on the local economy. Production multipliers are low compared to consumption multipliers. As expected, multipliers associated with non-farm tradables are stronger than those of farm tradables (3.17 versus 2.46), but the agricultural tradable multipliers measured are surprisingly high, probably as a consequence of low border/farm gate price transmission. Yet, farm non-tradables are more important than non-farm non-tradables in the overall size of the multiplier. Even when discounting these multipliers by 30 percent due to the assumption of fixed prices (see Delgado et al., 1997 for a discussion on such discounting practice), these are very high multipliers which signal the role of agriculture in generating and transmitting growth within the economy. The study for Ghana also produces simulations in which value added of farm activities is increased exogenously (for example, as a result of technical change and price incentives from better infrastructure). The conclusion is that the value of multipliers rises with higher farm value added. New technology, lower input costs and/or higher product prices are all factors that enhance agricultural growth's contribution to poverty reduction.

Growth multipliers in South Africa's communal areas are also positive but less than expected. At the margin, household budget share for staple crops is low, while it is substantially higher for vegetables, fruits, meat and consumer durables.[18] On the other hand and as previously discussed, a separate analysis of the impact of export-led growth based on unprocessed and processed agricultural commodities shows that interlinkages with other industries (chemicals, transport, wood and paper) result in a significant positive impact on labor income for those engaged in agriculture and in the broader rural economy.

The two RoA studies provide findings that are quite consistent with the overall growth multiplier literature. First, growth multipliers tend to be weaker when: (a) the labor supply has some inelasticity (that is, when underemployment in rural areas is low); (b) non-tradable goods are not a significant component of household expenditures; and (c) the share of non-tradables in overall production is limited. The linkages between agriculture and the rest of the economy increase, on the other hand, with public policies that strengthen the linkages between primary agriculture and downstream activities, including agro-industrial processors, packagers, and other industries which process raw materials produced by agriculture. For most developing small economy countries, such integrated growth would be hard to achieve if the economy is relatively closed. Forward and backward production multipliers acquire more importance[19] as agriculture becomes more integrated with world markets and with the rapid urbanization taking place in most countries.

1.4.3 The Food-price Channel

From a long-run perspective and for the global food system as a whole, the lowering of the real price of food represents agriculture's most fundamental contribution to welfare (for example, Johnson, 1997). In the RoA project, however, the perspective is that of individual countries, most of them price takers in world food markets. At the country level, one would expect that higher agricultural growth would lead to a reduction in poverty as a result of production expansion. For poor households which are net buyers of food, food expenditures usually represent a relatively high share of total household expenditures, thus lower food prices result in an increase in real income. The importance of food price levels is reflected in the fact that they are important in determining the poverty line in many countries; variations in food prices result in substantial changes in the prevalence of poverty at national and subnational levels. In other words, poverty lines are typically very elastic with respect to relative food prices and, depending on the distribution of income, changing food prices can translate into significant shifts in poverty indices. What is less surprising is to discover that relative food prices are often very loosely related to farm productivity over the medium to long term. Other intermediate factors might be much more important in decreasing food prices for consumers, *in primis* transportation and marketing costs.

In this section we examine findings from the Chile, Ghana, Mexico and South Africa case studies.[20] Before entering into details, some technical remarks are due. First, while most chapters focus on the food price index, that from Chile focuses on the real non-tradable component of the food price index, thus excluding the tradable component of food.[21] This is appropriate in the context of a very open economy like Chile's, where one expects a relatively high price transmission from border to domestic wholesale prices for commodities. By contrast, one expects that changes in domestic farm production would mostly be reflected in the price of non-tradable, rather than tradable foods. If no effect shows up on non-tradables, no effect should be expected on the aggregate food price index. Because of data limitation, this disaggregation, however desirable, could not be attempted in the other case studies. This implies that when the aggregate food price index is used, any effect of agricultural productivity growth through the price of non-tradable foods will be watered down. It should also be noted that the impact of changes in productivity growth on the price of non-tradable food products reflects the degree of their substitutability in consumption with respect to tradables. Overall, controlling for variables such as the real exchange rate, the approach of disaggregating the effect on the tradable and non-tradable component of the food price index allows a better understanding of how agricultural production expansion affects domestic food prices in the context of a broader macroeconomic and trade policy framework.

Second, besides a focus on the short- and long-term relationship between food prices and agricultural productivity, the South Africa case study also examines the impact on food price changes of agricultural productivity relative to that of marketing infrastructure. These findings can be used to help guide policy makers in prioritizing public investment for making food more affordable for the poor.

The main result that emerges from the analysis of the Chilean economy is that while the short-run impact on food prices of agricultural GDP is substantial, with an elasticity of –0.80, it is absorbed within a year, leaving a meager long-run elasticity of –0.18. The authors suggest that the difference between short- and long-run elasticities is influenced by the size of transaction costs, which determine the basket of non-tradables. The analysis also shows that, while in the short run the real price of non-tradable foods deviates from the price of tradable foods, in the long run the two prices are tied by an equilibrium relationship. Thus, the impact of agricultural GDP is limited when compared to other variables, in particular non-agricultural GDP and the real exchange rate. In the case of Chile, the food price channel is not a strong force in translating agricultural growth into sustained poverty reduction. An uncompensated 4.5 percent annual growth rate of GDP reduces the number of poor by 0.5 percent. The impact increases only slightly when the 4.5 percent growth rate is compensated.[22]

The Mexican study looks at the roles played by the real exchange rate and agricultural and non-agricultural GDP in determining the real food price index (which includes both tradables and non-tradables). Results show that the impact of agricultural GDP growth is insignificant, both in the long and short runs. The real exchange rate dominates, possibly a reflection of the high share of food tradables within the overall food basket on which the food price index is based.

The Ghana study also focuses on the elasticity of the food price index with respect to agricultural growth and looks at the effect of agricultural and non-agricultural labor productivity, minimum wages and food imports on real *urban* food prices. It is found that labor productivity growth in agriculture reduces urban food prices by the same proportion in the short run as in the long run, with an elasticity of 0.89 percent. On the other hand, a rise in the minimum wage and labor productivity in the non-farm sector exerts an upward impact on food prices, which suggests some supply inelasticity which could be associated with import restrictions and/or some degree of non-tradability of food products. The study reports a lack of correlation between food imports and domestic food prices during the period studied.[23]

The South Africa study examines the potential link between agricultural growth and food prices. South Africa has experienced considerable growth in the commercial farming sector but a rather stagnant or, in some cases, rapid decline in production in the former homelands – reflecting once again the dualistic nature of its agricultural economy. These former homeland areas are also home to the majority of the poorest population, who purchase most of their food requirements in small local stores and large retail chain outlets in major regional towns.

South Africa is characterized by a relatively high level of transport and communication infrastructures, is fairly open to trade, and has a deregulated policy environment. As a result, the pass-through from international to farm gate prices seems relatively strong, especially in the wheat and maize sectors. In South Africa, as in other countries, (real) exchange rate fluctuations are a very influential determinant of the domestic price fluctuations of basic staples such as wheat and maize, suggesting a substantial pass-through of international prices. However, due to the oligopsonistic nature of the food manufacturing and retail industry, and the mature marketing and distribution network, the trend in retail food prices tends to be divorced from farm gate prices, with fairly large farm to retail price spreads. This is largely related to a high value being added in these commercial supply chains. Price transmission in the supply chains also shows considerable asymmetry, with changes in farm commodity prices not always reflected in retail price trends. It is only when there are sharp commodity price increases that you see quick transmission, but true transmission of downward trends in commodity prices is not so evident. Since food inflation (increases in food retail prices) has been positive over most of the last 20 years (as high as 20 percent in 2002/03, as low as 0.2 percent in early 2004, and around 1 to 2 percent since then) the positive growth in agricultural production appears to have no real impact in reducing domestic food prices. Although the impact of increased agricultural productivity on urban food prices is at best modest, it does have a strong positive impact on raising food consumption and employment in rural areas.[24]

Overall, the results from the case studies are consistent with the hypothesis that trade openness impinges on the relationship between food prices and agricultural growth at the national level. More openness to trade contributes to a de-linking of food prices and local production food consumption, particularly for consumers in urban areas. While infrastructural development and transaction costs may reinforce the role of agricultural growth at the local level, at the national level – and especially in urban areas – the role of domestic agricultural growth in lowering the real price of food is limited, especially over the long run. The real exchange rate dominates the relationship, along with overall income growth (that is, non-agricultural growth) and the price of non-food products. Of course, this is not necessarily bad news if trade openness is associated with a decline in food prices. For segments of the small-farm sector, however, there is a risk of exclusion from growth and trade opportunities, thus the importance of reducing obstacles to farmers for integrating into the modern supply chains.

The South Africa study shows that where the cost of domestic interregional trade of food is high, infrastructure development (better roads in particular) is critical for exerting a significant downward pressure on food prices (besides stabilizing them at the national level). The lesson drawn from the South Africa case study is that the contribution of agriculture to lowering food prices must not be seen in isolation. Instead, it needs to be framed in the wider context of the transformation of the broader food system and, increasingly more relevant, an open economy.

1.4.4　A Growth Decomposition Approach to the Role of Agriculture in Poverty Reduction

In a seminal paper, Ravallion and Datt (1996) examined how the pattern of growth can influence the rate of poverty reduction. The methodology, which was applied to India, allows us to discern the role played by agriculture, manufacturing and services in reducing poverty (head count, depth and severity) at the national, rural and urban levels (see the technical appendix for more details). The approach yields reduced-form relationships that synthesize the joint effect of the various channels but do not allow the relative importance of the various channels to be discerned. It does, however, allow for deriving elasticities of poverty to sectoral growth that are useful in assessing the role of agriculture *relative* to other sectors.[25] Ravallion and Datt's analysis focused on India, for which a long time series of household income and consumption surveys, consistent in terms of data collection methodology, was available.

Four RoA countries applied this methodology, adapting it to their specific data availability, less substantial than in the Indian case. Indonesia and Mexico teams had access to surveys that are representative at the regional or provincial level and to regional data on GDP by sector. In the case of Ghana, data limitations prevented the use of the Ravallion–Datt approach, so the question was approached through a non-parametric decomposition of changes of poverty indicators at the national level attributable to the different sectors (Ravallion and Huppi, 1991; Datt and Ravallion, 1992). Chile used the results from the wage and employment channel analysis to simulate the impact of growth composition on poverty (discussed in Section 1.4.1 above).

Using regional panel data, the Indonesian case study measures the elasticity of three poverty indicators at the urban, rural and national levels with respect to growth in agriculture, industry and services, while controlling for inter-regional migration. Table 1.5 synthesizes the results, reporting only coefficients that are significant at the 10 percent level of confidence.

On the basis of these results, the contribution of agricultural growth to poverty reduction over the 1984–1996 period is estimated for each of the

Table 1.5   Elasticity of poverty to sectoral growth in Indonesia

Growth component	Head count			Poverty gap			Severity		
	Nat	Urb	Rur	Nat	Urb	Rur	Nat	Urb	Rur
Agriculture	−1.86	−1.13	−2.88	−0.66	−0.26	−1.02	−	−	−0.45
Industry	−	−1.90	−	−	−	−	−	−	−
Services	−	−	−	−	−	−	−	−	−
Population	0.12	−	0.10	0.05	−	0.05	0.02	−	0.02
Initial poverty	−0.11	−3.13	−0.14	−0.15	−0.17	−0.16	−0.17	−0.18	−0.17

Note: The table reports only results that are statistically significant at the 10% level of confidence.

*Table 1.6   Contribution of agricultural growth to poverty reduction in
Indonesia (percent poverty reduction according to three
poverty indicators)*

	Urban	Rural	Total
Head count	54.94	74.40	65.58
Poverty gap	36.05	57.15	51.13
Severity	–	49.22	–

three poverty indicators (see Table 1.6). The results show that agricultural
growth has been important in reducing the prevalence of poverty both in
rural and urban areas. Agricultural growth was also responsible for over 50
percent of the reduction in the depth of poverty in rural areas and for a
respectable 36 percent in urban areas. Interestingly, these figures are well
above the average share of agriculture in total GDP over the 1986–96 time
period.

Regional panel data were also used in the analysis for the Mexico study.
The study uses three definitions for poor households (food poor, between
non-food poor and moderate poor, and moderate poor), to measure the
impact of rural and urban growth on the incidence and depth of poverty.[26]
The analysis controls for possible endogeneity arising from the use of the
same survey data to compute dependent and independent variables. An
important limitation is that data availability precludes separating the GDP
of agriculture, industry and services at the regional level. Thus, growth is
decomposed into urban and rural growth. Nevertheless, the analysis shows
that the elasticity of regional rural consumption with respect to regional
agricultural GDP ranges between 0.75 and 0.87, implying that regional
rural consumption is a good proxy for agricultural growth. It then proceeds
to estimate the elasticities of poverty with respect to rural (that is, agricultural) and urban growth. The results are reported in Tables 1.7 and 1.8
(reporting only those with at least 10 percent significance).

Two main conclusions emerge from the Mexico report. First, due to the
high concentration of poor households in rural areas, the role of agricultural growth in reducing *national* poverty is substantial and stronger than
the role of urban income growth. Second, there are no inter-sectoral effects:
rural income growth reduces rural poverty and urban income growth
reduces urban poverty. Third, migration from rural to urban areas reduces
poverty in rural areas but does not increase poverty in urban areas; in other
words, rural areas are 'price takers' in urban labor markets. The latter result
supports the idea that in the case of Mexico, poverty is not urbanizing and
suggests that the recent wave of reforms aimed at liberalizing land markets

Table 1.7   Elasticity of poverty prevalence to sectoral growth in Mexico (according to three poverty levels)

	Food poverty			Midpoint between food and moderate poverty			Moderate		
	Total poverty	Urban poverty	Rural poverty	Total poverty	Urban poverty	Rural poverty	Total poverty	Urban poverty	Rural poverty
Urban growth	−0.88	−1.55	−	−	−0.4	−	−0.48	−0.73	−
Rural growth	−1.32	−	−1.52	−	−	−1.52	−0.56	−	−0.75

Table 1.8   Elasticity of food poverty to sectoral growth in Mexico (according to three poverty indicators)

	Head count			Income gap			Severity		
	Total poverty	Urban poverty	Rural poverty	Total poverty	Urban poverty	Rural poverty	Total poverty	Urban poverty	Rural poverty
Urban growth	−0.88	−1.55	−	−1.01	−1.89	−	−1.04	−0.91	−
Rural growth	−1.32	−	−1.52	−1.68	−	−2.09	−2.13	−	−1.08

in Mexico's *ejidos*, while favoring migration from rural areas, would not be expected to contribute significantly to growing poverty in urban areas.

In the case of Ghana, data limitations precluded such an extended analysis. Instead, the analysis measured the impact of agricultural growth on national poverty through two decomposition methods. The first method decomposes changes in national poverty indices into an income effect (keeping income distribution constant) and an inequality effect (keeping average income constant) (see Datt and Ravallion, 1992). The second method decomposes the same change in poverty indices into an intra-sectoral change in the same poverty index (keeping population constant) and a population shift (keeping the poverty index unchanged). A third element in this decomposition results from the interaction between the change in the poverty index and the shift in population, signaling whether population migrates from areas with worse poverty indices to areas with better-off poverty indices (see Ravallion and Huppi, 1991). These decompositions are done at the national as well as at the rural and urban levels.[27] The results show that in both urban and rural areas income growth has been the driving force behind the decline in poverty rates experienced during the 1990s. Yet, this growth has been accompanied by increasing inequality, the latter detracting from the positive effect of the former. Interestingly, the major reduction in poverty originated in the forest zone, where cacao is the driving economic activity. Looking at the decomposition of national poverty changes in intra-sectoral poverty and population movements, the report finds that the former accounts for roughly 80 to 88 percent of poverty reduction, while the latter is responsible for 11 to 18 percent of the overall effect. The interaction effect indicates that the population has shifted out of the food crop sector (mostly non-tradable) into the export crop sector, which is mainly represented by cocoa. These results are consistent with the notion that the liberalization of the cocoa sector that took place during the previous decade has had a significant positive impact on poverty in Ghana.

1.5   POLICY IMPLICATIONS AND AREAS FOR FUTURE RESEARCH

The link between agriculture and poverty has attracted the attention of development economists for a long time. A conceptual analysis of the link between agricultural growth and poverty reduction is part of the early literature in development. More recently, considerable progress has been made in using quantitative approaches to estimate some of the basic parameters, expressed, in most cases, in terms of fairly aggregated indicators. These were discussed earlier in the text.

In our view, the strength of this study is its contribution to the understanding of the channels through which agricultural growth can influence poverty, supported by a detailed quantitative analysis applied in a very diverse sample of countries. The sample of country case studies is small due to data limitations in several of the initially selected countries. Thus, although the six case studies selected from Asia, Africa and Latin America offer a range of farming conditions and levels of development, we should be very cautious in generalizing the main findings for the developing world.

The analysis of the link between agriculture and poverty presented in this volume comes from one of the seven modules covered in the RoA project. The other module studies for the 11 countries are available on the RoA website at www.fao.org/es/esa/roa. In this poverty synthesis we have emphasized the main findings supported by quantitative modeling. These findings are complemented in the RoA study by a set of country chapters, which introduce the context in which agriculture influences poverty in each of the six countries.

What have we found? First, at an aggregate level, the evidence for the 1990s shows that higher agricultural labor productivity is not always accompanied by a reduction in poverty, a finding which runs counter to a common perception. The six countries have performed differently, and to some extent counter to what the evolution in agricultural labor productivity would suggest. In South Africa and Mexico, where there was a strong increase in agricultural labor productivity, the incidence of poverty did not decline either at the rural or at the national level, and even showed a tendency to increase in South Africa. By contrast, the countries where the growth in agricultural labor productivity was modest – Ghana, India and Indonesia – experienced a reduction in poverty at the rural and national levels. Chile experienced high agricultural labor productivity growth and also benefited from a significant reduction in national and rural poverty. These findings are not an argument against achieving high growth in agricultural labor productivity, but demonstrate that other factors are also involved in rural poverty reduction.

As discussed above, the RoA project focused on three key channels that link agricultural growth to poverty trends in rural and urban areas:

- the labor market channel, through employment and wages of unskilled labor;
- the direct smallholder income effect coupled with growth multipliers; and
- the food price effect.

The main conclusion from this study is that it appears that the most positive role played by agricultural growth comes from labor market effects, specifically from growth in labor-intensive activities both on the farm and, importantly, in post-harvest agro-processing of primary farm products. In the long run, public policies that stimulate rapid growth in rural employment (farm and rural non-farm) emerge as the most powerful strategy through which agricultural growth can contribute to rural poverty reduction. For some developing countries, *not* necessarily all of them, the best hope for employment-intensive growth is associated with a specialization of their agricultural economy towards labor-intensive crops and production chains, perhaps as a result of a process of trade liberalization.

For the *labor market channel*, Chile, India, Mexico and South Africa provide evidence on how agricultural growth has positive economy-wide effects on the wages of the unskilled, and thereby on poverty. The results in Chile and Mexico show that agricultural growth had a significant impact on the demand for unskilled labor. The effect was relatively stronger in Chile, in part due to the definition of agricultural output, which included direct post-harvest employment in agro-processing, as opposed to being restricted to primary agriculture in Mexico. The South Africa study finds strong spillover effects of agricultural exports on employment and wages onto industries such as transportation, chemicals and manufacturing, and the impact is stronger when export agro-processed products are included. Thus in assessing the overall role of agricultural growth in poverty reduction, one should take into account both its direct and indirect effects via forward and backward linkages. Altogether, the country studies find that both the pattern of growth (degree of export orientation) and the degree of rural labor market mobility and integration are conditions which influence the impact of agricultural growth on (raising) labor income. These results suggest that the integration of agriculture into export markets, when it results in an expansion of labor-intensive activities, would induce a significant and positive rural employment effect.

It is important to note that for the labor market to be the key channel through which the benefits of agricultural growth reach the poor in both urban and rural areas, agriculture must be a relatively intensive user of unskilled labor. While this typically holds for countries at low levels of development, it is not clear that this continues to be the case as agriculture's share in total GDP declines. On the other hand, the share of unskilled labor in agriculture relative to the country's labor market probably declines with development. Thus, the role of agriculture in poverty reduction would, on balance, decline as countries develop. And this remains true even if one defines agriculture in its *extended* sense, that is, consolidating primary production with post-harvest activities, which augments the impact of agriculture on poverty reduction.

Net farm income plays an important role in pulling poor farmers out of poverty. Yet, the extent of its effectiveness depends on the competitiveness of agriculture in the relevant region and on the linkage between farm and non-agricultural activities. Two of the case studies (Chile and South Africa) empirically examined the *direct smallholder income channel*. The results for Chile show that, among low-income small farmers, the elasticity of total household income with respect to *farm-based* income growth is small, about 0.1. This can be attributed in part to the relatively low participation of low-income small farmers (as producers) in Chile's agro-export boom since the early 1980s. The South Africa study arrives at a similar finding, casting a doubt on the role of agriculture in lifting subsistence farmers out of poverty in the absence of a certain minimum level of commercialization of farming activities.

The basic message is that agriculture can offer a base for wealth accumulation if it becomes a stable and relevant source of income, sometimes achieved only by the relatively wealthier households among the small farmers. This conclusion points to the importance of growth in rural non-farm activities in the fight against poverty. In the Chilean, Indian, Mexican and South African cases, when off-farm job opportunities (partly related to processing of primary farm products) are available, the share of labor that farm households allocate to non-farm activities increases, thus increasing total household income.

Using a different approach, the studies on Ghana and South Africa estimated growth multipliers between agriculture and the rest of the economy, that is, the role of agriculture in generating and transmitting growth in the non-farm sector. Particularly for Ghana, the findings are consistent with the findings in linkages–multiplier literature which has emphasized consumption linkages. Agricultural growth multipliers are stronger when (a) non-tradable products represent a higher share of household expenditures and (b) rural labor supply is relatively elastic. The study for Ghana finds that the poorest farm households have relatively high budget shares for non-tradable products, higher than richer farm households, thus income growth of poor farmers induces consumption multipliers with spillover to the non-farm economy. By contrast, agricultural growth multipliers in South African communal areas though positive are small. It should be noted that in low-income countries, spillover effects from consumption multipliers dominate (over production multipliers). This changes as countries develop; in middle-income countries, production-related linkages dominate over consumption-related linkages, primarily through forward linkages. In developing countries, the nature of the contribution of agriculture through spillover effects varies with the level of development.[28]

Through its effects in lowering world prices for food products, the *food price channel* is perhaps the most fundamental contribution of agricultural growth to poverty reduction, both for low-income urban as well as rural consumers, for the world food system as a whole. It should be remembered that small farmers are often also net food buyers. However, the situation at the country level is different; most countries are price takers in world markets and are increasingly more open to imports of farm products. Thus, the distinction between the agricultural growth effects on domestic food prices of tradables compared to non-tradables is important in the final outcome. The main impact of growth would be reflected in the non-tradable component of the food price indices. The case studies do not find a strong long-run effect of agricultural growth on lowering domestic (aggregate) food prices at retail.

The RoA findings can be seen in the context of other evidence that has emerged on the role of agriculture and poverty reduction, discussed previously in the text. While they do not examine the channels of influence, the findings of the inter-sectoral analysis by Timmer (2002), Gardner (2005),

Bravo-Ortega and Lederman (2005), de Ferranti et al. (2005), Foster and Valdés (2006) and Christiansen et al. (2006), offer as a whole a quite consistent picture. These studies, although they diverge in terms of their findings on the magnitude of the impact of sectoral growth on poverty, they consistently support the view that non-agricultural growth is more important than agricultural growth in terms of the *direct* effect on poverty reduction in developing countries. On the other hand, when both direct and indirect growth effects are taken into account, the empirical evidence demonstrates that agricultural growth's impact on poverty is strong and, more importantly, when compared to non-agricultural growth it is also more *effective* in terms of poverty reduction. The positive impact of agricultural growth on poverty reduction is more than proportional to the relative importance of the sector in the economy.[29]

The World Bank study concludes that relative to its GDP share, agriculture has a greater impact on poverty reduction than non-agriculture, approximately 1.8 times its size in Latin America and the Caribbean (LAC) and 1.6 times its size for non-LAC countries. These are averages for the set of countries. The analysis also shows dispersion in the spillover effect, and, at least for the LAC region, strong cross-sector growth and poverty elasticities in those countries with the strongest inter-sectoral input–output linkages, particularly forward. Recent empirical evidence shows that rapid growth in the non-farm rural economy is crucial for creating employment and income opportunities for those who have limited economic prospects in farming alone. This finding on the growing complementarities between farming and the rural non-farm economy is corroborated in the RoA country studies. We do not conclude that agriculture can be always and everywhere the 'main' driver of growth and poverty, but for most developing countries, Timmer and the World Bank study suggest that the sector plays a significant and positive role in poverty reduction. This finding is consistent with the case-study analysis in the RoA project.

Can we attempt to derive practical policy implications from these findings? The RoA project cannot provide specific policy recommendations for strategies for rural development. From the beginning, the study's approach was positive rather than normative. Nevertheless, significant policy implications can be derived from empirical findings.

One is the critical importance of the poverty reduction and labor market link. The countries where this issue was examined rigorously indicate the importance of examining how public policies can enhance labor mobility and how to invest in schooling and training, and review labor legislation and labor practices so as to reduce transaction costs that inhibit employment within and across sectors. Investment in human capital can improve the integration of labor markets. From this point of view, quality and coverage of schooling in rural areas can be a strategic investment with social returns largely exceeding private benefits. However, it may also lead to a situation where part of the benefits do not accrue to agriculture, as the better-educated young migrate out of this sector.

Based on the findings on the role of agriculture and employment generation, one concludes that taxing agriculture is wrong! When resources can reallocate across activities and sectors, agriculture contributes to poverty reduction, and agriculture is responsive to economic incentives in the longer run.

Should we conclude that agriculture should be subsidized? Our answer is that agriculture should not receive preferential treatment with respect to other sectors. Border protection has a negative impact on the real income of food buyers (including many small farmers); input subsidies are often misallocated and leak to those that are not in need. Cash and non-cash income transfers are perhaps more attractive options, yet fiscal costs and targeting issues should be examined in detail. The arguments in favor of subsidization are weak, with the exception, in some countries, of a subset of very small farmers, but not for medium and large farmers.

These conclusions point strongly to a policy implication for the allocation of public expenditures. The de Ferranti et al., 2005 study mentioned above concludes that agricultural growth has positive direct and indirect effects on poverty reduction that are more than proportional to the share of the sector in the economy. Should the share of government expenditure in agriculture be 1.6 to 1.8 times the sector's share in GDP? This question goes beyond the scope of our analysis, and takes us to the issue of the effectiveness of rural public expenditures. There is a need to recognize that the way many governments allocate public monies for agriculture and the rural sector causes costly distortions in the sense that a high share of them are captured as subsidies and transfers as 'private' goods. The main concern is that there seems to be significant underinvestment in the provision of truly public goods such as education, infrastructure, research and technology, which compete for public monies with various subsidies and untargeted transfers. The existence of important indirect effects associated with agricultural growth means that particular caution must be taken when estimating the social returns of public projects in rural areas. Ultimately, the issue is not so much one of allocating public funds in relation to the total elasticity of poverty reduction to agricultural growth, but one of ensuring that all indirect (non-rural) effects of an increase in agricultural GDP are factored in when ranking projects by their social rates of return. This criterion applies for projects in both agriculture and non-agriculture. However, the results in the de Ferranti et al. (2005) study show that the spillover from non-agricultural to agricultural growth are considerably smaller. Assigning public investment funds according to the sector's share would not reflect these spillover impacts on growth and poverty reduction.

The results of the RoA country case studies provide further evidence to support existing literature for not taxing agriculture and for investing in efforts to improve the way rural and agricultural markets, with labor as key, work. The RoA case studies do not provide specific indications on how governments could or should intervene in addressing market and policy failures in agricultural markets. They do, however, suggest that governments should not look at the agricultural sector in isolation. Instead, they should look at agriculture in an extended way, taking into account forward and backward linkages with the rest of the economy and the influence that the rural labor market has on urban labor markets. All of the above is consistent with the notion that agricultural policy making should overcome the narrower sectoral view and adopt a more fully integrated perspective on the role of agriculture in the overall growth process.

NOTES

1. While on average growth is good for the poor, substantial variation in the relationship between growth and poverty reduction exists. Thus, the poor's share of total income can decrease while poverty is reduced (Demery and Squire, 1996).
2. Although the phenomenon of urban poverty is increasing at an accelerated pace (Ravallion, 2001).
3. This conclusion echoes Gardner's (2005) questioning of the agriculture-as-engine-of-growth vision on the basis of his review of the historical experience of the US (see Gardner, 2002), whereby rural income growth has historically been driven by non-farm income growth rather than by farm income growth.
4. The reader might be interested in the recent (unpublished) work by Christiansen et al. (2006) where the authors explore the relationships between poverty rates on one hand and agricultural and non-agricultural growth on the other. The results, although tentative, show a fairly large impact of agricultural growth on poverty reduction, which, although surprisingly high, supports the findings with respect to the direction of effects in Bravo-Ortega and Lederman (2005) and this book. A survey of several quantitative studies on the agricultural-poverty relationship is found in Valdés and Foster (2006).
5. For example, Ravallion and Datt (1996) offer evidence that in the case of India, rural–urban migration does not play a major role in reducing poverty, while yield increases do. Yet, yield increases may occur for many reasons other than increases in inputs or increased productivity. As the inverse farm-size productivity literature shows, labor, credit and land market imperfections have an impact on yields by altering the relative use of factors at the farm level in a more or less systematic way. As development occurs, the impact of such imperfections on yields may also be affected.
6. In Chapter 2, the interested reader will find a more thorough discussion of the importance of these channels. What follows is a synthesis of that discussion.
7. This question begs the one of which growth rates one has in mind. Here one could resort to historical or projected rates.
8. Short-term effects may also bear important policy issues in those cases where prices and wages are sticky and transitory price shocks may have long-term impacts on real wages.

9. Arable land is defined as: 'Land under temporary crops (double-cropped areas are counted only once), temporary meadows for mowing or pasture, land under market and kitchen gardens and land temporarily fallow (less than five years). The abandoned land resulting from shifting cultivation is not included in this category. Data for "Arable land" are not meant to indicate the amount of land that is potentially cultivable' (FAOSTAT, 2005). This definition excludes land planted with forests for commercial exploitation.

   In the case of Chile, while FAO's statistics show a slight reduction in arable land, statistics computed by ODEPA (2001) show that total area, which includes crops, pastures, and planted forest area, has slightly increased over the same period. Here we rely on FAO's statistics for definitional consistency with the other countries.

10. The agricultural population is defined as all persons who depend on agriculture, hunting, fishing or forestry for their livelihood. This estimate includes all persons actively engaged in agriculture and their non-working dependants (FAO).

11. Countries with abundant rural labor (CARL), have been defined by Tomich et al. (1995) as those countries where both labor productivity in agriculture and per capita GDP are low and more than 50 percent of the labor force is employed in agriculture.

12. See Chapter 2 for a more detailed discussion on this point.

13. Details of the functional form used and related derivations can be found in the technical appendix.

14. The difference in elasticity depends on the assumptions concerning the elasticity of supply of unskilled labor with respect to wages.

15. Here we refer to the poverty gap and squared poverty gap indices.

16. In Chile, agrarian reform is not a realistic option today. The country underwent a massive agrarian reform program between 1965 and 1973, which was fiscally expensive and had no direct positive effect on agricultural productivity or the modernization of agriculture. An evaluation/assessment of agrarian reforms cannot be based on one case only, but it serves as a warning about how extraordinarily complex it is to make agrarian reform work.

17. A key issue is how goods are classified as non-tradables. A typical approach, followed in the Ghana study, is to consider non-traded goods as non-tradables. One should bear in mind, though, that some goods are non-traded because of the existence of policy barriers and not because of their intrinsic nature, which might affect the cost of transacting them on the market.

18. In the South African context, durables represent a significant leakage as they are typically not produced in the local economy.

19. A paper by O'Ryan and Miller (2004), which is part of the RoA study in Chile, computes three different types of multipliers under different assumptions regarding the linkages to include and the flexibility of non-tradable prices. The computation of the three multipliers is carried out using a computable general equilibrium (CGE) model calibrated for Chile.

20. The India study finds real food prices to have a significant impact on poverty. Yet, it does not examine how agricultural growth affects food prices.

21. In the Chile study, food prices (real price of non-tradable food products) depend on agricultural GDP, non-agricultural GDP, the real price of non-food products, and the real exchange rate.

22. This counterintuitive result can be explained on the grounds that non-agricultural output, required to fall in order to compensate for the increase in agricultural output, is strongly correlated with non-tradable food prices.

23. This result could depend on the existence of food import policies aimed at stabilizing internal prices. This would make the food imports variable endogenous with respect to food prices.

24. Since international prices are only one component of the final domestic price of a given commodity, it is difficult to be definitive on the degree of responsiveness of domestic to international prices in the South Africa study. One could think of the domestic price as being the product of the world price, the exchange rate, policy interventions, and residual factors such as imperfections in domestic market structures. One would need to

decompose the change in the domestic prices in the changes in the rest of the prices in order to assess the contribution of each factor.
25. An important caveat concerning the approach is that the estimated reduced-form para- meters are unstable and tend to change with the underlying institutional and policy contexts. See Lucas's (1976) seminal contribution on this issue.
26. The analysis is based on the existence of two poverty lines: the food poverty line and the moderate poverty line.
27. Data from the Living Standards Measurement Surveys of 1991/92 and 1998/99.
28. See, for example, the report *Beyond the City: The Rural Contribution to Development*, by de Ferranti et al. (2005).
29. It is important to note that for developed countries, the same study finds a negative effect of agricultural growth on non-agricultural GDP and a negative impact of the same on the average income of the poorest quintile of the population.

REFERENCES

Adelman, I. and C. Morris (1973), *Economic Growth and Social Equity in Developing Countries*, Stanford, CA: Stanford University Press.
Bell, C. and P. Hazell (1980), 'Measuring the indirect effects of an agricultural project on its surrounding region', *American Journal of Agricultural Economics*, **62**: 75–86.
Bigsten, A. and J. Levine (2004), 'Growth, income distribution and poverty: a review', in A. Shorrocks and R. van der Hoeven (eds), *Growth, Inequality, and Poverty*, Oxford: Oxford University Press, pp. 251–76.
Bravo-Ortega, C. and D. Lederman (2005), 'Agriculture and national welfare around the world: causality and heterogeneity since 1960', Policy Research Working Paper 3499, World Bank, Washington, DC, USA.
Christiansen, L., L. Demery and J. Kühl (2006), ' The role of agriculture in poverty reduction – an empirical perspective', mimeo, World Bank, Washington, DC.
Danielson, Anders (2001), 'When do the poor benefit from growth, and why?', Working Papers 2001: 12, Department of Economics, Lund University.
Datt, G. and M. Ravallion (1992), 'Growth and redistribution components of changes in poverty measures: a decomposition with applications to Brazil and India in the 1980s', *Journal of Development Economics*, **38**: 275–95.
Datt, G. and M. Ravallion (1998), 'Why have some Indian states done better than others at reducing rural poverty?', *Economica*, **65**: 17–38.
de Ferranti, D., G.E. Perry, W. Foster, D. Lederman and A. Valdés (eds) (2005), *Beyond the City: The Rural Contribution to Development*, Washington, DC: World Bank, Latin American and Caribbean Studies.
Delgado, C.L., J. Hopkins and V.A. Kelly (1997), 'Agricultural growth linkages in Sub-Saharan Africa', IFPRI Research Report 107, Washington, DC, USA.
Demery, L. and L. Squire (1996), 'Macroeconomic adjustment and the poverty in Africa: an emerging picture', *World Bank Research Observer*, **11**(1): 39–59.
Dollar, D. and A. Kraay (2002), 'Growth is good for the poor', *Journal of Economic Growth*, **7**(3): 195–225.
FAOSTAT (2005), Food and Agriculture Organization, http://faostat.fao.org/.
FAO–World Bank (2001), *Farming Systems and Poverty: Improving Former's Livelihoods in a Changing World*, edited by J. Dixon, A. Gulliver and D. Gibbon, Rome and Washington, DC, FAO and World Bank.

Foster, W. and A. Valdés (2006), 'Chilean agriculture and major economic reforms: growth, trade, poverty and the environment' (ed.), *Région et Développment*, **23**: 187–214.

Gardner, B. (2002), *American Agriculture in the Twentieth Century*, Cambridge, MA: Harvard University Press.

Gardner, B. (2005), 'Causes of rural economic development', in D. Colman and N. Vink (eds), *Reshaping Agriculture's Contribution to Society*, Proceedings of the 25th International Conference of Agricultural Economists, Durban, Oxford: Blackwell, pp. 21–41.

Hazell, P.B.R. and S. Haggblade (1989), 'Farm–nonfarm growth linkages and the welfare of the poor', Paper Presented at the World Bank/IFPRI Poverty Research Conference, 2 October, Airlie House, VA, USA.

Jayne, T.S., D. Mather and E. Mghenyi (2005), *Smallholder Forming in Difficult Circumstances: Policy Issues for Africa*, Proceedings of the Research Workshop on the Future of Small Farms, 26–29 June, Wye, UK.

Johnson, D. Gale (1997), 'Agriculture and the wealth of nations', Richard T. Ely Lecture, *American Economic Review*, **87**(2): 1–12.

Johnston, B.F. and J. Mellor (1961), 'The role of agriculture in economic development', *American Economic Review*, **51**(4): 566–93.

Krueger, A., M. Schiff and A. Valdés (1988), 'Agricultural incentives in developing countries: measuring the effect of sectoral and economywide policies', *World Bank Economic Review*, **2**(3): 255–71.

López, R. and A. Valdés (eds) (2000), *Rural Poverty in Latin America*, New York: St. Martin's Press.

Lucas, R.E. (1976), 'Econometric policy evaluation: a critique', *Carnegie-Rochester Conference Series on Public Policy*, **1**: 19–46.

Mellor, J.W. (1976), *The New Economics of Growth: Strategy for India and the Developing World*, Ithaca, NY: Cornell University Press.

O'Ryan, R. and S. Miller (2004), 'The role of agriculture in poverty alleviation, income distribution and economic development: a CGE analysis for Chile', www.fao.org/es/esa/roa.

ODEPA (Oficina de Estudios y Política Agraria) (2001), 'Una Política de Estado Para la Agricultura Chilena. Período 2000–2010', Ministerio de Agricultura, Santiago.

Ravallion, M. (2001), *On the Urbanization of Poverty*, Washington, DC: World Bank.

Ravallion M. and G. Datt (1996), 'How important to India's poor is the sectoral composition of economic growth', *World Bank Economic Review*, **10**(1): 1–25.

Ravallion, M. and M. Huppi (1991), 'Measuring changes in poverty: a methodological case study of Indonesia during an adjustment period', *World Bank Economic Review*, **5**(1), 57–84.

Reardon, T., J. Berdegué and G. Escobar (2001), 'Rural nonfarm employment and incomes in Latin America: overview and policy implications', *World Development*, **29**(3): 395–409.

Schultz, T.W. (1993), *The Economics of Being Poor*, Cambridge, MA: Blackwell.

SOFT (2000), (The State of Food Insecurity in the World) *Food Insecuity: When People Live with Hunger and Fear Starvation*, Rome: Food and Agriculture Organization.

Timmer, C.P. (2002), 'Agriculture and economic development', in B.L. Gardner and G.C. Rausser (eds), *Handbook of Agricultural Economics*, Vol. 2A, Amsterdam: North-Holland, pp. 1487–546.

Tomich, T., P. Kilby and B.F. Johnston (1995), *Transforming Agrarian Economies: Opportunities Seized, Opportunities Missed*, Ithaca, NY and London: Cornell University Press.

Valdés, A. and W. Foster (2006), 'Reflections on the role of agriculture in pro-poor growth', *World Development* (forthcoming).

Warr, Peter G. (2002), 'Poverty reduction and sectoral growth: evidence from Southeast Asia', mimeo, Australian National University, Canberra.

Warr, Peter G. and Wang Wen-Thuen (1999), 'Poverty, inequality and economic growth in Taiwan', in Gustav Ranis Sheng-Cheng Hu and Yun-Peng Chu (eds), *The Political Economy of Taiwan's Development into the 21st Century: Essays in Memory of John C.H. Fei*, Volume 2, Cheltenham, UK and Northampton, MA, USA: Edward Elgar, pp. 133–65.

World Bank (2004), *World Development Indicators*, Washington, DC: World Bank, available at www.worldbank.org.

2. Agricultural growth and poverty reduction

Ramón López

2.1 INTRODUCTION

This chapter does two things. First, it provides an overview of the mechanisms through which agricultural growth reduces poverty and it examines the key conditions affecting the intensity of the impact of agricultural growth on poverty. Second, it reviews other conceptual analyses for methodological guidance that can be used in empirical analyses.

If the focus of this chapter were purely on the 'poverty externalities' of agriculture, it could be argued that the discussion should be restricted to how agricultural growth impacts the poor outside the agricultural sector. This would be justified by the fact that agricultural value added already includes the increased income of poor farmers and poor farm workers. However, for the sake of comprehensiveness, we shall also consider the impact of agricultural growth on the poor who depend directly on agriculture.[1] This has the added benefit of allowing us to compare agriculture with other sectors in terms of the distribution of the sectoral value added and answers the question: is agricultural income better distributed than income generated in other sectors?

In the context of this study, we cannot comprehensively and exhaustively cover the enormous variety of structural conditions and policies that affect the poverty impact of agricultural growth. Rather, we focus on selected issues that we believe are important for future empirical studies. Although market and government policy failures are often key factors behind the persistence of poverty in most countries, in this analysis we consider market failures mostly in an implicit manner. The emphasis is on the identification of conditions under which agricultural growth affects poverty *changes*, not on what determines poverty.

2.2   AGRICULTURE AND THE POOR

Poverty is usually more widespread and more intense in rural than in urban areas. In most developing countries the majority of the poor still live in rural areas. Agriculture and agricultural-related activities provide most of the employment in rural areas. The high rural poverty rates may thus imply that agricultural jobs are poorly paid and that the sector tends to employ mostly unskilled workers, which constitute the majority of the poor. It also means that increasing agricultural growth may have a large positive impact on poverty. It has been shown, however, that returns to schooling in rural areas are indeed low (López and Valdés, 2000). This may imply that the returns to schooling in agriculture are also quite low. People in rural areas can obtain higher returns to schooling mainly by migrating into urban areas.

In a sense, agricultural growth can alleviate poverty only temporarily. Poverty may be reduced as labor productivity in agriculture expands, but the potential of this sector (and any other sector, for that matter) to permit unskilled workers to attain truly adequate standards of living is limited. Unskilled workers that achieve incomes above the poverty line usually remain highly vulnerable to even moderate economy-wide, sectoral and household-specific shocks. Indeed the long-term solution to poverty is not through higher incomes for unskilled workers, but through more schooling and technical training to make the unskilled become skilled workers.

2.2.1   The Structure of Agriculture and the Rural Sector

The rural sector is not homogeneous. For our purposes, there are at least three important rural sectors to recognize, at least in middle- and low-income countries: (i) the farm subsistence or semi-subsistence, mostly self-employed sector that produces a combination of food staples and commercial goods; (ii) the commercial farm sector comprising medium- and large-size farmers that gives employment to a significant part of the rural landless. This sector usually exploits the best lands and uses modern technologies; and (iii) the rural non-farm sector.

Sector (i) includes indigenous communities, a significant proportion of whose land is held in common property, minifundistas and rural frontier households. Sector (ii) usually provides seasonal employment to an important part of the rural labor force, many of them coming from sector (i). Thus, sectors (i) and (ii) are not independent from each other since many small-farm households in sector (i) complement their cultivation income through work in the commercial sector. Moreover, at times, the commercial sector has been developed by appropriating large tracts of land from sector

(i) using both legal and illegal means. In certain areas this process of land concentration is still taking place.

Sector (ii) is the one that provides the backward and forward linkages of agriculture into the input-provider sectors as well as the agricultural processing and service sectors (Mellor and Desai, 1985; Timmer, 1992). Importantly, these 'linkage industries' tend also to be quite intensive in unskilled labor. Sector (ii) has traditionally been the focus of government support (irrigation, credit, tax incentives and so on) and policies, while in most cases only part of sector (i) (usually the segment considered to have agriculture potential) receives limited public support, mainly in the form of technical assistance and some credit.

Sector (iii), the rural non-farm sector, varies quite significantly in size across countries, but in some places it can be as important as agriculture itself in terms of GDP and employment. This sector not only includes industries that provide agricultural inputs and process agricultural outputs but also covers a vast array of services and small manufacturing activities that are not directly dependent on agriculture (Lanjouw, 2000). Despite its large size, sector (iii) is rarely the focus of public policies and support programs.

2.2.2 Agricultural Growth and the Real Wage of the Unskilled in Non-farm Rural Areas and Urban Sectors

With the exception of the informal service sector and construction, agriculture is generally the most unskilled labor-intensive sector in the economy. Because of this, agriculture often provides the basic opportunity cost for unskilled workers for the whole economy. Unskilled workers in urban areas, workers employed in the rural non-farm sector and the unemployed have, as a last resort, the possibility of returning to the farm sector where they may find work. Thus, a very important role of agriculture is the provision of an opportunity cost or floor wage for the unskilled working outside agriculture in both the rural or urban sectors. This effectively contributes to setting wage rates for the unskilled in *all* sectors of the economy, not only in agriculture. Increasing agricultural growth and productivity is likely to benefit both urban and rural poor by inducing higher real wages for the unskilled in urban as well as rural areas.

By considering agriculture as dictating, or at least playing a key role in the determination of the market wage rate for unskilled labor for the whole economy, we place the importance of agriculture for poverty alleviation in the right perspective. Since, as shown by profiles of the poor around the world, most of the poor are unskilled workers and depend on their wage income for their survival, a fast-growing agriculture could dramatically help alleviate poverty in rural as well as urban areas. This general equilibrium effect, which gives agriculture a crucial role in setting economy-wide unskilled wages, may explain the large elasticities of poverty with respect to agricultural growth estimated by several studies (see, for example, Ravallion and Datt, 1996 with evidence for India or Kakwani, 1993, for Côte d'Ivoire).

An interesting finding of some empirical studies is that the effect of agriculture growth in reducing *urban* poverty is also very large, almost 50 percent as large as its effect on rural poverty itself (Ravallion and Datt, 1996). Although the general equilibrium wage effect is rarely fully recognized, it is evident that the direct effect of migration alone cannot account for such a large reduction of urban poverty. The indirect effect of migration via the market wage rate is perhaps more important. In a more recent study on India, Datt and Ravallion (1998) found that growth of agricultural productivity led to large wage increases and that the wage mechanism explains an important share of the poverty-reducing effect of agricultural productivity. By contrast, Balisacan (1993) shows that the accelerated agricultural growth of the 1960s and 1970s in the Philippines had a relatively small poverty-reducing effect due to the fact that real wages failed to increase. Thus, fast agricultural growth may not cause increases in real wages if other factors (for example, rapid increase of the labor force or certain policy and market failures) operate against it. Studies by Bardhan (1984) and Van de Walle (1985) confirm the importance of real wages for the unskilled as a key factor in decreasing poverty.

If agricultural growth is based mostly in the commercial sector and not in the rest of the farm economy, it is possible that this wage effect would be considerably dampened. This is particularly the case when a high concentration of land may lead to oligopsonistic rural labor markets. Some Indian evidence provided by Bardhan (1984) shows that the poverty-reducing effect of agricultural growth may be weaker as a consequence of these factors.

There are studies that document a significant decline in poverty without rising real wage rates for the unskilled. Lipton (1993) provides evidence for Indonesia, Egypt and Kenya for 1950–75 where real farm wages show no clear upward trend while rural poverty falls. Ravallion and Huppi (1991) show a similar pattern for Java in the 1980s. However, as Lipton and Ravallion (1995) conclude, this evidence shows not that 'poverty incidence is unaffected by the real wage rate for unskilled labor, *ceteris paribus*, but rather that other variables also matter to the outcome for the poor' (p. 592).

2.2.3 Non-wage Effects on Poverty of Agricultural Growth

Direct effects on smallholders

Apart from the wage effect, agricultural growth has a direct effect on small-holders (who are generally poor) to the extent that productivity increases through such mechanisms as green revolution new technologies, public investment in agricultural infrastructure and improvement of agricultural terms of trade.

There are many examples of rapid agricultural growth based on the economic growth of the smallholder sector. In Asia, in certain parts of India, Indonesia, China, Korea and others where wealth distribution, particularly land distribution, is not too concentrated and rural population density is high, agriculture is largely based on small farmers. In these cases, agricultural income growth and smallholders' income growth tend to be positively correlated, so agricultural growth is closely associated with increased productivity of small farmers.

In other countries, however, particularly in Latin America and Africa, overall agricultural growth and small-farmer productivity increases are less correlated. In countries with highly inequitable rural wealth and land distribution, power is highly concentrated among the large commercial farmers who are often able to induce the state to allocate public resources to their advantage. This is frequently translated into allocations of public support that are heavily biased toward the commercial farm sector. Public investments in irrigation, agricultural research, technological diffusion and rural infrastructure often target the commercial farm sector rather than the smallholders. Furthermore, credit market failures prevent smallholders' access to adequate levels of liquid capital necessary to respond to economic incentives via expanded investments. These land market imperfections combined with policy failures induce a highly segmented land market that prevents smallholders from expanding their landholdings even if they are able to obtain a higher marginal and average productivity of the land (Carter and Zegarra, 2000).

Thus, we can hypothesize that the direct poverty-reducing effect of agricultural growth on poor farmers is likely to decrease where land is more concentrated. One may also postulate that poverty reduction is more dependent on the real wage effect as land and other assets in the rural sector are more concentrated. When rural assets are highly concentrated, agricultural growth tends to be focused mostly on the commercial farm sector. In this case, the dominant factor is likely to be an increased labor demand from the commercial farm sector which causes wages to increase even if the supply of labor (mostly from the smallholder sector) is not much affected by agricultural growth. Real wages may rise in both cases, whether or not land and other rural assets are concentrated. However, the increase in real wages can be considerably reduced if the high concentration of rural assets leads to oligopsonistic labor market structures. In this case the poverty-reducing effect of agricultural growth would be much more modest. Thus, poverty reduction is less dependent on the wage effect when rural assets are more equitably distributed than when they are not.

The vast majority of the analyses that measure the impact of agricultural growth on poverty have focused on countries such as India, Indonesia, China, and others that have a relatively more equitable distribution of land and other rural assets. The findings in these cases are that the poverty-reduction effect of agricultural growth is still large even if real wages are kept constant. In this respect, the above-mentioned study by Balisacan (1993) in the Philippines is very important. The Philippines is one of the few countries in Asia where the highly biased land distribution is more akin to that prevailing in Latin America than that in other Asian countries. Unlike the findings for other Asian countries, where poverty has declined despite that fact that real wages have not increased, Balisacan shows that the failure to increase real wages in the Philippines is a key reason for poverty's low response to agricultural growth. The contrast between the case of the Philippines and that of other Asian countries supports the hypothesis of an inverse (direct) relationship between the relative import-ance of the small farmers' (wage) effect and agricultural growth in poverty reduction.

Rural non-farm 'linkage' effects

An important segment of the rural non-farm sector (sector (iii)) is linked to the farm sector because the former is a major provider of agricultural inputs and processor of farm products. But, perhaps more importantly, it is because the rural non-farm sector produces services and non-agricultural goods whose demand levels are heavily dependent on the income of farmers and farm workers (Lanjouw, 2000). Much of the non-farm sector com-prises small industries and service providers that exploit rural 'market niches' that may exist as a consequence of high transportation costs and relatively small volumes of consumption, which give local industries some advantages over large non-rural providers.

Employment and the income levels of local suppliers are thus closely linked to the performance of the agricultural sector. Many non-farm-level suppliers have low skills and are poor. Thus, an additional contribution of agriculture to reducing poverty is caused by the increased demand from agriculture that contributes to raising the income of poor non-farm rural producers.

Food price and 'linkage' effects

A third channel by which agricultural growth affects poverty is its effect on food prices as well as its effect on related industries (fertilizers, pesticides, equipment, food processing and so on). Higher agricultural output causes lower real food prices (benefiting the urban poor, while mitigating benefits to poor farmers) and increases demand for inputs, and the supply of raw food to agro-processing sectors. These are the so-called 'linkage effects'. It is important to note that the vehicle for these linkages is mostly, but not exclusively, prices. Increased agricultural production raises the demand for fertilizer, for example, and this benefits domestic producers of fertilizers mainly because the price of fertilizers increases. There may also exist, in the short run, a non-price effect if capacity is underutilized due to 'price stickiness' or other market imperfections.

In general, both the food-price effect and the linkage effect of agricultural growth are greatly diminished by the degree of openness to international trade. The more open an economy is, the smaller the domestic food-price effect and the less dependent the suppliers of agricultural inputs and agro-processors from domestic agriculture.[2] This dependence may still exist to some degree in an open economy, given that transportation costs introduce a price range (world price ± transportation costs) over which the domestic price may fluctuate. The more advanced the transportation infrastructure (ports, roads and so on) servicing international trade and the less geographically isolated a country is, the narrower this range is. Thus, in middle-income countries (such as most of Latin America), which are characterized by highly open trade regimes and relatively good transportation infrastructure, the food price and linkage effects as poverty-reducing mechanisms associated with agricultural growth are not likely to be large. At the time when most of the data used by recent studies were obtained (typically from 1960 to the early 1990s), countries such as India and China were largely closed to international trade. This explains the relatively important food price mechanism behind poverty reduction that is implicit in some of these studies.

2.2.4 Sectoral Policies and the Efficiency of Agricultural Growth to Reduce Poverty

The larger the subsistence sector (subsector (i)) the greater the downward pressure exerted on the wages paid by commercial agriculture and the 'linkage sectors'. Similarly, the more forsaken subsector (i) is in terms of infrastructure, policies and other forms of public support, the less likely it is that agricultural growth will include such a sector. That is, the direct poverty-reducing effects of agricultural growth on smallholders is likely to be weaker. Further, labor productivity in sector (i) will increase by less, thus rendering more precarious the negotiating ability of this sector's workers elsewhere in the economy. Additionally, agricultural growth that is based on policies that neglect sector (i) will directly benefit fewer farm households and, therefore, the linkage effect on the rural non-farm sector is going to be

weaker. This is because most of the demand for the rural non-farm production comes from relatively poor farm households as wealthier households usually are able to buy from national providers instead of rural ones.
Thus, policy neglect of sector (i) implies that the poverty-reducing effect of
agricultural growth on the rural non-farm sector is likely to be weak.

Another point to be considered is that policies which artificially reduce
the cost of machinery and equipment in the commercial farm sector (such
as credit subsidies, investment subsidies, tax exemptions and so on) cause
the sector to become less labor intensive and more capital intensive. In such
a policy environment, growth of the commercial agricultural sector will be
less effective in increasing smallholder income and the unskilled market
wage rate and, therefore, less effective in reducing poverty.

Traditional macro policies (documented, for example, by Krueger et al.,
1988) consisting of taxing agriculture through exchange rate overvaluation
and trade protectionism coupled with partial compensation via sectoral
policies such as tax exemptions, credit subsidies and investment subsidies,
could not have been worse for the poor. The macro biases slowed down
agricultural growth while the compensating sectoral policies (mostly targeting the commercial farm sector) made growth more capital intensive and
less unskilled labor intensive. Although most countries have removed anti-
agriculture macro biases, sectoral policies that induce an artificially high
capital intensity of commercial agriculture remain in place. Additionally,
in several countries sectoral policies generate incentives that favor capital-
intensive activities such as cattle operations and discriminate against labor-
intensive crops (Heath and Binswanger, 1996).

As for most other sectoral policies, public support of agricultural
research tends to serve mostly commercial agriculture. Public research is
highly limited and generally neglects the needs of sector (i). This, of course,
prevents productivity growth in this sector and reduces the potential for
subsistence and semi-subsistence farmers to increase their income and
attain higher wages elsewhere in the economy. The same is true of public
investment in irrigation and other infrastructure, which are mostly directed
to commercial farmers neglecting sector (i). Agricultural growth can
become more pro-poor if public investments are allocated in a more balanced way. It is not clear whether this more balanced allocation of public
investment and other forms of support would imply a trade-off with the
overall rate of growth of agriculture. That is, whether a reallocation of
public resources from sector (ii) to sector (i) would necessarily entail slower
growth of agriculture. This is an important question that requires country-
level study. What is clear is that removing the remaining policy distortions
that favor capital-intensive technologies in commercial agricultural is both
pro-poor and pro-efficiency and perhaps pro-growth too.

2.3 MEASUREMENT ISSUES

2.3.1 Poverty Measures and Approaches

Numerous empirical studies evaluating the poverty effects of agricultural growth permit us to draw some important methodological lessons. First, some general features. Most studies rely on periodical household surveys covering time spans of longer than one and a half decades. They evaluate elasticities of poverty with respect to agricultural growth; some, such as Ravallion and Datt (1996), compare the impact of agricultural growth with that of other sectors and growth of total GDP. The vast majority of the studies estimate elasticities of poverty with respect to sectoral growth mostly using, alternatively, three measures of poverty: head count ratio (HC), poverty gap (PG) and Foster–Grear–Thorbecke (FGT) ($\alpha = 2$). The HC measures only the proportion of people below the poverty line; PG also includes the distance between the poverty line and the average consumption of the poor; FGT ($\alpha = 2$) is also a poverty gap measure but, because of its quadratic nature, it accounts for income distribution within the poor (alternatively, some studies use a Sen index which incorporates a Gini index of the poor in combination with the gap).

2.3.2 Methodologies and Empirical Findings

Two approaches have been used for estimating the impact of economic growth (both sectoral and national) on poverty: (a) a reduced-form econometric approach where various factors, including agricultural growth, are used as explanatory variables of a poverty equation. Limited efforts are made to separate the various mechanisms by which such factors affect poverty; (b) a statistical decomposition analysis where changes of additive measures of poverty are decomposed into changes due to variation in mean consumption levels and changes in inequality.

Reduced-form econometric approaches
One of the most important methodological concerns regarding the econometric approach is the possibility of biases arising from simultaneity in the determination of growth and poverty and from omitted variables. Instrumental variables, sometimes combined with fixed effects, are the prime methods used to deal with these potential biases.

The article by Bell and Rich (1994) is one of the most important from the point of view of the approach used. This paper distinguishes itself by explicitly accounting for the issue of serial dependence of the poverty variable that may reflect the existence of chronic poverty among an important segment of society. Their estimation is, therefore, dynamic by allowing lagged poverty levels as explanatory variables in the poverty equation. This allows the authors to estimate short- and long-run poverty elasticities, showing that the latter tend to be much larger than the former. This large difference between short- and long-run elasticities suggests not only the existence of structural or chronic poverty but also that agricultural growth, if sustained over time, can be effective in reducing even structural poverty. An additional feature, also incorporated by other authors, is the emphasis on controlling for inflation as an important variable that increases poverty.

Another important study is that of Ravallion and Datt (1996) for India. It formally tests the hypothesis that agricultural (primary sector) growth is as effective in reducing poverty as overall economic growth. The study also compares the poverty-reduction effect of agricultural growth to those of industry (secondary sector) and services (tertiary sector). The authors find that agricultural growth is statistically much more effective in reducing poverty than either total growth or secondary sector growth. They found elasticities of national poverty with respect to agricultural growth of the order of –1.2 to –1.9. Most strikingly, they estimated elasticities of about –0.4 to –0.5 for *urban* poverty with respect to agricultural growth, thus confirming the importance of the economy-wide wage and perhaps food-price effects of agriculture. By contrast, growth of the secondary sector appears to increase rather than reduce poverty. An important advantage of Ravallion and Datt's methodology is that the estimated elasticities incorporate *all* direct and indirect effects of growth on poverty, including income distribution and general equilibrium effects.

Statistical decomposition analyses
Other studies focus on a statistical decomposition of poverty changes between the effect of changes in mean consumption or income and the effect of changes in inequality. The study by Kakwani (1993) in Côte d'Ivoire is representative of this approach (see also Thorbecke and Jung, 1996, for Indonesia). This approach relies less on reduced-form econometrics and more on statistical calculations based on the household sample data. Kakwani, however, estimates a Lorenz curve as an intermediate step to facilitate the calculations. The problem with this approach is that it is very difficult to estimate the effect of growth on inequality. Indeed, most measures of inequality are valid only under certain assumptions. Also, it is difficult in practice to precisely estimate the effect of growth on whatever measure of inequality is used.

For this reason, Kakwani just simulates the effect of changing inequality on poverty but does not derive the effect of growth on the Lorenz curve (Kakwani's estimate of the Lorenz curve is purely definitional, relating the income shares to population shares; she does not try to establish relationships to growth or other economic variables). In any case, Kakwani found that poverty is very sensitive to economic growth, assuming a constant level of inequality. But poverty was found to be even more sensitive to changes in inequality – three times more sensitive. Hence, economic growth accompanied by even modest increases in inequality can be deleterious for the poor.

Additionally, agricultural growth is even more influential in reducing poverty than overall growth. Changes in the terms of trade in favor of agriculture were extremely positive for poverty alleviation in Côte d'Ivoire. A very important observation made by Kakwani is the following: the main reason why poverty is so sensitive to mean income (elasticity with respect to mean income was about –3.0) is that there is a large clustering of the population's income in the neighborhood of the poverty line. Moreover, the even greater effect of agriculture is mostly because the poor are largely concentrated in rural areas. The nature of the approach does not allow the estimation of indirect effects of agricultural growth. For example, the analysis simply measures how household income in rural areas increases due to a 1 percent increase in agricultural income in the absence of redistribution. It does not account for indirect effects explicitly, in particular for the real wage effect of agricultural expansion. This may grossly underestimate the effect of agriculture on poverty reduction.

2.4 CONCLUSION

The empirical evidence on the effect of economic growth on poverty alleviation suggests that the effect is large, with elasticities that often exceed one. At the same time, studies coincide in indicating that poverty is highly sensitive to changes in income distribution. The effect of sectoral growth is less frequently estimated, but the few studies that have dealt with this issue indicate that agricultural growth is one of the most pro-poor forms of economic growth. Unfortunately, the sectoral evidence covers only a handful of countries, mostly located in Asia. There is a dearth of empirical sectoral studies for Latin American and sub-Saharan African countries.

The importance of broadening the spectrum of countries analyzed is high because, as shown in this chapter, the effectiveness of agricultural growth as a poverty-reducing mechanism depends on a number of factors that tend to be quite heterogeneous across countries. One example is rural wealth distribution, including land distribution, which impinges upon the degree of heterogeneity of farm producers. The more homogeneous the structure of producers in agriculture, the more effective agricultural growth is in reducing rural poverty. Since the majority of the studies concern India and other Asian countries where the structure of agriculture tends to be more homogeneous than in most other continents, it is an open question whether the estimated high poverty elasticities are also valid for countries such as Brazil or Colombia where agriculture is highly segmented and growth is likely to be based on the richer commercial farm sector rather than on smallholders.

Another important factor affecting poverty impacts is the degree of openness to trade and transportation costs. The more closed to trade an economy is and the higher the transportation costs are, the more likely it is that the food price and other linkage effects of agriculture will be high. A significant part of the data used in estimating the poverty elasticities in Asia corresponds to periods when the economy was relatively closed. An important question is whether these estimated large elasticities would apply to countries that are more open, and even whether they would apply to the formerly closed countries now that they have become open.

A third obvious factor, not discussed in the text, is the size of agriculture, and particularly its importance in terms of employment share in national employment. In middle-income economies, such as most of the large economies in Latin America, agriculture is much less important a source of employment than in most countries where previous studies have been developed. This is another reason why the existing elasticities may not apply to Latin America. Fourth, policies such as credit subsidies, allocation of public investment, and special tax treatment mainly to large commercial farmers are likely to affect the responsiveness of poverty to agricultural growth. The implication of this discussion is that in choosing countries for case studies, diversity in the above set of conditions should be taken into account.

Finally, future studies should carefully consider the following important issue that is outside the scope of this chapter: after measuring elasticities of poverty reduction with respect to agricultural growth, the question of how to value the welfare impact of such a poverty-reduction effect remains. One way of doing this is to consider poverty as an explicit element of a social welfare function. The key question is what such social welfare function should be, particularly what is the weight to be attributed to the income of the poor? One possibility is to measure aggregate income change, using as weights the population shares by deciles or quintiles and *not* the income value shares. This, of course, significantly increases the weight of the poor as their income value shares are much lower than their population shares. If such a social welfare function is used and if agricultural growth is more pro-poor than the rest of the economy, then the newly measured contribution of agriculture to social welfare would be higher than that using conventional national accounts data. The poverty-reduction value of agricultural growth would be approximately equal to the difference between its contribution to the new social welfare function and the conventional social welfare as measured by income in national accounts. In any case, this is just one way of valuing the enhanced poverty-reduction contribution of agriculture. There are certainly many other ways of doing this, depending on the specification for the social welfare function chosen.

Those skeptical about using explicit social welfare functions to value poverty alleviation, can use contingent valuation methods. To do this, it is necessary to use willingness-to-pay surveys by (non-poor) people for poverty reduction. Then the value of poverty reduction could be interpolated from the figures obtained by such surveys.

NOTES

1. Since the approach consists in decomposing the various mechanisms or effects by which agricultural growth affects the poor, if one wants to isolate the truly external poverty effects this can be done by simply subtracting the effect on the agricultural poor. Besides, as we shall see, most of the 'poverty externalities' are the result of market effects; that is, they are properly pecuniary externalities.
2. One could also claim that the wage effect is also greatly weakened by openness to international trade. This argument relies on factor price equalization (FPE) where commodity prices dictate factor prices. However, FPE relies on assumptions that are empirically highly implausible. The FPE hypothesis is often rejected by most empirical studies. Even within the confines of FPE, factor prices can be affected by productivity growth.

REFERENCES

Balisacan, A. (1993), 'Agricultural growth, landlessness, off-farm employment, and rural poverty in the Philippines', *Economic Development and Cultural Change*, **43**(3): 534–59.

Bardhan, P. (1984), *Land, Labor and Rural Poverty*, New York: Columbia University Press.

Bell, C. and R. Rich (1994), 'Rural poverty and aggregate agricultural performance in post-independence India', *Oxford Bulletin of Economics and Statistics*, **56**(2): 111–33.

Carter, M. and E. Zegarra (2000), 'Land markets and the persistence of rural poverty: post-liberalization policy options', in López and Valdés (eds), pp. 65–85.

Datt, G. and M. Ravallion (1998), 'Farm productivity and rural poverty in India', *Journal of Development Studies*, **34**(4): 62–85.

Heath, J. and H. Binswanger (1996), 'Natural resource degradation effects of poverty are largely policy-induced: the case of Colombia', *Environment and Development Economics*, **1**(1): 65–84.

Kakwani, N. (1993), 'Poverty and economic growth with application to Côte d'Ivoire', *Review of Income and Wealth*, **75**(4): 121–39.

Krueger, A., M. Schiff and A. Valdés (1988), 'Agricultural incentives in developing countries: measuring the effects of sectoral and economy-wide policies', *World Bank Economic Review*, **2**(3): 255–71.

Lanjouw, P. (2000), 'Rural non-agricultural employment and poverty in Latin America', in López and Valdés (eds), pp. 99–119.

Lipton, M. (1993), 'Land reform as commenced business: the evidence against stopping', *World Development*, **21**(4): 641–57.

Lipton, M. and M. Ravallion (1995), 'Poverty and policy', in J. Behrman and T.N. Srinivasan (eds), *Handbook of Development Economics*, London: Elsevier Science, pp. 2551–657.

López, R. and A. Valdés (eds) (2000), *Rural Poverty in Latin America*, London: Macmillan and New York: St Martin's Press.

Mellor, J. and G. Desai (1985), *Agricultural Change and Rural Poverty*, Baltimore, MD: Johns Hopkins University Press.

Ravallion, M. and G. Datt (1996), 'How important to India's poor is the sectoral composition of growth?', *World Bank Economic Review*, **10**(1): 1–26.

Ravallion, M. and M. Huppi (1991), 'Measuring changes in poverty: a methodological case study of Indonesia during an adjustment period', *World Bank Economic Review*, **5**(1): 57–84.

Thorbecke, E. and H. Jung (1996), 'A multiplier decomposition method to analyze poverty alleviation', *Journal of Development Economics*, **48**(2): 279–300.

Timmer, C.P. (1992), 'Agriculture and economic development revisited', *Agricultural Systems*, **40**(1): 21–58.

Van de Walle, D. (1985), 'Population growth and poverty: another look at the Indian time series', *Journal of Development Studies*, **21**(3): 429–39.

PART II

Country case studies

3. Chile

Ramón López and Gustavo Anríquez

3.1 INTRODUCTION

The objective of this chapter is to quantitatively analyze the role of agriculture in reducing poverty. Following the methodology proposed by López (2002), we consider three channels by which agricultural growth can affect poverty, namely its effects on the real wage of unskilled workers (and/or its possible effect in reducing their unemployment), the direct impact of agricultural growth upon the income of poor farmers and its effect on real food prices. The latter effect is mostly relevant for food items that are not traded. That is, for commodities that due to large transaction costs or to government policies have endogenous domestic prices.

We first econometrically estimate the impact of agricultural growth on the real wage of unskilled workers, its employment level, real food prices and income of poor farmers. Next we simulate how such changes impact the income of the poor and how they affect the extent and depth of poverty. We consider a benchmark case based on the current situation and then using the same methodology we simulate how poverty would have changed if agricultural and agro-processing output had been higher than it actually was. Also, we consider how increasing the share of agriculture and agro-processing in total GDP would affect poverty. The idea is to test the hypothesis that a shift in the composition of national output toward agriculture (keeping total national output constant) is pro-poor and to measure the quantitative importance of such effect if the hypothesis is not rejected.

The remainder of the chapter is organized as follows: Section 2 provides a general overview of the evolution of poverty in Chile over the last decade and a half. This section also discusses general economic trends. Section 3 presents the econometric estimates of the labor demand equations which are the basis for most of the exercise. Section 4 reports on the estimates of food prices and some estimates of the contribution of agriculture to the income of poor farmers. In each section we present poverty simulations separating each of the three channels mentioned above. We also present the consolidated effects of all mechanisms on extent and depth of poverty. Section 7 concludes.

3.2   POVERTY PROFILE (1987–2000)

During the 1990s the Chilean economy underwent a period of fast economic expansion which translated into a successful poverty-reduction experience. As shown in Table 3.1, except for the last two years of the century,
which showed a slowdown, per capita GDP experienced rapid growth.
Agricultural growth, however, slowed down from 1994 onward.

As seen in Table 3.2, most poverty measures show a sharp reduction. We
focus on the FGT (Foster–Greer–Thorbecke) class of poverty indicators.
See the technical appendix for the definition of the FGT indices of poverty
and a discussion of their merits and weaknesses.

We measure poverty using the official poverty line developed by the
Economic Commission for Latin America and the Caribbean (ECLAC)
and the Chilean Ministry of Planning (Table 3.2). Additionally, for
international comparison purposes in Table 3.3 we measure poverty
using a standard poverty line equivalent to US$2 per day. The following
discussion centers on the first two indicators. The official poverty line
is equal to two minimum food baskets for urban areas. A separate
food basket is calculated for rural areas, where food prices are lower,
and the poverty line is calculated as 1.75 times the value of the rural
basket of food, as it is assumed that the cost of services is lower in rural
areas.

At the beginning of the period less than one-fifth of the population was
considered rural, and by the end of the period the proportion of rural
population fell to about one-sixth. This is in part due to a change of
definition of rural locations that took place in 1996. Prior to 1996, locations with fewer than 2000 inhabitants were considered rural. From 1996
onwards the definition of rural changed to locations with fewer than 1000
inhabitants or between 1000 and 2000, where less than 50 percent of the

*Table 3.1   Income growth: national and agricultural related sectors
           (annual %)*

	87/90	90/92	92/94	94/96	96/98	98/2000
Per capita GDP growth	5.4	8.3	4.6	7.4	4.2	0.8
Agricultural per capita GDP growth	7.3	4.5	2.7	1.7	−0.1	0.7
Agriculture + food processing per capita GDP growth	5.7	6.8	3.3	3.2	−0.4	N/A

Table 3.2   Poverty and inequality

	1987	1990	1992	1994	1996	1998	2000
Total population							
Poverty							
Head count – FGT(0)	46.08	38.46	32.43	27.4	23.13	21.62	20.58
Income gap	42.55	38.36	34.93	35.31	33.65	34.48	34.52
Poverty gap – FGT(1)	19.61	14.75	11.33	9.67	7.78	7.46	7.1
FGT(2)	11.18	7.86	5.57	4.96	3.83	3.78	3.71
Inequality							
GINI	56.74	0.5523	54.97	55.18	55.22	55.88	55.83
Coefficient of variability	1.6789	1.8636	1.8027	3.3318	1.7495	1.8556	1.9319
Rural population							
% rural	19.47	18.55	18.04	16.54	16.12	14.57	14.14
Poverty							
Head count – FGT(0)	53.47	39.37	33.37	30.8	30.57	27.57	23.82
Income gap	40.15	37.06	32.42	33.5	33.37	32.88	34.62
Poverty gap – FGT(1)	21.47	14.59	10.82	10.32	10.2	9.06	8.25
FGT(2)	11.52	7.83	5.03	5.11	4.95	4.33	4.28
Inequality							
GINI	49.02	57.73	50.69	50.38	49.27	49.69	51.08
Coefficient of variability	2.0213	2.6651	2.1475	2.2339	1.7090	3.1124	2.8564

Note: Authors' calculations using CASEN surveys.

Table 3.3   Internationally comparable poverty measures (US$2 per day poverty line)

Total population	1987	1990	1992	1994	1996	1998	2000
Head count – FGT(0)	43.62	33.22	26.04	23.91	20.23	18.79	17.57
Income gap	42.7	37.53	33.74	34.49	33.96	34.7	34.95
Poverty gap – FGT(1)	18.62	12.46	8.79	8.25	6.87	6.52	6.14
FGT(2)	10.61	6.55	4.25	4.23	3.41	3.33	3.25

Note: Authors' calculations using CASEN surveys. A 2 US dollars of 1994 per day line was used for the above calculations.

economically active population is employed in secondary (industry) and tertiary (services) activities. Thus, rural numbers are not strictly comparable between 1987–94 and 1996–2000.[1]

As shown in Table 3.2, the incidence of poverty shows a marked reduction; in less than a decade from 1987 to 1996 it was halved from

46 to 23 percent. The poverty gap and the FGT(2) indicators have also shown similarly impressive reductions during the period. However, looking at the income gap, one can see that this indicator fell during the 1987–92 period; after that it remained relatively stable at around 34–35 percent. This indicates that the reductions of the FGT(1) and FGT(2) indicators after 1992 are due mainly to reductions of the incidence of poverty, and not to reductions in its depth. Rural poverty, on the other hand has shown a similarly fast reduction pattern. Except for the 1994–96 period, rural poverty has fallen throughout the 1990s even during the last two years of the century when the economy overall slowed down.

Although it has been a stated objective of the governments of the period, there have not been important improvements in inequality. The more broadly used Gini coefficient shows a slight improvement from 1987 to 1992, but followed by an increase in inequality from 1994 onwards. The coefficient of variability that applies a greater weight to distances in the upper tail, that is to the richest, shows a steady increase in the period. The exception is 1994, with an extremely low inequality level that may be due to a mis-sampling of the wealthiest in the 1994 CASEN (Caracterización Socioeconómica Naciona) survey.

3.3   ESTIMATING THE WAGE, PRICE AND DIRECT INCOME EFFECTS

3.3.1   The Structure of Labor Demand

We postulate that producers in the economy minimize the cost of production. There are two outputs being produced, agriculture and agroprocessing (Q_a), and everything else (Q_n). These outputs are produced using three variable factors of production, unskilled labor (L_u), skilled labor (L_s), and capital (K). Producers are assumed to be competitive, facing exogenously given factor prices (w_u for unskilled labor, w_s for skilled labor and w_r for the rental price of capital). The three factors of production are also assumed to be mobile across the two productive sectors and are allocated in such a way that their marginal products are equalized across the sectors. Under these assumptions cost minimization implies that there exists an aggregate dual cost function, $C(w_u, w_s, w_r; Q_a, Q_n; t)$, where t stands for the level of technology. The cost function must satisfy certain properties: it is non-decreasing, linearly homogeneous and concave in factor prices, and non-decreasing in each of the outputs (Diewert, 1971).

We specify a multi-output generalized Leontief (GL) form for the cost function, which is considered to be a flexible functional form (ibid.). GL is flexible because it does not impose a priori any form of separability or any restrictions on the elasticities of substitution among the factors of production. This is, in contrast for example with the highly popular Cobb–Douglas function, which a priori imposes that the marginal rate of substitution of all input pairs are independent of other inputs (separability) and that all elasticities of substitution are equal to one. Similarly, the constant elasticity of substitution (CES) function imposes all the above restrictions except that it allows for non-unitary but identical elasticity substitution among all input pairs. Imposing these restrictions reduces the reliability and usefulness of empirical estimates that rely on functional forms that are not flexible.

A specification for the multi-output GL is the following:

$$C = Q_a \sum_i \sum_j b_{ij}(w_i w_j)^{1/2} + Q_n \sum_i \sum_j c_{ij}(w_i w_j)^{1/2} + t Q_a \sum_i b_i w_i$$
$$+ t Q_n \sum_i c_i w_i + Q_a Q_n \sum_i d_i w_i, \tag{3.1}$$

where b_{ij}, c_{ij}, b_i, c_i and d_i $(i, j = u, s, r)$ are coefficients. The GL cost function a priori imposes linear homogeneity only in factor prices. All other properties of the cost function could in principle be tested. The implicit demand equations for unskilled and skilled labor are derived from (3.1) using Shephard's lemma:

$$L_s = \sum_j b_{sj}(w_j/w_s)^{1/2} Q_a + \sum_j c_{sj}(w_j/w_s)^{1/2} Q_n$$
$$+ b_s t Q_a + c_s t Q_n + d_s Q_a Q_n \tag{3.2}$$

$$L_u = \sum_j b_{uj}(w_j/w_u)^{1/2} Q_a + \sum_j c_{uj}(w_j/w_u)^{1/2} Q_n$$
$$+ b_u t Q_a + c_u t Q_n + d_u Q_a Q_n. \tag{3.3}$$

The linear homogeneity property of $C(\cdot)$ in (3.1) leads to factor demands that are homogeneous of degree zero in all factor prices. Also using Shephard's lemma, one could derive the demand for capital. However, we have data only for the price of capital but not for its quantity demanded. Therefore, we omit the equation for capital demand although we do use its rental price on the right-hand side of labor demand equations. Equations

(3.2) and (3.3) can be jointly estimated after imposing the symmetry conditions, $b_{ij}=b_{ji}$ and $c_{ij}=c_{ji}$.

3.3.2 Estimation Procedure

The labor demand equations (3.2) and (3.3) are estimated using data from CASEN surveys for the 1990–96 period. We have data for each one of the 13 regions of the country and for each one of the four years in which the survey was implemented (1990, 1992, 1994, 1996). That is, we have a regional data panel of 52 observations (13 regions × 4 periods) for each of the equation variables, except for the rental price of capital for which we have only annual prices for the whole country (but see below for an explanation of why this price can still be used in the panel estimates). We have data of total unskilled and skilled labor used in each region over the period; also from the CASEN survey we estimated wages for each one of the two types of labor. The distinction between skilled and unskilled labor was based on years of schooling: workers with schooling of less than eight years (primary and compulsory school in Chile) were considered 'unskilled' while workers with greater schooling are labeled 'skilled'. From other sources we were able to calculate regional GDP separated between agriculture and non-agricultural industries.

Also from non-CASEN sources we obtained implicit unit values of imported capital goods. The unit values for imported capital goods were used as proxies for the domestic price of capital.[2] These prices do not vary across regions and, in fact, the price of capital is not likely to change much across regions of the country. Despite the lack of variability across regions we still have enough variability of the *relative* factor prices to allow us to estimate cross-demand elasticities, for example, elasticities of labor demand with respect to the price of capital. This is due to the homogeneity condition derived from the theoretical restrictions arising from the assumption of cost minimization. As can be seen in (3.2) and (3.3), the two labor demand equations are explained by factor price ratios. The rental price of capital appears as w_r/w_s in (3.2) and w_r/w_u in (3.3). These ratios vary not only over time but, given that w_s and w_u change across regions as well, also across regions.

Table 3.4 shows the estimated coefficients for equations (3.2) and (3.3). In estimating these equations we have used a seemingly unrelated system (SUR). As can be seen in the table, the goodness-of-fit of the system is highly satisfactory as shown by the high level of significance of most coefficients. Moreover, the estimated coefficients are consistent with several of the properties of a cost function. The estimated cost function is monotonically increasing and concave in factor prices, and increasing in each one of the outputs.

Table 3.4   Estimates of the multi-output cost function (restricted SUR method)

	Coefficient	Standard error
b_{11}	571.65*	303.11
b_{12}	3.1445**	1.3778
b_{13}	−87.94	74.05
c_{11}	5.9092	36.0636
c_{12}	−0.0837	0.1926
c_{13}	4.5720	8.0695
b_1	−0.2865*	0.1516
c_1	−0.0029	0.0181
d_1	−2.4E−07	2.25E−07
b_{21}	3.1445**	1.3778
b_{22}	951.0**	280.0
b_{23}	−339.8**	93.5
c_{21}	−0.0837	0.1926
c_{22}	−113.50**	33.15
c_{23}	56.36**	10.42
b_2	−0.4734**	0.1397
c_2	0.0565**	0.0165
d_2	1.21E−06**	2.06E−07

Note: * significance at the 10% level; ** significance at the 5% level.

3.3.3   The Elasticities: Effects of Changes in Agricultural Output Level

Table 3.5a shows the elasticities of demand for unskilled and skilled labor implicit in the estimated coefficients and evaluated at sample means. It also presents the standard errors of these elasticities (note that the elasticities are functions of several coefficients) and their degree of statistical significance. As can be seen, the two labor demand equations are downward sloping with similar own-price elasticities of the order of −0.28.[3] Unskilled and skilled labor are substitute inputs as shown by the fact that the cross-price elasticities are both positive; the elasticity of unskilled labor demand with respect to skilled labor wage rate is about 0.63 while the elasticity of skilled labor demand with respect to the unskilled wage rate is about 0.21. All own prices as well as cross-demand elasticities are statistically significant at least at 10 percent.

Somewhat surprisingly, unskilled workers appear to be complements with capital, with an elasticity of labor demand with respect to the rental price of capital of −0.35. Skilled workers on the other hand, are marginally

Table 3.5a *Estimated labor demand elasticities (evaluated at sample means)*

	Unskilled labor	Skilled labor	Capital	Agricultural output	Non-agricultural output
Unskilled labor	-0.28*	0.63***	-0.35	0.66***	0.37***
	(0.1682)	(0.2103)	(0.2375)	(0.0906)	(0.0706)
Skilled labor	0.21***	-0.28**	0.07	0.43***	0.67***
	(0.0693)	(0.1126)	(0.1060)	(0.0490)	(0.0402)

Note: Standard errors in parentheses. *** Significant at the 1% level; ** Significant at the 5% level; * Significant at the 10% level.

Hypothesis tests

I. $H_0: \varepsilon_{uQ_a} - \varepsilon_{uQ_n} > 0$

$z: \dfrac{0.29}{0.1527} = 1.91**$

II. $H_0: \varepsilon_{sQ_a} - \varepsilon_{sQ_n} < 0$

$z: \dfrac{-0.25}{0.0842} = -2.92***$

III. $H_0: \varepsilon_{uQ_n} - \varepsilon_{sQ_n} > 0$

$z: \dfrac{0.24}{0.0670} = 3.55***$

IV. $H_0: \varepsilon_{uQ_n} - \varepsilon_{sQ_n} < 0$

$z: \dfrac{-0.30}{0.0508} = 5.91***$

Table 3.5b *Effects of technical change on labor demand (evaluated at sample means)*

	Technical change	Total output
Unskilled labor	-0.11***	1.04***
	(0.0294)	(0.0557)
Skilled labor	-0.02	1.10***
	(0.0162)	(0.0309)

Note: Standard errors in parentheses. *** Significant at the 1% level, ** Significant at the 5% level, * Significant at the 10% level.

substitutes for capital with an elasticity of skilled labor demand with respect to the rental price of capital of about 0.10. These elasticities, however, turn out not to be statistically significantly different from zero. That is, the two kinds of labor are neither substitutes for nor complements with capital. This suggests that the concern so often found in the literature about the potential displacement of labor by capital does not appear to be empirically grounded. In fact if the (Hicksian) elasticities of labor to capital price are zero, the output scale effect induced by a cheaper cost of capital should lead to an increased demand for labor.

The most important empirical finding is the asymmetric response of the two types of labor to output expansion in the agricultural and non-agricultural production. The demand for unskilled workers is much more sensitive to an expansion of agriculture than skilled workers. In fact, the elasticity of unskilled labor demand with respect to agricultural output is almost 0.67 compared to an elasticity for skilled labor of only 0.37. Additionally, unskilled labor demand is more responsive to agricultural than to non-agricultural output; while skilled labor exhibits opposite responses. The demand for unskilled labor is only about 50 percent as responsive to non-agricultural output as the demand for skilled labor. As shown in Table 3.5, all four labor demand elasticities with respect to output are statistically significant at the 1 percent level. Moreover, the null hypothesis that unskilled labor demand is more responsive to agricultural than non-agricultural output is accepted (not rejected) at the 5 percent level of significance and the hypothesis that skilled labor demand is more responsive to non-agricultural than to agricultural output is accepted at the 1 percent level. These results imply that increasing the share of agriculture in total output while keeping total output constant would lead to an expansion of employment of unskilled workers. That is, agricultural-based economic growth is more favorable for unskilled (usually poor) workers than economic growth with a stagnant agricultural sector.

Table 3.5a also suggests that the output scale elasticities (for example, the sum of the elasticities with respect to Q_a and Q_n) are remarkably close to 1 for the case of unskilled labor and about 1.1 for the case of skilled workers. In fact the output scale elasticities are not statistically different from 1. This suggests a very close link between overall economic growth and labor demand, with skilled labor demand being only slightly more responsive than unskilled labor demand. Thus, the apparent difficulties of the economy to create jobs is not necessarily related to low labor/output intensities.

What can explain the sluggish process of job creation over time despite relatively rapid output expansion may be technical change. Table 3.5b shows the effects of technical change (crudely measured here by a time trend) on the two labor demands. The impact of technological change on unskilled labor demand is indeed very large, negative and highly significant, while its effect on the demand for skilled workers is not statistically different from zero. That is, technical change seems to be heavily biased against unskilled labor. A possible reason for this could be the much discussed technological dependence of the Chilean economy. Chile expends little effort on research and development or the adaptation of new technologies. This means that it must rely on imported new technologies with little adaptation of them to the factor endowment reality of the country. Since most imported technologies come from developed countries, they tend to be heavily biased against labor which is a much more expensive factor there than in Chile.

3.3.4   Effect of Changes in Output Mix or Composition

To estimate the effect of a change in the *composition* of production towards the agricultural sector we proceed as follows: total output can be approximated by the following aggregator:

$$Q = Q_a^\gamma Q_n^{1-\gamma},$$

where γ is the weight of agriculture and agro-processing in aggregate output and $1 - \gamma$ is, of course, the corresponding share of all other sectors. Logarithmic differentiation yields:

$$d \ln Q = \gamma d \ln Q_a + (1 - \gamma)d \ln Q_n.$$

To consider the pure composition effect we allow a compensated change of Q_a so that Q does not change. This means that $d \ln Q = 0$. Hence, we get that to maintain total output constant the expansion of agriculture has to be compensated by a corresponding fall of Q_n. Hence,

$$\left. \frac{d \ln Q_n}{d \ln Q_a} \right|_{dQ=0} = \frac{-\gamma}{1-\gamma}.$$

Thus, the compensated logarithmic effect of Q_a on L_u is:

$$\left. \frac{d \ln L_u}{d \ln Q_a} \right|_{dQ=0} = \frac{\partial \ln L_u}{\partial \ln Q_a} + \frac{\partial \ln L_u}{\partial \ln Q_n} \left. \frac{\partial \ln Q_n}{\partial \ln Q_a} \right|_{dQ=0}. \tag{3.4}$$

From our estimates (Table 3.5) we have that $\partial \ln L_u / \partial \ln Q_a = 0.66$ and $\partial \ln L_u / \partial \ln Q_n = 0.37$. Also the share of agriculture/agro-processing in total GDP (γ) over the period was about 0.15. Hence,

$$\left. \frac{d \ln L_u}{d \ln Q_a} \right|_{dQ=0} = 0.66 - 0.37 \cdot \frac{0.15}{0.85} = 0.6.$$

That is, a 1 percent compensated increase in agricultural output (which needs a $0.15/0.85 = 0.17$ percent fall in non-agricultural output) induces an increase in the demand for unskilled workers of the order of 0.6 percent. In other words a 1 percent increase in the share of agriculture keeping total output constant raises the demand for unskilled workers by 0.6 percent.

3.3.5 Simulating Poverty Impacts of Agriculture through Labor Demand Mechanisms: The Assumptions

In this subsection we use the previous results to evaluate the impact of agricultural growth on poverty as measured by the head count index and the income gap of the poor relative to the poverty line. We do not have reliable estimates of unskilled labor supply elasticities for Chile. We have been able to find only one study for Chile that estimates a labor supply elasticity, Mizala et al., 1999. This means that we have little information to compare and evaluate the reliability of the findings in this study. For this reason we alternatively use two extreme assumptions that give the boundaries of these effects, and next we contrast them using the Mizala et al. estimate for the labor supply elasticity. In the first extreme case we assume that labor supply elasticity is zero, that is, supply of labor is fixed in which case only the wage rate changes. At the other extreme, labor supply is assumed completely elastic, in which case the wage rate is fixed and, as a consequence, the labor market may not clear and unemployment may prevail. In this second case the full adjustment is absorbed by employment change. This latter assumption is consistent, for example, with labor market regulations or binding minimum wages. Finally, we use the Mizala estimates of labor supply elasticity (1.8), which allows for wages and employment to adjust simultanously.

Fixed supply of unskilled workers
If the supply of unskilled labor is fixed and the wage rate adjusts to clear the labor market we have that the unskilled wage elasticity with respect to agricultural output is 2.35. This result is based on the elasticities provided in Table 3.5. That is, a 1 percent increase in agricultural output, *ceteris paribus*, will cause an increase in the wage rate of the unskilled of 2.35 percent. This elasticity is directly related to the size of the elasticity of L_u with respect to Q_a and inversely related to the own-price elasticity of unskilled labor demand.

The elasticity of the unskilled wage with respect to non-agricultural output is estimated in a similar way. Given the estimated elasticities in Table 3.5, we have that $\partial \ln w_u / \partial \ln Q_n = 1.32$. That is, the effect of non-agricultural output on the unskilled wage rate is only about 60 percent the value of the corresponding agricultural output elasticity.

The compensated wage effect of agricultural/agro-processing output keeping total output in the economy constant can be estimated as:

$$\frac{d\ln w_u}{d\ln Q_a} = \frac{\partial \ln w_u}{\partial \ln Q_a} + \frac{\partial \ln w_u}{\partial \ln Q_n}\frac{\partial \ln Q_n}{\partial \ln Q_a}\bigg|_{dQ=0}$$

$$= 2.35 - 1.3 \cdot \frac{0.15}{0.85} = 2.12. \tag{3.5}$$

That is, a change in the composition of GDP that increases the share of agriculture/agro-processing by 1 percent leads to an increase in the wage rate of the unskilled of 2.1 percent.

Fully elastic supply of unskilled workers
The above estimates will provide an upper bound of the poverty effect of agricultural growth. If the supply elasticity of labor is elastic instead of inelastic as assumed above, the wage effect of agricultural growth is smaller. In fact the larger is the labor supply elasticity, *ceteris paribus*, the smaller is the wage effect. The lower bound for the poverty effect occurs when the labor supply elasticity is infinity, in which case we only have an employment effect instead of a wage/employment effect. In this case the effect is an increase in employment with an elasticity equal to 0.66, while the compensated employment effect is 0.6.

The intermediate case
If the labor supply elasticity is neither 0 nor infinity, the wage effect of increasing agricultural output becomes:

$$\frac{d\ln w_u}{d\ln Q_a} = -\frac{\partial \ln L_u/\partial \ln Q_a}{\partial \ln L_u/\partial \ln w_u - \partial \ln L_u^s/\partial \ln w_u} = 0.43,$$

where $\partial \ln L_u^s/\partial \ln w_u$ is the labor supply elasticity. In addition, in this case there is also an employment effect which is:

$$\Delta \ln L_u = \frac{\partial \ln L_u^s}{\partial \ln w_u}\frac{d\ln w_u}{d\ln Q_a}\Delta \ln Q_a.$$

Simulation Results

From the previous analysis we estimated the elasticities of unskilled wage rates and employment with respect to agricultural growth. It was assumed that all unskilled and skilled workers benefited from their corresponding wage increase, which is translated into higher per capita household income.

The increased employment effect on the other hand, was simulated by adding the average wage rate per skill level to the incomes of those who are economically unemployed, and who are able to become employed. The number of individuals who become 'employed' in such a manner is determined by the corresponding labor elasticities. Also, each additional individual 'employed' will increase household income which may lead the household out of poverty (for example, the number of poor declines by the number of individuals in the household) or the increased household income may not be sufficient to bring its per capita income above poverty or the household may be already above the poverty line. Each new worker was randomly selected from the pool of unemployed. Thus, the household per capita income increases through these two channels, namely wage and employment effects. With this new household income profile we performed the new estimates for head count poverty, poverty gap and so on.

The first column of Table 3.6 provides the benchmark poverty situation in Chile in the year 2000. It includes head count poverty, the income gap of the poor, and also the proportion of the vulnerable population, defined as those whose income is less than the poverty line plus 20 percent, as well as their mean proportional income surplus above that line. The next three vertical blocks (I, II and III) in Table 3.6 show the simulation results under the three alternative assumptions for the case where agricultural output increases 4.5 percent, which has been the actual growth rate until the late 1990s. Within each block we present the uncompensated and compensated (constant aggregate output) effects. Blocks I and III show the simulation results under alternative extreme assumptions of fixed supply of unskilled labor (in which case the effect of agricultural growth is reflected on wage increases only) and an infinitely elastic supply consistent with unemployment caused, for example, by a binding minimum wage (in which case the effect of agricultural growth occurs via greater employment). In Block II we present the intermediate case that assumes a labor supply elasticity of 1.8 obtained from Mizala et al. (1999) (in which case agricultural expansion causes both higher wages and greater levels of employment).

The largest poverty-reduction impact of agricultural expansion occurs, as expected, in the case where the elasticity of labor supply is zero, that is when labor supply is fixed. The smallest poverty-reduction impact occurs when labor supply is fully elastic (for example, when minimum wages are binding and fully enforced) while the effect is intermediate (and closer to the infinite labor supply case as the supply elasticity assumed is rather high) when labor supply elasticity is assumed to be 1.8. Thus the poverty-reduction (measured by head count) change for the uncompensated agricultural growth fluctuated between 10 percent when labor supply is fixed (from 20.58 to 18.46 percent) and 7 percent (to 19.12 percent) when labor

Table 3.6   Effects of agricultural expansion on poverty: labor market effects

	2000 Bench-mark	I Wage effects only†		II Wage and employment effects§		III Employment effects‡	
		(1)	(2)	(1)	(2)	(1)	(2)
Poverty							
Head count (%)	20.58	18.46	18.80	19.02	19.30	19.12	19.45
Income gap (%)	34.52	34.35	34.35	33.66	33.72	33.70	33.69
FGT(1)	7.10	6.34	6.46	6.40	6.51	6.44	6.55
FGT(2)	3.71	3.34	3.40	3.29	3.35	3.31	3.36
Vulnerable groups, poverty line + 20%							
Head count (%)	7.34	6.82	6.97	7.14	7.17	7.10	7.22
Income surplus (%)	9.81	10.00	10.01	9.84	9.90	9.80	9.80
Per capita income (100s Ch.$2000)	1383	1462	1443	1412	1406	1404	1399
Income change (%)		5.7	4.4	2.3	1.7	1.6	1.2

Notes:
(1) Uncompensated simulations.
(2) Compensated simulations.
†   Wage effect under the assumption that labor market clears and supply of unskilled labor is fixed, i.e., labor supply elasticity is zero.
§   Employment expansion and wage effect using estimated labor supply elasticity of 1.8 from Mizala et al. (1999).
‡   Employment expansion effect under the assumption that labor supply is fully elastic and unemployment prevails, i.e., labor supply elasticity is infinity.

supply is fully elastic. In the intermediate case, head count poverty falls by 7.6 percent (to 19.02 percent). Thus, under the various assumptions about labor supply elasticity we have a fairly narrow range between 7 and 10 percent. The income gap is reduced but only very slightly from 0.5 percent in the fixed labor supply case to about 2.3 percent in the other two cases. Interestingly, unlike head count poverty, the poverty gap tends to fall faster when there is an employment effect than when there is a pure wage effect. Poverty vulnerability is also reduced slightly in all three cases while the income surplus of the non-poor but vulnerable groups also marginally increases.

The compensated effects (for example, the case when there is only a change in the composition of output in the form of agriculture but not an expansion of aggregate output) follow similar patterns, but of course are of a smaller magnitude. Poverty also falls within a narrow range between

5.5 percent when labor supply is fully elastic and 8.6 percent when labor supply is fixed. In any case these effects are still quite large, suggesting that a more agricultural-based growth is clearly pro-poor.

3.4   FOOD PRICES AND AGRICULTURAL GROWTH

In this section we examine the hypothesis that agricultural growth helps to reduce the real price of food products that are not tradable. Evidence would suggest that in Chile most of the agricultural growth has been outward oriented with expansion of tradable goods and processed agricultural products. However, whether or not this growth has spillovers to non-tradable food prices remains an empirical question that we address by analyzing time series of prices.

To determine the marginal effect of agricultural growth on food prices we explain the path of the real non-tradable food price index (*PINTF*) as a function of external factors, real exchange rate (*RER*), and internal factors: real non-food price index (*PINF*), agricultural output (Q_a) and non-agricultural output (Q_n):

$$PINTF_t = \alpha + \delta \cdot t + \beta_1 RER_t + \beta_2 PINF_t + \beta_3 \ln Q_{at} + \beta_4 \ln Q_{nt} + \mu_t, \quad (3.6)$$

where α is a constant, and μ_t a random error term. The first problem we have to deal with before estimating (3.4) is that some or all series are expected to be non-stationary. For example, if both agricultural and non-agricultural output have a long-run growth rate, with yearly deviations from those levels then by definition $\ln Q_a$ and $\ln Q_n$ are non-stationary series, integrated of order $1 - I(1)$: $\Delta \ln Q_n = a + \eta_t$, where a is a constant and η_t is a mean zero random perturbation. The use of non-stationary series in regressions yields invalid, spurious correlation results, usually red-flagged by an R^2 approaching to 1 as sample size grows.

Thus, we run a battery of unit root tests on our series to detect the presence of integrated time series. The results presented in Table 3.7 suggest as expected that the logs of agricultural and non-agricultural output are I(1): neither the Phillips–Perron nor the Advanced Dickey Fuller (ADF) tests reject the null hypothesis for the series in levels, but strongly reject the null for the series in first differences. There is strong evidence that the rest of the time series are also I(1). In spite of our small sample size (1976–2000), most of the test results are strong, except for the Phillips–Perron test on the levels of the non-food real price index which is almost rejected at the 10 percent level, and the tests for the first differences of the real exchange rate which at the 5 percent level are inconclusive. The unit root tests performed on the

Table 3.7   Food price equation: unit root tests

Series	Levels			First difference		
	Phillips–Perron	ADF	Interpolated 5% critical level	Phillips–Perron	ADF	Interpolated 5% critical level
Non-tradable real food prices	−2.813	−1.909	−3.600	−3.789	−3.962	−3.000
Real exchange rate	−1.330	−2.155	−3.600	−3.089	−2.977	−3.000
Non-food real prices	−3.129	−2.378	−3.580	−7.454	−7.398	2.989
Log agricultural output	−2.857	−1.209	−3.580	−5.721	−5.676	2.989
Log non-agricultural output	−1.652	−2.194	−3.580	−3.867	−3.793	2.989

Note: In both tests H_0: the series has a unit root. A trend term was used in the tests for the series in levels. Three lags were used in both set of tests to control for autocorrelation.

second differences of the real exchange rate reject the null (ADF = −5.44), which would altogether suggest that *RER* is I(2). Other researchers have also found evidence of aggregate price levels being I(2) (for example, Clements and Mizon, 1991; Miller, 1991). However, it turns out that this result may be due to the low power of the ADF test. In fact, both Clements and Mizon, and Miller carry out their subsequent analysis assuming that aggregate prices are I(1). We also treat *RER* as I(1), given that the test results are not overwhelming, and our sample size is very small.

Assuming that all of the time series are integrated of order 1 we test for cointegration among series. We carried out full information maximum likelihood procedures, as suggested by Johansen (1991), not rejecting the hypothesis that the series cointegrate. However, here we report the Phillips and Ouliaris (1990) single-equation procedure, because we attempt to explain only one series, and the power of the full information method is very low with small samples like ours. The Phillips and Ouliaris procedure amounts to testing for the stationarity of the residual of (3.6), μ_t. The ADF and Phillips–Perron tests of −6.22 and −4.83, respectively, lie below the asymptotic critical value at 5 percent of −4.49.[4] Therefore, we conclude that the residual of (3.6) is stationary, and equivalently the time series cointegrate, with [1 β] as a cointegrating vector.

Cointegration first of all means that the results of estimating (3.6) are not spurious. Cointegration means that two or more series that are non-stationary, although they may deviate from each other in the short run, have a long-run equilibrium; that is, in spite of the deviations, they move

Table 3.8 Non-tradable real food prices: estimated long-run effects

	Coefficient	Std error	*t*-stat
Constant	247.16***	34.83	7.10
Trend	−0.1426***	0.0211	−6.77
Real exchange rate	0.0232***	0.0040	5.85
Non-food real prices	2.8425*	1.6155	1.76
Log agricultural output	−0.5620*	0.2749	−2.04
Log non-agricultural output	2.7893***	0.5332	5.23

Notes:
$R^2 = 0.67$.
Observations: 24; 1977–2000.
Std error of regression $= 0.4947$.
*** Significant at the 1% level, ** Significant at the 5% level, * Significant at the 10% level.
Durbin–Watson stat.: 1.83; critical values at 5% (0.925–1.902).
Newey–West standard errors presented.

together. A classic and intuitive example of cointegration is given by aggregate consumption and income series. Both are usually non-stationary, but cointegrate as they have a long-run equilibrium, given by a long-run share of income devoted to consumption. The fact that our series cointegrate indicates that they too have a long-run equilibrium. That is, the real price of non-tradable food may deviate from the real price of non-food goods, the real exchange rate, and agricultural and non-agricultural output, but in the long run the five move together.

The results of estimating (3.4) are presented in Table 3.8. We find some intuitive results: the real price of food is positively correlated with the real price of non-food goods, the real exchange rate and the non-agricultural output. The relationship of our interest, between agricultural output and the price of non-tradable food goods is negative, as hypothesized; however, this relationship is not as strong as the effect of non-agricultural output with a coefficient almost significant at the 5 percent level. The estimated coefficient of –0.56, evaluated at the sample mean, translates to a long-run elasticity of non-tradable food prices to agricultural output of –0.18.

Furthermore, as in the previous section, we can calculate the compensated elasticity of non-tradable food prices to agricultural output:

$$\frac{d\ln PINTF}{d\ln Q_a}\bigg|_{dQ=0} = \frac{\partial \ln PINTF}{\partial \ln Q_a} + \frac{\partial \ln PINTF}{\partial \ln Q_n}\frac{\partial \ln Q_a}{\partial \ln Q_n}$$

$$= -0.18 + 0.9 \cdot (-0.15/0.85) = -0.34.$$

This compensated elasticity is higher than the uncompensated one because non-agricultural output, which is required to fall in a constant total output agricultural expansion, is strongly correlated with non-tradable food prices.

We proceed to estimate the error-correction representation to analyze the short-run relationships, by estimating:

$$\Delta PINTF_t = a + \gamma_1 \Delta RER_t + \gamma_2 \Delta PINF_t + \gamma_3 \Delta lnQ_{at} + \gamma_4 \Delta lnQ_{nt}$$
$$+ \lambda \hat{\mu}_{t-1} + \varepsilon_t, \tag{3.7}$$

where a is a constant, $\hat{\mu}_t$ is the estimated residual from (3.6), and ε_t is a random perturbation. In (3.7), the γ_i represent the short-run relationships, as opposed to the long-run relationships captured in the first regression. The estimated coefficient of λ of -0.97 represents the proportion of the short-run deviation in $t-1$ that is offset by a movement in $PINTF_t$; that is, almost all of the departure from the long-run equilibrium is eliminated within a year. The results of estimating (3.7) are presented in Table 3.9, where we can see that the signs of the short-run relationships are equivalent to the long run presented in Table 3.8. An important result is that the short-run effect of agricultural output on non-tradable food prices is much larger than the long-run effect. This may be due to the fact that when prices go up some commodities in the non-tradable food price index start being traded in the international market. That is, the price of some of these commodities may leave the range of transaction costs. But initially non-traded commodities can become tradable only after some adjustment period has elapsed. This result suggests that increases in the growth rate of agricultural

Table 3.9   *Change in non-tradable real food prices (error correction representation): estimated short-run effects*

	Coefficient	Std error	t-stat
Constant	-0.1475***	0.0195	-7.55
Change real exchange rate	0.0226***	0.0029	7.94
Change non-food real prices	3.4377***	0.9098	3.78
Change log agricultural output	-0.9367**	0.3984	-2.35
Change log non-agricultural output	3.2451***	0.3708	8.75
Lagged error	-0.9665***	0.1365	-7.08

Notes:
$R^2 = 0.68$.
Observations: 23; 1978–2000.
Std error of regression $= 0.4763$.
*** Significant at the 1% level, ** Significant at the 5% level, * Significant at the 10% level.
Durbin–Watson stat.: 1.81; critical values at 5% (0.895–1.920).
Newey–West standard errors presented.

output has a strong short-run (1 year) effect in decreasing the real price of non-tradable food, but this effect is reduced after one year as the long-run equilibrium is re-established. For the poverty simulations presented below we use the estimated long-run elasticities.

3.4.1 Food Price Poverty Effects: Simulations

The reduction of non-tradable food prices affects poverty twofold. First, the price fall increases real incomes; at the same time the cost of the food basket that is used to measure poverty becomes lower, that is, the poverty line falls. The change in real income from a reduction in food prices can be calculated using the weights from the national consumer price index (CPI) which reflects consumption patterns for society as a whole. According to the consumption survey used to construct the 1998 base year CPI, 27 percent of household budgets is spent on food. Thus, if the price of food falls 1 percent, then real incomes grow by: $1/(1 - 1\% \cdot 27\%) - 1 = 0.3\%$.

An additional effect of food price changes is its impact upon the poverty line. The poverty line which as explained earlier is equal to two food baskets is of course quite sensitive to changes in the price of food. We used the same estimates to evaluate the fall in the poverty line as a consequence of a reduction of food prices.

With the information on the changes in real income and the poverty line, we simulate the effect of an expansion of agriculture by 4.5 percent, both by itself, and by holding total output constant. Table 3.10 shows the result of this exercise. In the first column we show the benchmark poverty measures for the year 2000; the second column presents poverty effects of food price reductions following an expansion of the agricultural sector. The results suggest that through the price effect a 4.5 percent growth of agriculture would at most reduce the incidence of poverty by about 0.5 percent, and would leave the vulnerability (as measured by the population with per capita income up to 20 percent above the poverty line) of those almost poor relatively unchanged.

As can be seen in Table 3.10, unlike the labor market effect, the price effect is larger in the compensated case than in the uncompensated one. The reason is that in the compensated case non-agricultural output falls, causing a further reduction of agricultural prices (note in Table 3.8 that the coefficient of non-agricultural output in agricultural prices is positive).

3.5 DIRECT EFFECTS ON POOR FARMERS

The direct poverty effect via the income of poor farmers was also measured. We found that even under the most optimistic assumptions this effect is

Table 3.10   Effects of agricultural expansion on poverty: food price effect

	2000 benchmark	Food price effects	
		(1)	(2)
Poverty			
Head count (%)	20.58	20.43	20.33
Income gap (%)	34.52	34.49	34.42
FGT(1)	7.10	7.05	7.00
FGT(2)	3.71	3.68	3.65
Vulnerable groups, poverty line + 20%			
Head count (%)	7.34	7.29	7.23
Income surplus (%)	9.81	9.78	9.83
Per capita income (100s Ch.$2000)	1,383	1,383	1,384
Income change (%)		0.1	0.1

Notes:
(1) Uncompensated Simulations.
(2) Compensated Simulations.

negligible. To determine the importance of agricultural/agro-processing output in the income of poor farmers we estimated a regression where both off-farm income as well as agricultural output explain total household income of poor farmers, so as to determine the relative shares of each component (Table 3.11). The use of this simple approach is mostly due to the fact that we lack information on key variables affecting poor farmers' income such as landholdings as well access to other assets. Nonetheless, the estimated elasticity of 0.1 seems plausible when one considers the increasing importance of non-farm employment and incomes in rural Chile reported by Berdegué et al. (2001). These authors show that the importance of non-farm income has been growing in rural areas, adding up to 41 percent of overall rural income. This does not mean that the share of agricultural-related income in total poor farmers' income is only 10 percent. In fact a significant part of their remaining income is still derived from agricultural activities outside their own farm. We note that the effects of off-farm agricultural output sources on poor farmers occur essentially via wage and off-farm agricultural employment levels. These effects are ignored here because they are already accounted for in the labor market analysis.

Furthermore, the incidence of subsistence farming in Chile is very limited. About 1.4 percent of those working are considered to be subsistence farmers in the country. As a consequence, the exercise of simulating increases in poor farmers' income as a result of agricultural growth provided a negligible effect on poverty.

Table 3.11   Estimates for the participation of agricultural income in poor farmers' per capita income

	Coefficient	Std error
Log off-farm per capita income	0.9911***	0.0596
Log of agricultural product	0.1219**	0.0577

Notes:
$R^2 = 0.99$.
Observations: 31.
Std error of regression = 3.6921.
*** Significant at the 1% level, ** Significant at the 5% level, * Significant at the 10% level.
White's robust standard errors shown.

	Coefficient	Std error
Log off-farm per capita income	1.013***	0.0568
Log of agricultural product + Ag. processing output	0.0984*	0.0535

Notes:
$R^2 = 0.99$.
Observations: 31.
Std error of regression = 3.7743.
*** Significant at the 1% level, ** Significant at the 5% level, * Significant at the 10% level.
White's robust standard errors shown.

Table 3.12   Consolidated effects of agricultural growth of 4.5% on poverty

	Upper bound	Wage and employment effects	Lower bound
Uncompensated	−11.0	−9.4	−7.8
Compensated	−9.9	−8.8	−6.7

3.6   CONSOLIDATED RESULTS

We finally consolidate the poverty-alleviating effects of an agricultural expansion of 4.5 percent in Table 3.12. The most striking result is that there is not a big difference between the compensated and uncompensated effects of agricultural expansion on poverty. In the uncompensated case, the labor market effects dominate for a reduction of the incidence of poverty between 7.8 and 11 percent. In fact the labor market effect explains more than 90 percent of the total poverty reduction while the food price effect explains the remaining 10 percent. The composition change effects of agricultural expansion are also clearly pro-poor. An increase in the share of agriculture by 4.5 percent reduces poverty by 6.7 to 9.9 percent. In this latter case, however, the price effects play a more important role, explaining about 15 percent of total poverty reduction.

3.7   CONCLUSION

This chapter has evaluated the role of agricultural growth in reducing poverty in Chile. The analysis is broad enough to allow for economy-wide mechanisms including wage changes and food price changes that affect poverty among both rural and urban households. It also measures the direct impact of agricultural expansion on the income of farmers who are poor and also upon those who are not poor but are near poor. An important result is that while the economy-wide effects taking place via food prices and especially the labor market are quantitatively important, the direct income effects on farmers are almost negligible.

The pro-poor role of agricultural expansion appears to be quite dramatic: agricultural growth tends to improve all measures of poverty significantly with head count falling between 8 and 11 percent as a consequence of a 4.5 percent increase in agricultural output. That is, the elasticity of poverty reduction with respect to agricultural growth falls within the range of 1.8 to 2.4, substantially larger than elasticities normally found for aggregate growth in Chile, which is of the order of 0.8 to 1.2 (Contreras, 2003; World Bank, 2002). That is, agricultural growth not only has a large impact on poverty but also its effect is much greater than the effect of expanding other sectors in the economy.

This latter result is corroborated by our finding that the *compensated* effect of agricultural growth is also positive and large. In fact, a 4.5 percent increase in agricultural output, keeping total output constant, leads to poverty reductions in the range of 6.7 to 9.9 percent. That is, the compensated elasticity of poverty reduction is within the 1.5 to 2.2 range. Interestingly, our estimates are highly consistent with the aggregate output elasticities of around 1 found by Contreras. Given that the share of agriculture plus agro-processing in national outputs is about 0.15, we have that a 1 percent compensated rise in agricultural output means that the rest of the economy must contract by about 0.17 percent. If the aggregate poverty elasticity is about 1 as estimated by other studies, the 0.17 percent contraction by the non-agricultural sector should cause an increase of poverty by less than 0.17 percent. Also the 1 percent rise in agricultural output should, according to our estimates, reduce poverty by about 2 percent. Hence, the net (compensated) elasticity should be above 1.8, well within the range that we predict for the elasticity of poverty reduction with respect to agricultural growth.

Over the period of analysis, employment of unskilled workers has increased on average only by 0.44 percent per annum. This despite the fact that real aggregate output rose by 7.7 percent per annum. According to our estimates, however, the biggest obstacle for faster employment of unskilled workers is not a low responsiveness to output expansion. It is not due to ever higher real wages for the unskilled either; real wages for the unskilled increased by only 2.4 percent per annum compared to 3.6 percent for skilled workers and 1.8 percent for capital. In fact, this moderate wage increase causes only a very small negative impact on unskilled labor demand compared to the very dramatic increase that expanding output caused. The real source for slow unskilled job creation is the enormous bias of technological change against unskilled workers. This also constitutes a significant obstacle to a faster rate of poverty reduction. This result thus underlines another cost associated with the low priority given to investments in research, development and especially technological adaptation in Chile.

NOTES

1. Also, note that Chile uses a rather narrow definition of rural compared, for example, to the 10,000 inhabitants threshold used in Switzerland.
2. See Appendix 3A for more details regarding the data.
3. This value is highly consistent with previous estimates of (own-price) labor demand elasticities obtained by studies for Chile that have usually ranged between –0.2 and –0.4 (see for example, Riveros, 1985 and Fajnzylber and Maloney, 2000).
4. Critical value from Phillips and Ouliaris (1990); furthermore, the 2.5 percent critical value is –4.77, and the 1 percent critical value is –5.04.

REFERENCES

Berdegué, Julio, Eduardo Ramírez and Thomas Reardon (2001), 'Rural non farm employments and incomes in Chile', *World Development*, **29**(3): 411–25.

Clements, Michael P. and Grayham E. Mizon (1991), 'Empirical analysis of macroeconomic time series: VAR and structural models', *European Economic Review*, **35**(4): 887–917.

Contreras, Dante (2003), 'Poverty and inequality in a rapid growth economy: Chile 1990–1996', *Journal of Development Studies*, **39**(3): 181–200.

Diewert, W.E. (1971), 'An application of the Shephard duality theorem: a generalized Leontief production function', *Journal of Political Economy*, **79**(3): 481–507.

Fajnzylber, Pablo and William Maloney (2000), 'Labor Demand in Colombia, Chile and Mexico: Dynamic Panel Modeling', mimeo, World Bank, Washington, DC.

Johansen, Søren (1991), 'Estimation and hypothesis testing of cointegration vectors in Gaussian vector autoregressive models', *Econometrica*, **59**(6): 1551–80.

López, Ramón (2002), 'Agricultural growth and poverty reduction', Prepared for FAO-RoA project as a methodological background paper.

Miller, Stephen M. (1991), 'Monetary dynamics: an application of cointegration and error-correction modeling', *Journal of Money, Credit and Banking*, May: 139–54.

Mizala, Alejandra, Pilar Romaguera and Paulo Henríquez (1999), 'Female labor supply in Chile', Documento de Trabajo 58, Centro de Economía Aplicada, Universidad de Chile.

Phillips, P.C.B. and S. Ouliaris (1990), 'Asymptotic properties of residual based tests for cointegration', *Econometrica*, **58**: 165–93.

Riveros, Luis (1985), 'Determinación de Salarios y Eficiencia del Mercado Laboral en la década del 70', *Cuadernos de Economía*, **22**(65): 123–43.

World Bank (2002), 'Poverty and Income Distribution Dynamics in a High-Growth Economy: The Case of Chile, 1987–98', Report No. 22037-CH, Washington, DC.

APPENDIX 3A   DATA

The measures of agricultural and total output, both at the national level, as well as the regional level come from the national accounts maintained by Chile's Banco Central. We used the accounts with constant figures with 1986 as base year. We additionally developed an indicator of agricultural processing value added. The development of this series required two main data sources, the Chilean economy's input–output matrix (1996), and the yearly 'Encuesta Nacional de la Industria Anual' ENIA (1980–98).[1] With the aid of the input–output matrix we first identified the industrial sectors that use agricultural output as their main input. Examples of these sectors include the meat-processing, milk-processing and wine industries. With the aid of the ENIA surveys we determined the share of total industrial value added due to these agricultural processing industries. Finally, the product of this latter share and the national accounts industrial GDP gave us a yearly figure of agricultural processing value added both at the national level (1980–98), and the regional level (1980–96).[2]

The section on employment effects of agriculture required the use of three inputs, unskilled labor, medium- and high-skilled labor, and capital inputs. The monthly wages for the unskilled and skilled sectors were calculated using CASEN national surveys. The division between skilled and unskilled labor was given by the years of education of labor: workers with eight or fewer years of education were considered unskilled. The cost of capital inputs was proxied by the cost of imported capital goods given by the index of imported capital goods (Banco Central).

The section on non-tradable food prices required the creation of a price index of non-tradable goods. The index was created using nominal prices of non-tradable food goods such as tomatoes, potatoes, eggs, bread, carrots and so on (monthly: 1975–2000). A Laspeyres index was constructed using weights from the national CPI (base year 1998), and was deflated by the national CPI to obtain real prices. The non-food real price index was constructed by using the ratio of non-food component of the national CPI, divided by the national CPI. For the regression analysis we used the yearly average of the price indices. The real exchange rate was obtained from the Banco Central, and it is defined as the nominal exchange rate times the ratio of foreign inflation to national inflation.

For the section on poor farmers, we calculated household income for those households where the head was identified as a subsistence farmer by the CASEN national survey. Next, we separated household income between that which is generated on the farm, and that which comes from off-farm activities.

NOTES

1. The input–output matrix is available in Banco Central (2000). ENIA surveys performed by the Instituto Nacional de Estadísticas (INE), are available in print at their public library.
2. More details on the development of the agricultural processing value added are available in Anríquez et al. (2003).

REFERENCES

Anríquez, Gustavo, William Foster and Alberto Valdés (2003), 'Agricultural growth linkages and the sector's role as buffer', Roles of Agriculture Project Paper, FAO, Rome, available at http://ftp.fao.org/es/ESA/ROA/pdf5_Buffer/Buffer_Chile. pdf.
Banco Central (2000), 'Matriz de Insumo-Producto de la Economía Chilena', Banco Central, Santiago, Chile, www.bcentral.cl/Publicaciones/matriz/MIP1996.htm.

4. Mexico

Isidro Soloaga and Mario Torres

4.1 INTRODUCTION

There has been a lively debate on agriculture's poverty alleviation role in recent years. Research outcomes vary, depending largely on methodology and data used. For example, Ravallion and Datt (1996) found that agricultural growth has a significant effect in reducing not only rural but also urban poverty in India. Similar findings were reported for the Ivory Coast (Kakwani, 1993) and Indonesia (Thorbecke and Jung, 1996). Some other evidence for India, however, points to weak poverty-alleviating effect of agricultural growth in areas with high inequality in land distribution (Bardhan, 1985; Gaiha, 1987). Thus, differences in initial conditions alter findings.

There is therefore a strong justification for a systematic investigation of the agricultural growth–poverty relationship. This requires identification of the main channels through which agricultural growth impacts poverty and an understanding of the conditions under which these channels operate effectively. According to López (see Chapter 2), the main channels through which agricultural growth contributes to poverty reduction are:

1. a general equilibrium effect through the increase of unskilled labour wage rate;
2. an increase in smallholders' income;
3. higher agricultural output leading to lower food prices; and
4. forward/backward linkage effects which spur non-farm income growth and investment in agro-industries and other downstream activities.

Whether these channels exist and their effectiveness when they do, are largely contextual issues. The measurement of agriculture's effectiveness in reducing poverty and the clarification of the nature of some of the agriculture–poverty linkages in Mexico are the main goals of this chapter. Their knowledge will help policy makers to design a more comprehensive and effective poverty-reduction strategy.

Section 2 illustrates the evolution of poverty in Mexico, emphasizing its rural and urban components. Section 3 focuses on modeling the main links through which agricultural growth translates into reduction of rural and urban poverty. We applied the Ravallion and Datt (1996) methodology to regional data, and conducted a sensitivity analysis to check for the robustness of our results. Section 4 discusses the data used, and Section 5 the empirical results. Section 6 explores the channels by which agricultural growth impacts on poverty levels. Section 7 is devoted to a discussion of the empirical results and their policy implications.

4.2 EVOLUTION OF POVERTY AND OTHER STATISTICAL INDICATORS

Poverty remains at high levels in Mexico. Although a clear negative trend was observed between 1996 and 2002, by the year 2000 about 18 percent of the population still falls below the food poverty line (see Figure 4.1). Rural poverty (35.2 percent) is more than double the national level (14.4 percent), while urban poverty is considerably lower (7.5 percent). From 1989 and up to 1994, urban and rural poverty levels followed different paths: while urban poverty levels fell by 6.5 percentage points (from 18.4 percent in 1989 to 11 percent in 1994) rural poverty increased by 8 percentage points (from 41.8 percent in 1989 to 49.8 percent in 1994). Since the 1995 macroeconomic crisis, urban and rural poverty has followed similar paths. The impact of the crisis can be clearly seen: overall food poverty jumped from 21.5 percent in 1994 to 29.7 percent in 1996, whereas rural poverty rose to 60.5 percent (from 49.8 percent two years before), and urban poverty reached 18.2 percent in 1996, 7.2 percentage points higher than in 1994. Since 1996, the decrease in urban poverty has been higher than the decrease in rural poverty rates: while rural poverty fell to 35.2 percent, urban poverty more than halved to 7.5 percent, whereas total poverty fell to 14.4 percent.

Poverty levels are not evenly distributed and rather vary a lot across the different regional areas of Mexico (see Appendix 4A1 for the definition of geographic areas). Poverty levels are relatively low in the North, in the Pacific, and in Mexico City (between 10 and 14 percent on average since 1994) and high (between 29 and 45 percent on average since 1994) in the other four regions (Golfo, Centro, Centro-Norte and Sur) (see Figure 4.2).

There are also huge variations within each region. Figure 4.3 shows that rural poverty is always higher across all the regions: on average for all years in the sample and for all regions, rural poverty is about three times higher than urban poverty.

Table 4.1 shows by region the urban–rural composition of the population, of total consumption and of three measures of poverty. For Mexico

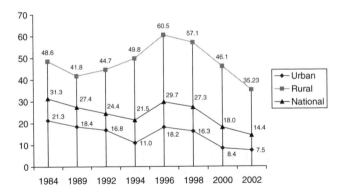

Source: Own, based on INEGI and World Bank.

Figure 4.1   Poverty in Mexico: extreme (food) poverty lines

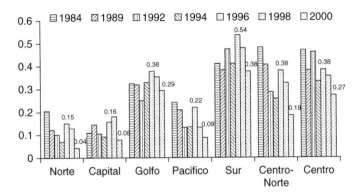

Source: Own, based on INEGI and World Bank.

Figure 4.2   Poverty in Mexico: regional extreme (food) poverty levels

as a whole (average 1984–2002) 32.1 percent of the population live in rural areas, consume only 19.5 percent of total Mexican consumption, and house 54.3 percent of the total number of extremely poor people in Mexico. In the four regions with the highest level of poverty (Golfo, Sur, Centro and Centro-Norte), rural areas contribute with more than 60 percent or the total number of poor people, which means that poverty in those areas is, above all, rural poverty. The same situation can be found when considering other measures of poverty (FGT(1) and FGT(2)). By region, the highest incidence of rural poverty can be found in the south, where 50.3 percent of the population living in rural areas share only 32 percent of total regional consumption, and house 69 percent of the region's poor people.

Country case studies

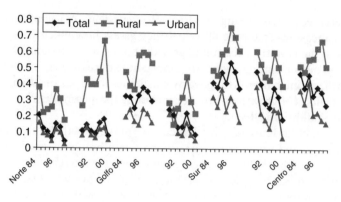

Source: Own, based on INEGI and World Bank.

Figure 4.3   *Poverty in Mexico: rural and urban poverty within each region,
1984–2000*

Table 4.1   *Shares of population, consumption and poverty (total Mexico
and by region, average 1984–2002)*

	Share in total population		Share in total consumption		Share in head count poverty FGT(0)		Share in poverty gap FGT(1)		Share in squared poverty gap FGT(2)	
	Urban	Rural	Urban	Rural	Urban	Rural	Urban	Rural	Urban	Rural
Total	0.679	0.321	0.805	0.195	0.457	0.543	0.393	0.607	0.345	0.655
Norte	0.844	0.156	0.911	0.887	0.596	0.404	0.510	0.490	0.444	0.556
Capital	0.906	0.094	0.965	0.035	0.658	0.342	0.583	0.417	0.516	0.484
Golfo	0.586	0.414	0.764	0.236	0.352	0.648	0.292	0.708	0.256	0.744
Pacífico	0.736	0.264	0.797	0.203	0.520	0.480	0.457	0.543	0.393	0.607
Sur	0.497	0.503	0.679	0.321	0.310	0.690	0.250	0.750	0.219	0.781
Centro-Norte	0.593	0.407	0.767	0.233	0.374	0.626	0.315	0.685	0.280	0.720
Centro	0.593	0.407	0.750	0.250	0.394	0.606	0.342	0.658	0.308	0.692

Source: Own estimates.

4.3   EMPIRICAL MODEL

This section addresses the nature of intra- and inter-sectoral effects of
growth on poverty. We follow the approach presented in Ravallion and Datt
(1996), who utilized a reduced-form econometric approach where agricultural and non-agricultural growth are used as explanatory variables of

a poverty equation. Using a series of consistent, consumption-based poverty measures spanning 40 years, they assess how much India's poor shared in the country's economic growth, taking into account its urban–rural and output composition. An important feature of their methodology is that the estimated growth–poverty elasticities incorporate *all* direct and indirect effects of growth on poverty, including the income distribution and general equilibrium effects.

Their main findings are: (i) rural consumption growth reduced poverty in both rural and urban areas; (ii) urban growth brought some benefits to the urban poor, but had no impact on rural poverty; and (iii) rural-to-urban population shifts had no significant impact on poverty. Decomposing growth by output sectors, they found that ouput growth in the primary and tertiary sectors reduced poverty in both urban and rural areas but that secondary sector growth did not reduced poverty in either.

Ravallion and Datt's methodology uses Foster, Greer and Thorbecke (FGT) (see Foster et al., 1984) decomposable measures for poverty and considers two sectors, urban and rural. We extend their model to capture the regional dimension of the dataset we shall use here. The average level of poverty in region i in period t is given by:[1]

$$P_{it} = n_{it}^u P_{it}^u + n_{it}^r P_{it}^r, \tag{4.1}$$

where n^k and P^k are the population shares and poverty meassures, respectively, for sectors $k = u, r$ (urban and rural). Similarly, mean consumption can be written as:

$$\mu_{it} = n_{it}^u \mu_{it}^u + n_{it}^r \mu_{it}^r, \tag{4.2}$$

where μ^k is the mean for sector k. Let $s_k^P = n_k P_k / P$ and $s_k^\mu = n_k \mu_k / \mu$ be the sector shares of total poverty and total consumption. The growth rate in the poverty measure can be decomposed by taking the total differential of equation (4.1):

$$d\ln P_{it} = s_{uit}^P d\ln P_{it}^u + s_{rit}^P d\ln P_{it}^r + (s_{uit}^P - s_{rit}^P n_{it}^u / n_{it}^r) d\ln n_{it}^u. \tag{4.3}$$

Equation (4.3) shows that the average rate of poverty reduction is made up of the intra-sectoral gains to the poor, given by the share-weighted rates of poverty reduction within each sector $(s_k^P d\ln P^k)$, and the independent contribution of the rate of urbanization. The second term can be interpreted as poverty reduction attributable to the 'Kuznets process', where population shifts from the 'traditional' rural to the 'modern' urban sector.

Note that the coefficient $d \ln n_u$ can also be written as $(P^u - P^r)n^u/P$, indicating that urbanization under the Kuznets process will reduce poverty only if poverty is greater in rural areas than in urban areas. Similarly, the differential of equation (4.2) gives:

$$d \ln\mu_{it} = s^P_{uit}d \ln\mu^u_{it} + s^P_{rit}d \ln\mu^r_{it} + (s^P_{uit} - s^P_{rit}n^u_{it}/n^r_{it})d \ln n^u_{it}. \qquad (4.4)$$

By combining (4.3) and (4.4), Ravallion and Datt tested whether the composition of growth matters for poverty reduction:

$$\Delta\ln P_{it} = \pi_u s^\mu_{uit-1}\Delta\ln\mu_{uit} + \pi_r s^\mu_{rit-1}\Delta\ln\mu_{rit}$$
$$+ \pi_n(s^\mu_{rit-1} - s^\mu_{uit-1}n_{rit-1}/n_{uit-1})\Delta\ln n_{rit} + \Delta\varepsilon_{it} \qquad (4.5)$$
$$(t = 2\ldots, T)$$

where the πs are parameters to be estimated, Δ is the discrete time difference operator, and ε is the error term that accounts for other – not controlled-for – factors that influence measured poverty. Note that by using first differences, time-invariant region-specific effects are being eliminated. π_u and π_r coefficients can be interpreted as the impact of (share-weighted) growth in the urban and rural sectors, respectively, while π_n shows the impact of the population shift from rural to urban areas.[2]

We would like to test whether economic growth in one sector affects distribution in other sectors. We can use equation (4.3) to decompose the rate of growth in average poverty, and estimate the following system of equations:

$$s^P_{uit}\Delta\ln P^u_{it} = \pi_{u1it}s^\mu_{uit}\Delta\ln\mu^u_{it} + \pi_{u2it}s^\mu_{rit}\Delta\ln\mu^r_{it}$$
$$+ \pi_{u3it}(s^\mu_{rit} - s^\mu_{uit}n^r_{it}/n^u_{it})\Delta\ln n^r_{it} + \Delta\varepsilon_{uit} \qquad (4.6)$$

$$s^P_{rit}\Delta\ln P^r_{it} = \pi_{r1it}s^\mu_{uit}\Delta\ln\mu^u_{it} + \pi_{r2it}s^\mu_{rit}\Delta\ln\mu^r_{it}$$
$$+ \pi_{r3it}(s^\mu_{rit} - s^\mu_{uit}n^r_{it}/n^u_{it})\Delta\ln n^r_{it} + \Delta\varepsilon_{rit} \qquad (4.7)$$

$$(s^P_{rit} - s^P_{uit}n^r_{it}/n^u_{it})\Delta\ln n^r_{it} = \pi_{n1it}s^\mu_{uit}\Delta\ln\mu^u_{it} + \pi_{n2it}s^\mu_{rit}\Delta\ln\mu^r_{it}$$
$$+ \pi_{n3it}(s^\mu_{rit} - s^\mu_{uit}n^r_{it}/n^u_{it})\Delta\ln n^r_{it} + \Delta\varepsilon_{nit}, \qquad (4.8)$$

where $\pi_j = \pi_{uj} + \pi_{rj} + \pi_{nj}, j = 1, 2, 3$. If we sum equations (4.6), (4.7) and (4.8) we obtain equation (4.4). Equation (4.6) shows how the composition of growth and population shifts affect urban poverty. In turn, equation (4.7) shows how rural poverty is being affected, and equation (4.8) shows the impact on the population shift component of $\Delta \ln P$. From the last three equations only two of them needed to be estimated, the third coming from using the additive restriction $\pi_{nj} = \pi_j - \pi_{rj} - \pi_{uj}, j = 1, 2, 3$. The elasticities of the poverty measures to the sector means can be readily obtained by multiplying the regression coefficients by the relevant consumption or income shares.

In this chapter we apply Ravallion and Datt's approach to Mexican data. Lacking a long panel of poverty measures, we estimate equations (4.5), (4.6) and (4.7) using combined regional and time-series household data. That is, we estimate total rural and urban poverty changes *by region* instead of for the whole country. This allows us to sufficiently increase the number of observations to perform econometric analysis.[3]

Our dependent variable is the FGT index of poverty (1, 2 and 3).[4] For our sensitivity analysis we have taken three indicators: (i) 'food-consumption poverty', where the poverty line is equivalent to the income needed to satisfy a specific minimum caloric intake per capita; (ii) 'moderate poverty', where the poverty line is equivalent to the previous one *plus* the income needed to develop certain activities (food poverty line times 2 in urban areas, food poverty line times 1.75 in rural areas); and (iii) poverty levels of people situated between the 'food-consumption poverty' and the 'moderate poverty'.

By its nature, FGT(i) indices cannot capture non-income measures of well-being and we say nothing here about how responsive these dimensions may be to growth. Regarding the choice of consumption versus income, there are indications that current consumption is a better indicator of current level of living than current income (Ravallion, 1994), and this is the metric we use for our measures.

4.4 DATA

We use comparable household data coming from the National Institute for Statistics, Geography and Informatic (its acronym in Spanish is INEGI: Instituto Nacional de Estadistica, Geografia e Informatica) for years 1984, 1989, 1992, 1994, 1996, 1998, 2000 and 2002. Each INEGI household survey (ENIGH: *Encuesta Nacional de Ingresos y Gastos de los Hogares*) is representative at three levels: (i) national level; (ii) 'urban' areas (that is, localities with population above 2500 inhabitants); and (iii) 'rural' areas (that is, localities with population below 2500 inhabitants).

The poverty lines and poverty levels used in this chapter are the same as those used by the World Bank in its poverty studies on Mexico, and are presented in Table 4.2. To make comparison with results from other countries feasible, we also converted the poverty lines to dollar terms using the average official exchange.[5]

Table 4.2   Poverty lines

	1984	1989	1992	1994	1996	1998	2000	2002
Rural (Mexican $ per month)	4.233	68.81	124.75	163.89	313.33	390.30	443.22	473.71
Urban (Mexican $ per month)	4.969	86.40	167.96	170.28	317.77	445.47	484.80	520.61
Exchange rate	4.89	2.551	3.098	3.394	7.56	9.46	9.3683	9.889
Rural (US$ per day)	0.88	0.90	1.34	1.61	1.38	1.38	1.58	1.60
Urban (US$ per day)	1.02	1.13	1.81	1.67	1.40	1.57	1.72	1.75

Sources: Up to 2000: López-Acevedo et al. (1999), and World Bank (2001).

As mentioned above, to get enough degrees of freedom we use the regional estimates of poverty as in Soloaga and Torres (2003).[6] They estimated poverty levels at the estate level (32 in Mexico) as well as at the regional level (seven regions in Mexico following INEGI's regionalization). The complete set of estimates and their corresponding standard errors are available from the authors on request. Because the estimates at the state level showed excessive standard errors (see Table 4.3), in what follows we present estimates using data at the regional level.

4.5   ECONOMETRIC RESULTS

For each poverty measure we have estimated two sets of regressions in first differences, one by ordinary least squares (OLS) and the other by instrumental variables (IV). The IV approach was needed because the dependent and independent variables are estimated from the same survey data. This can produce a bias because measurement errors in the survey can impact on both variables; if the mean is underestimated, poverty will tend to be overestimated. The full set of instruments used is listed in Appendix 4A2. In most of the cases, the Durbin–Wu–Hauman (DWH) tests of exogeneity of independent variables indicated that the OLS approach would bring consistent estimates. Nonetheless, we report here both set of results.

Table 4.4 resumes our estimations for FGT(0) poverty measures. The upper panel shows the impact of urban and rural growth on total poverty (columns 3 and 4), on urban poverty (columns 5 and 6) and on rural poverty (columns 7 and 8). The first line in each panel indicates the value of the coefficient, the second its *t*-statistic and the third the elasticity computed at mean value levels. For clarity, bold indicates statistical significance.

Table 4.3   Coefficient of variation for poverty indicators

	Coefficient of variation for head count poverty index (H): standard error of H/mean H, average over 1984–2002		
	National level*	Regional level**	State level**
Total poverty	0.0476	0.1234	0.3043
Urban poverty	0.0835	0.1951	0.384
Rural poverty	0.0502	0.1334	0.247

Notes:

* By design, the ENIGH surveys are statistically representative only at national levels.
** Estimates following Howes and Lanjouw (1998).

Source: Soloaga and Torres (2003).

Following column 4 (IV estimation is indicated by the DWH test, and the Sargan test for exogeneity of instrument indicates that they are appropriated; the full set of results is listed in Appendix 4A2), we find that growth in both sectors, urban and rural, impacted negatively on total poverty levels, although growth in rural areas seems to have a stronger impact. Column 5 and 7 (the DWH test indicates that this is appropriated) show that, contrary to Ravallion and Datt's (1966) findings for India, there are no inter-sectoral effects: urban growth has an impact only on urban poverty (elasticity 1.35) and rural growth has an impact only on rural poverty (elasticity 0.87).

When considering the poverty level of people between the food and the moderate poverty lines, we find that while urban or rural growth had no impact on overall poverty, urban and rural growth impacted negatively on urban poverty (elasticities of 0.25 and 0.27, respectively), and had no impact on rural poverty. In rural areas, only migration from the countryside to urban areas reduced poverty.

Finally, when considering moderate poverty, we find that urban and rural growth reduced total poverty about equally (similar elasticities), and, again, that there are no inter-sectoral effects: urban growth reduces only urban poverty (elasticity of 0.58) and rural growth reduces only rural poverty (elasticity of 0.53). Population shifts from rural to urban areas reduce poverty in rural areas.

When considering other measures of poverty, the rural growth impact on poverty is stronger. For instance, for food poverty, the impact of rural growth on FGT(1) doubles that of urban growth (see Table 4.5). Clearly, rural growth has more power than urban growth in impacting on the poorest of the poor.

This set of estimates suggests that there is an important role for rural growth when considering the goal of poverty reduction. Urban and rural

Table 4.4 Condensed results from estimations.[1]

		Total poverty (3) OLS	Total poverty (4) IV	Urban poverty (5) OLS	Urban poverty (6) IV	Rural poverty (7) OLS	Rural poverty (8) IV
Food poverty							
Urban	coeff	−0.95	−1.09	−0.77	−0.88	−0.14	−0.15
growth	*t*-statistic	(−4.21)	(−2.89)	(−4.53)	(−3.31)	(−1.16)	(−1.01)
π_1	elasticity	−0.76	−0.88	−1.35	−1.55	−0.21	−0.22
Rural	coeff	−2.80	−6.78	−0.59	−2.11	−2.43	−4.24
growth	*t*-statistic	(−2.61)	(−2.50)	(−0.68)	(−1.11)	(−2.91)	(−2.74)
π_2^2	elasticity	−0.55	−1.32	−0.25	−0.90	−0.87	−1.52
Population	coeff	0.04	−0.46	−0.33	−0.17	0.42	0.36
shift π_3	*t*-statistic	−0.05	(−0.36)	(−0.59)	(−0.19)	−2.71	−0.84
Population between food poverty and moderate poverty							
Urban	coeff	−0.14	−0.21	−0.22	−0.30	0.07	0.08
growth	*t*-statistic	−1.18	−1.16	−2.34	−2.14	1.56	0.97
π_1	elasticity	−0.11	−0.17	−0.25	−0.34	0.20	0.23
Rural	coeff	−0.73	−0.16	−1.00	−1.07	0.29	0.86
growth	*t*-statistic	−1.20	−0.12	−2.08	−1.05	0.63	1.21
π_2^2	elasticity	−0.14	−0.03	−0.27	−0.29	0.20	0.59
Population	coeff	0.08	0.54	0.24	0.45	−0.36	−0.19
shift π_3	*t*-statistic	0.21	0.86	0.77	0.92	−1.74	−0.76
Moderate poverty							
Urban	coeff	−0.47	−0.60	−0.44	−0.55	−0.03	−0.04
growth	*t*-statistic	(−4.21)	(−2.89)	(−4.53)	(−3.31)	(−1.16)	(−1.01)
π_1	elasticity	−0.38	−0.48	−0.58	−0.73	−0.06	−0.08
Rural	coeff	−2.02	−2.88	−0.89	−1.30	−1.06	−1.52
growth	*t*-statistic	(−2.61)	(−2.50)	(−0.68)	(−1.11)	(−2.91)	(−2.74)
π_2^2	elasticity	−0.39	−0.56	−0.29	−0.42	−0.53	−0.75
Population	coeff	0.10	0.20	−0.32	0.26	−0.08	0.14
shift π_3	*t*-statistic	−0.05	(−0.36)	(−0.59)	(−0.19)	−2.71	−0.84

Notes:
1. Dependent variables: first panel: food poverty FGT(0); second panel: FGT(0) between food and moderate poverty lines; third panel: moderate FGT(0).
2. The elasticity of regional rural consumption growth to regional agricultural GDP growth is high. Depending on model specifications it varies from 0.75 to 0.87.

Source: Own estimates.

growth have about equal power in reducing total food and moderate poverty at the country level. Importantly for policy implications, rural growth has an inter-sectoral impact on that part of the population that is situated between the food and the moderate poverty lines, reducing the proportion of poor people not only in rural areas but also in urban areas. Also,

Table 4.5 *Impact of growth on poverty (estimates, t-statistics and elasticities)*

Poverty index	Impact on total poverty		Impact on urban poverty		Impact on rural poverty	
	OLS(1)	**IV(2)**	**OLS(3)**	IV(4)	**OLS(5)**	**IV(6)**
Impact of urban growth						
FGT(0)	−0.95	−1.09	−0.77	−0.88	−0.141	−0.151.11
	(−4.21)	(−2.89)	(−4.53)	(−3.31)	(−1.16)	(−1.01)
	−0.76	**−0.88**	**−1.35**	−1.55	−0.21	−0.22
FGT(1)	−1.18	−1.26	−0.84	−0.92	0.18	−1.49
	(−4.02)	(−2.48)	(−4.69)	(−3.27)	(−0.2)	(−0.74)
	−0.95	**−1.01**	**−1.72**	−1.89	0.23	−1.97
FGT(2)	−1.29	−1.29	−0.34	−0.39	0.15	−0.35
	(−3.55)	(−2.06)	(−4.16)	(−3.25)	(−0.38)	(−0.41)
	−1.03	**−1.04**	**−0.78**	−0.91	0.19	−0.43
Impact of rural growth						
FGT(0)	−2.80	−6.78	−0.59	−2.11	−2.43	−4.24
	(−2.61)	(−2.50)	(−0.66)	(−1.11)	(−2.91)	(−2.74)
	−0.55	**−1.32**	−0.25	−0.90	**−0.87**	**−1.52**
FGT(1)	−3.19	−8.63	−0.29	−0.27	−3.73	−6.50
	(−2.13)	(−2.38)	(−1.52)	(−1.11)	(−3.32)	(−2.95)
	−0.62	**−1.68**	−0.14	−0.13	**−1.20**	**−2.09**
FGT(2)	−4.14	−10.93	−0.17	−0.19	−2.24	−3.62
	(−2.25)	(−2.44)	(−1.68)	(−1.42)	(−3.56)	(−3.02)
	−0.81	**−2.13**	−0.10	−0.11	**−0.67**	**−1.08**

Notes: The first line for each FGT index shows coefficients from regressions from Appendix 4A2.

The second line shows the *t*-statistics. The third line shows elasticities at mean points. The upper panel shows the impact of urban growth on total, urban and rural poverty, the lower panel the impact of rural growth on total, urban and rural poverty.

The Durbin–Wu–Hausman (DWH) test for endogeneity for IV estimates showed that for total poverty (first two columns) IV is indicated. For urban poverty (third and fourth columns) OLS give consistent estimates, whereas for rural poverty (fifth and sixth columns) OLS consistency is not rejected at the 95 percent confidence level, but is rejected at the 90 percent confidence level (*p*-value of the DWH test was 0.092). The main difference in results for these last two columns is the impact of urban growth on rural poverty (it is not statistically significant in OLS estimates but it is significant under IV estimates). A full set of results and tests are presented in Appendix 4A2.

The bold indicates by column, which one is the appropriated model (IV or OLS), and by line, which parameters are statistically significant in the appropriated model. See Table 4.1 for mean values of consumption and poverty used to construct the elasticities. At mean values, urban consumption is 85.6% of total consumption, urban share of total poverty FGT(0) is 41.8%, 34.3% of FGT(1), and 0.297 of FGT(2).

Source: Own estimates.

*Table 4.6   Impact of urban–rural growth on poverty: 1984–2002
(Elasticities by region)*

	Poverty region total		Poverty region urban		Poverty region rural	
	OLS(1)	IV(2)	OLS(3)	IV(4)	OLS(5)	IV(6)
Urban growth						
Total effect	−0.76	**−0.88**	**−1.35**	−1.55	−0.87	−3.13
Norte	−0.86	**−1.00**	**−1.18**	−1.34	−0.02	−0.02
Capital	−0.91	**−1.06**	**−1.13**	−1.29	−0.01	−0.01
Golfo	−0.72	**−0.84**	**−1.67**	−1.91	−0.10	−0.10
Pacífico	−0.75	**−0.87**	**−1.18**	−1.35	−0.06	−0.06
Sur	−0.64	**−0.74**	**−1.68**	−1.92	−0.15	−0.16
Centro-Norte	−0.72	**−0.84**	**−1.58**	−1.80	−0.09	−0.09
Centro	−0.71	**−0.82**	**−1.46**	−1.67	−0.09	−0.10
Rural growth						
Total effect*	−0.55	**−1.32**	**−0.06**	−0.06	**−0.87**	**−1.52**
Norte	−0.25	**−0.60**	**−1.32**	−4.76	**−0.54**	**−0.93**
Capital	−0.10	**−0.24**	**−1.66**	−5.95	**−0.25**	**−0.43**
Golfo	−0.66	**−1.60**	**−0.69**	−2.49	**−0.89**	**−1.54**
Pacífico	−0.57	**−1.38**	**−0.97**	−3.50	**−1.03**	**−1.79**
Sur	−0.90	**−2.17**	**−0.58**	−2.08	**−1.13**	**−1.97**
Centro-Norte	−0.65	**−1.58**	**−0.72**	−2.59	**−0.90**	**−1.58**
Centro	−0.70	**−1.69**	**−0.73**	−2.61	**−1.00**	**−1.75**

Notes: * First line from Table 4.5.
The bold indicates by column, which one is the appropriated model (IV or OLS), and by
line, which parameters are statistically significant in the appropriated model. For the impact
of rural growth on rural poverty (fifth and sixth columns) OLS consistency is not rejected at
the 95% confidence level, but is rejected at the 90% confidence level (*p*-value of the DWH
test was 0.092). See full set of results and tests in Appendix 4A2.

Source: Own estimates based on Table 4.5.

judging for the elasticities of the poverty gap and of the squared poverty
gap indices of poverty, rural growth seems to be more powerful than urban
growth in impacting on the poorest of the poor.

   Table 4.6 shows results by region for FGT(0). While the impact of urban
growth on total poverty is within a relatively small range (lowest elasticity
of 0.74 in the Sur region, and highest elasticity of 1.06 in the Capital
region), the impact of rural growth showed more variation. Not surprisingly, the impact follows the share of rural population in each region (see
Table 4.1, above, for population and consumption shares by region): higher
elasticity in the three poor and relatively more rural regions of Sur, Golfo,

Centro and Centro-Norte – between 1.58 and 2.17 – and lower elasticities in the other less poor and more urbanized Norte, Capital and Pacifico regions – between 0.24 and 1.38. As mentioned above, regression results did not show inter-sectoral effects (that is, urban growth affected only urban poverty and rural growth affected only rural poverty). Interestingly, both urban and rural growth had a bigger impact on urban and rural poverty, respectively, in those areas where the share of urban population is relatively smaller (Sur, Golfo, Centro and Centro-Norte).

4.6 EXPLORING THE CHANNELS

4.6.1 Income Distribution

To explore plausible channels for the effects found in our regressions, we regress the change between surveys in the Gini index logs on the growth rates in both urban and rural means. The results suggest that growth in rural areas decreases the Gini coefficient at both the national and urban levels. Interestingly, it has no effect on the Gini in rural areas (that is, rural growth is distribution neutral in rural areas):

$$\Delta Gini\ Total = 0.25\Delta \ln mean(urban) - 0.22\Delta \ln mean(rural) \quad (4.9)$$

$$\Delta Gini\ Urban = 0.23\Delta \ln mean(urban) - 0.21\Delta \ln mean(rural). \quad (4.10)$$

In both regressions, coefficients are statistically significant at 1 percent with R-squared of 0.37 and 0.24, respectively.

Rural consumption growth has been decreasing inequality in urban areas, while urban growth has been exacerbating it. This suggests that rural growth has a general equilibrium effect on urban areas, derived perhaps from a Harris–Todaro-like effect by deterring migration.

4.6.2 Relative Wages Effect[7]

We postulate that producers minimize the cost of production. There are two outputs being produced, agricultural (Q_a) and non-agricultural products (Q_n). These outputs are being produced in competitive markets using three variable factors of production, unskilled labor (L_u), skilled labor (L_s), and capital (K). The three factors of production are supposed to be mobile across the two productive sectors and are allocated efficiently.

We specified a generalized Leontief cost function which, using Shephard's lemma, brings the implicit demand equations for unskilled and skilled labor:

$$L_s = \sum_j b_{sj}(w_j/w_s)^{1/2}Q_a + \sum_j c_{sj}(w_j/w_s)^{1/2}Q_n + b_s t Q_a + c_s t Q_n + d_s Q_a Q_n$$

(4.11)

$$L_u = \sum_j b_{uj}(w_j/w_u)^{1/2}Q_a + \sum_j c_{uj}(w_j/w_u)^{1/2}Q_n + b_u t Q_a + c_u t Q_n + d_u Q_a Q_n.$$

(4.12)

The demand for capital is not derived. Equations (4.11) and (4.12) can be jointly estimated after imposing the symmetry conditions, $b_{ij} = b_{ji}$ and $c_{ij} = c_{ji}$.

The labor demand equations (4.11) and (4.12) are estimated using data from Encuesta Nacional de Hogares Survey (ENE) for the 1996–2001 period. We constructed data for the seven INEGI regions for all six years for all the variables in equations (4.11) and (4.12) except for the rental price of capital, for which we used the annual price of capital goods for the whole country. We have used data for total unskilled and skilled labor in each region over the period, and, from the same ENE surveys, we estimated wages for each of the two types of labor. Workers with less than 8 years of schooling were considered as 'unskilled' labor, while workers with more schooling were considered 'skilled'. From INEGI, we also calculated regional GDP separated into agricultural and non-agricultural industries.

Table 4.7 shows the estimated coefficients for equations (4.11) and (4.12) we have used a SUR approach for greater efficiency.

Table 4.8 shows the elasticities of demand for unskilled and skilled labor implicit in the estimated coefficients and evaluated at sample means. It also presents the standard errors of these elasticities (note that elasticities are functions of several coefficients) and their degree of statistical significance. The two labor demand equations are downward sloping, with unskilled labor demand being relatively more elastic (–1.3) to its own price than the skilled labor demand equation (–0.55). Unskilled and skilled labor are substitutes (cross-elasticities are both positive: 0.28 and 0.42, respectively). Almost all demand elasticities are statistically significant at least at 10 percent. Only the response of skilled labor to agricultural output turned out to be not statistically significant. Both types of labor appear to be substitutes for capital.

We have run this model to see what the impact of agricultural/non-agricultural growth is on the demand of skilled/unskilled workers. Results show that growth in the agricultural output has an impact on the demand for unskilled workers, whereas growth in the non-agricultural sector increases demand for both types of labor with a higher elasticity for the demand of skilled workers (0.88 versus 0.57, the differences being statistically significant).[8]

For the purpose of this chapter, agricultural growth seems to have an

Table 4.7 Estimates of the multi-output cost function

Parameter	Coefficient	Standard errors	Significance
Skilled labor demand equation			
b11	−0.039	0.036111	
b12	−0.02	0.025974	
b13	0.217	0.131515	
c11	0.004	0.002198	
c12	0.004	0.002685*	
c13	−0.005	0.009434*	
b1	0.0024	0.001644	
c1	−0.0001	0.000197	
d1[a]	0.0037	0.004933	
constant ls	19835	19446.08	
Unskilled labor demand equation			
b21	−0.02	0.025974	
b22	−0.18	0.036437***	
b23	0.575	0.130682***	
c21	0.004	0.002685	
c22	−0.005	0.004386	
c23	0.013	−0.01182	
b2	0.008	0.001914***	
c2	0.001	0.001493	
d2[a]	0.35	0.072917***	
Constant	125,776	11,518***	

Notes:
(a) Coefficients for d1 and d2 were multiplied by 1,000,000 to fit the table.
(b) Significance levels: *** 1%, * 10%.

Source: Own estimates.

impact on unskilled labor demand. Higher demand for unskilled labor would presumably have a quantity effect on poor people, taking into account that this is their relative abundant resource. If this higher demand for unskilled workers is translated into higher wages for unskilled workers, this would also add a price effect for the agricultural growth impact on the standard of living of poor people.

4.6.3 Relative Prices Effect

In this subsection we examine the hypothesis that agricultural growth helps to reduce the real price of food products. To determine the marginal effect

Table 4.8   Estimated labor demand elasticities

	Prices			Growth	
	Unskilled labor	Skilled labor	Capital	Agricultural output	Non-agricultural output
Unskilled	−1.30***	0.28***	1.05***	0.22*	0.57***
labor demand	(0.1253)	(0.0024)	(0.1246)	(0.1130)	(0.0086)
Skilled	0.42***	−0.55***	0.27**	0.06	0.88***
labor demand	(0.0242)	(0.1309)	(0.1265)	(0.1349)	(0.0072)

Note: Standard errors in parentheses. Level of significance: *** at 1%; ** at 5%; and
* at 10%.

of agricultural growth on food prices we explain the path of the real food price index (RFP, measured as the food, beverage and tobacco consumer price index (CPI) divided by the GDP implicit price index) as a function of external factors, real exchange rate (RER, measured as the current exchange rate inflated by the US Wholesale Price Index (WPI) and deflated by the Mexican GDP implicit price index) and average nominal tariffs, and internal factors, agricultural output (Q_a, from Mexican national accounts) and non-agricultural output (Q_n, from Mexican national accounts):

$$RFP_t = \alpha + \delta t + \beta_1 RER_t + \beta_2 \ln Q_{at} + \beta_3 \ln Q_{nt} + \mu_t. \qquad (4.13)$$

Several econometric issues arise in estimating this equation. Some or all of the variables in equation (4.13) are expected to be non-stationary and could lead to spurious correlation results. Thus, we run a battery of unit root tests to detect the presence of integrated time series. It turned out that all variables in (4.13) are integrated of order 1–I(1). We then ran the Phillips and Oularis single-equation procedure to explain variation in RFP. The Dickey–Fuller (DF) test for cointegration gives a value of −3.26, which is below the asymptotic critical value at 5 percent (2.986) – the critical value at 1 percent is −3.716. Therefore we conclude that the residual of (4.13) is stationary, and equivalently the time series cointegrate. This means that in the long run the four variables move together.

For the case of Mexico, the RER seems to have the most important role in determining relative food prices. See Table 4.9 for long-run effects.

For this and other specifications we tried, results strongly suggest that what matters for real food price behavior is real exchange rate movements.[9] The coefficient for agricultural growth, although it has the expected negative sign, was statistically not different from zero. We have also estimated the

Table 4.9   *Estimated long-run effects, 1970–2001 (dependent variable real food prices)*

Variable	Coefficient	Std error	Statistical significance
RER	0.146	0.038	***
$\ln Q_a$	−0.021	0.399	Not significant
$\ln Q_{na}$	0.047	0.206	Not significant

Note: Statistical significance: *** 1%. R-squared 0.45. Number of obs. 32.

Source: Own estimates.

Table 4.10   *Agricultural income as a percentage of total income and number of people in each category*

	Share of agricultural income in total income	Number of people in each category (millions of persons)
Food poverty	0.35	14.6
Rural areas	0.46	8.8
Urban areas	0.18	5.7
Moderate poverty	0.20	42.7
Rural areas	0.39	16.7
Urban areas	0.08	26.0
Poverty between both lines	0.14	28.1
Rural areas	0.33	7.9
Urban areas	0.06	20.2

Source: Own estimates.

short-run relationships by way of an error the correction representation, with the same outcome: agricultural growth had no real impact on real food prices. In summary, we conclude this subsection by stating that all the price–growth relationships investigated showed that it is not through lowering food prices that agricultural growth has an impact on poverty levels.

4.6.4   Sources of Income of Poor People

Finally, we describe here the sources of income of the different categories of people. Table 4.10 shows that for moderately poor people, 20 percent of income comes from agricultural sources (for example, from wages or from self-employment in agricultural activities) and the remaining 80 percent from urban sources. For the people classified under food poverty, the share of income from agricultural sources rises to 35 percent, whereas for those that fall between both poverty lines, the share of agricultural income is 14 percent.

Agricultural income is about 46 percent of total income of the rural food-poor people, whereas it is only 18 percent in urban areas for the same group. For people below the moderate poverty line, the share of agricultural income as a percentage of total income is 39 percent in rural areas and 8 percent in urban areas. For people between both poverty lines, the share of income coming from agriculture as a percentage of total income is 33 percent in rural areas, and only 6 percent in urban areas.

4.7 CONCLUSIONS

Poverty levels have been diminishing in Mexico since the late 1990s, although several regions still show high levels of poverty, and they are extremely high in some rural areas. This chapter has addressed the issue of the linkages between sectoral growth (urban/rural) and poverty levels. It was found that although both types of growth impacted negatively on poverty levels in Mexico, rural growth seems to have a higher power in improving consumption per capita of the poorest of the poor. Moreover, the only inter-sector linkage found was the one that connects rural growth with urban poverty for those people above the food poverty line but below the moderate poverty line.

Exploring plausible channels, we found that rural growth enhances equality of income distribution at total and urban levels, while urban growth does exactly the opposite. But this is still a general equilibrium effect. Thus, we further explored labor market issues. We found that rural growth impacted positively on labor demand for unskilled workers: on this base, *ceteris paribus* it is better for poverty alleviation to have rural growth. We also explored the issue of relative prices, although no impact of rural/urban growth was found here. Everything seems to be driven by the real exchange rate behavior. The share of agricultural to total income is relatively more important for poor people in rural areas, and most of the food-poor people live in rural areas. This may be at the root of our findings.

NOTES

1. We follow their presentation closely.
2. If what matters is overall growth, then $\pi_u = \pi_r = \pi_n = \pi$ and equation (4.5) reduces to: $\Delta \ln P_{it} = \pi \Delta \ln \mu_{it} + \Delta \varepsilon_{it}$.

3. The problem is that inter-regional migration is not taken into account. Since poverty rates are very different among Mexican regions, incorporating inter-regional migration would provide complementary information by measuring how sectoral growth affects poverty as poor people migrate from say high to lower poverty regions. Lack of data prevents us from taking migration flows into account, although below we discuss its likely impact on our results.

4. The FGT(0) (head count) measures the proportion of people below the poverty line; FGT(1) (poverty gap) includes the distance between the poverty line and the average consumption of the poor; FGT (2) accounts for income distribution within the poor. See the technical appendix for a definition of the FGT indices.

5. The poverty lines for 2002 were obtained by inflating figures for 2000 with the implicit prices used in SEDESOL's rural and urban poverty lines for 2000 and 2002, respectively (SEDESOL, 2002).

6. To calculate the FGT class of poverty indicators and their standard errors, Soloaga and Torres (2003) used the SEPOV command from STATA (Jolliffe and Semykina, 1999). This command follows Howes and Lanjouw's (1998) methodology, and allows for the statistical sampling design of each ENIGH to be incorporated into the estimates for the standard errors.

7. This subsection closely follows López and Anriquez's presentation for the Chilean case (see Chapter 3, this volume).

8. This issue may explain the positive impact of urban growth on the Gini coefficient: urban growth as a greater impact on skilled than on unskilled labor demand.

9. We tried other formulations. For instance, we have included dummy variables for the 1982 and 1995 macroeconomic crises. We have included non-agricultural prices in the right-hand side of the equation. We have also reduced the period to 1980–2001 to be able to use the average tariff information available. Results were consistent: what matters is the real exchange rate.

BIBLIOGRAPHY

Ahuja, V., B. Bidani, F.H.G. Ferreira and M. Walton (1997), *Everyone's Miracle?*, Washington, DC: World Bank.

Anand, Sudhir and Ravi Kanbur (1985), 'Poverty under the Kuznets process', *Economic Journal*, **95** (supplement): 42–50.

Atkinson, Anthony (1987), 'On the measurement of poverty', *Econometrica*, **55**: 749–64.

Bardhan, Pranab Kumar (1985), 'Poverty and trickle-down in rural India', in J.W. Mellor and G.M. Desai (eds), *Agricultural Change and Rural Poverty*, Baltimore, MA: Johns Hopkins University Press.

Datt, Gaurav and Martin Ravallion (1992), 'Growth and redistribution components of change in poverty measures: a decomposition with applications to Brazil and India in the 1980s', *Journal of Development Economics*, **38**: 275–95.

Datt, Gaurav and Martin Ravallion (1998a), 'Why have some Indian states done better than others at reducing rural poverty?', *Economica*, **65**: 17–38.

Datt, Gaurav and Martin Ravallion (1998b), 'Farm productivity and rural poverty in India', *Journal of Development Studies*, **34**: 62–85.

Deininger, Klaus and Lyn Squire (1996), 'A new data set measuring income inequality', *World Bank Economic Review*, **10**(3): 565–91.

Deininger, K. and L. Squire (1998), 'New ways of looking at old issues', *Journal of Development Economics*, **57**: 259–87.

Dollar, D. and A. Kraay (2002), 'Growth is good for the poor', *Journal of Economic Growth*, **7**(3): 195–225.

ECLAC (1997), *Panorama Social de América Latina*, Santiago, Chile: Economic Commission for Latin America and the Caribbean.

Fields, Gary (1989), 'Changes in poverty and inequality in developing countries', *World Bank Research Observer*, **4**: 167–86.

Foster, James, J. Greer and Erik Thorbecke (1984), 'A class of decomposable poverty measures', *Econometrica*, **52**: 761–5.

Foster, James and Anthony Shorrocks (1998), 'Poverty orderings', *Econometrica*, **56**(1): 173–7.

Foster, J. and M. Székely (2001), 'Is economic growth good for the poor? Tracking low incomes using general means', Working Paper, Inter-American Development Bank, WP-453, Washington, DC.

Friedman, Jed (2005), 'How responsive is poverty to growth? A regional analysis of poverty, inequality, and growth in Indonesia, 1984–1999', in R. Kanbur and T. Venebles (eds), *Spatial Inequality and Development*, Oxford: Oxford University Press.

Gaiha, Raghav (1987), 'Impoverishment, technology and growth in rural India', *Cambridge Journal of Economics*, **11**(1): 23–46.

Greene, William (2000), *Econometric Analysis*, 4th edn, Basingstoke and New York: Macmillan.

Harris, John R. and Michael P. Todaro (1970), 'Migration, unemployment and development: a two sector analysis', *American Economic Review*, **60**(1): 126–42.

Howes, Stephen and Jean Olson Lanjouw (1997), 'Making poverty comparisons taking into account survey design: how and why?', Living Standards Measurement Study Working Paper no. 129, World Bank, Washington, DC.

Howes, Stephen and Jean Olson Lanjouw (1998), 'Does sample design matter for poverty rate comparisons?', *Review of Income and Wealth*, **44**: 99–109.

Instituto Nacional de Estadística, Geografía e Informática (INEGI) and Comisión Económica para América Latina y el Caribe (CEPAL) (1993), *Magnitud y Evolución de la Pobreza en México, 1984–1992*, Informe Metodológico, México.

Jolliffe, Dean and Anastassia Semykina (1999), 'Robust standard errors for the Foster–Greer–Thorbecke class of poverty indices', *Stata Technical Bulletin Reprints*, Vol. 9, pp. 200–203.

Kakwani, N. (1993), 'Statistical inference in the measurement of poverty', *Review of Economics and Statistics*, **75**(4): 632–9.

Kanbur, Ravi (1987), 'Structural adjustment, macroeconomic adjustment and poverty: a methodology for analysis', *World Development*, **15**: 1515–26.

Krueger, Anne O., Maurice Schiff and Alberto Valdés (1988), 'Agricultural incentives in developing countries: measuring the effect of sectoral and economywide policies', *World Bank Economic Review*, **2**: 255–71.

Kuznets, Simon (1955), 'Economic growth and income inequality', *American Economic Review*, **45**: 1–28.

Levy, Santiago (1991), 'Poverty alleviation in Mexico', Policy, Research and External Affairs Working Paper, WPS 678, World Bank, Washington, DC.

Lipton, Michael (1977), *Why Poor People Stay Poor: Urban Bias and World Development*, London:Temple Smith.

Lipton, M. and Martin Ravallion (1995), 'Poverty and policy', in Jere Behrman and T.N. Srinivasan (eds), *Handbook of Development Economics*, Vol. III, Amsterdam: North-Holland, pp. 2202–614.

Londoño, J.L. and Miguel Székely (2000), 'Persistent poverty and excess inequality', *Journal of Applied Economics*, **3**(1): 93–134.

López-Acevedo, Gladys, Angel Salinas and Quentin Wodon (1999), 'A profile of poverty in Mexico: 1984–1996', Mexico: Poverty and Public Policy Background Paper no. 1, World Bank, Washington, DC.

Lustig, Nora and Miguel Székely (1997), 'México: Evolución Económica, Pobreza y Desigualdad', Inter-American Development Bank.

Mellor, John (2001), 'Meeting the OECD Poverty Targets: An Approach Paper for USAID', Agricultural Policy Development Research Report No. 3, Abt Associates Inc., MA, USA.

Ram, Rati (1995), 'Economic development and inequality: an overlooked regression constraint', *Economic Development and Cultural Change*, **3**: 425–34.

Ravallion, Martin (1994), *Poverty Comparisons*, Chur: Harwood Academic.

Ravallion, Martin and Benu Bidani (1994), 'How robust is a poverty profile?', *World Bank Economic Review*, **8**: 75–102.

Ravallion M. and S. Chen (1997), 'What can new survey data tell us about recent changes in distribution and poverty?', *World Bank Economic Review*, **11**(2): 357–82.

Ravallion Martin and Shaohua Chen (1999), 'When economic reform is faster than statistical reform, measuring and explaining inequality in rural China', Oxford Bulletin of Economic Statistics, **61**(1): 33–56.

Ravallion, Martin and Gaurav Datt (1996), 'How important to India's poor is the sectoral composition of economic growth', *World Bank Economic Review*, **10**(1): 1–25.

Ravallion, Martin and Monika Huppi (1989). 'Poverty and undernutrition in Indonesia during the 1980s', World Bank Policy Research Working Paper 286, World Bank, Washington, DC.

Ravallion, Martin and Monika Huppi (1991), 'Measuring changes in poverty: a methodological case study of Indonesia during an adjustment period', *World Bank Economic Review*, **5**(1): 57–84.

Robinson, Sherman (1976), 'A note on the U-hypothesis relating income inequality and economic development', *American Economic Review*, **66**: 437–40.

SEDESOL (2002), 'Medición de la pobreza: variantes metodológicas y estimación preliminar', Documentos de Investigación 1, Secretaría de Desarrollo Social, Mexico, available at www.sedesol.gob.mx/publicaciones/libros/medicion.pdf.

Sen, Amartya (1981), *Poverty and Famines: An Essay on Entitlement and Deprivation*, Oxford: Oxford University Press.

Soloaga, Isidro and Mario Torres (2003), 'Crecimiento y Pobreza. El caso de México', Documento de Trabajo, Centro de Investigación en Economía y Políticas Públicas, CIEPP-UDLAP.

Székely, Miguel (1998), *The Economics of Poverty, Inequality and Wealth Accumulation in Mexico*, Basingstoke: Macmillan.

Székely, Miguel, Nora Lustig, Martin Cumpa and Antonio Mejía (2000), 'Do we know how much poverty there is?, Working Paper 437, Inter-American Development Bank, Washington, DC.

Thorbecke, Erik and Hong-Sang Jung (1996), 'A multiplier descomposition method to analyze poverty alleviation', *Journal of Development Economics*, **48**: 279–300.

Timmer, C. Peter (1996), 'Food security strategies: the Asian experience', FAO Agricultural Policy and Economic Development Series, 3, FAO, Rome.

Timmer, C. Peter (1997), 'How well do the poor connect to the growth process',

CAER II Discussion Paper No. 17, Harvard Institute for International Development (HIID), Cambridge, MA.

Wodon, Quentin (1999), 'Growth, poverty, and inequality. A regional panel for Bangladesh', Policy Research Working Paper 2072, World Bank, Washington, DC.

Wodon , Quentin (2000), *Poverty and Policy in Latin America and the Caribbean*, Washington, DC: World Bank.

Wooldridge, M. Jeffrey (1999), *Introductory Econometrics: A Modern Approach*, Cincinnati, OH: South-Western College Publishing.

World Bank (1990), *World Development Report 1990: Poverty*, Oxford and New York: Oxford University Press for the World Bank.

World Bank (1999), *World Development Indicators*, Washington, DC: World Bank.

World Bank (2001), 'Country Assistance Strategy Progress Report of the World Bank Group for the United Mexican States', World Bank, Washington, DC.

World Health Organization (1985), 'Energy and Protein Requirements', WHO Technical Report Series 724, Geneva.

APPENDIX 4A1

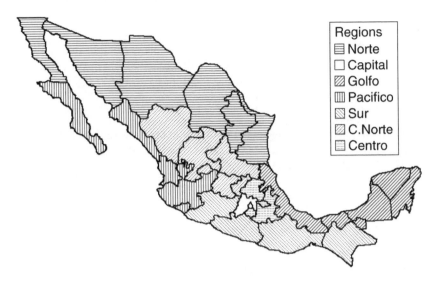

Norte: Baja California, Sonora, Chihuahua, Choahuila, Nuevo León and Tamaulipas
Capital: Mexico and Distrito Federal
Golfo: Veracruz, Tabasco, Campeche, Yucatan and Quintana Roo
Pacífico: Baja California Sur, Sinaloa, Nayarit, Jacisco and Colima
Sur: Michoacan, Guerroro, Oaxaca and Chiapas
Centro Norte: Durango, Zacatecas, San Luis Potosí, Aguas Calientes, Guanajuato
and Queretaro
Centro: Hidalgo, Pueblo,Tlaxcala and Morelos

Figure 4A1.1   Regions and states

Country case studies

APPENDIX 4A2   POVERTY IMPACT OF SECTORAL GROWTH: ESTIMATES WITH REGIONAL DATA

In Tables 4.5, 4.6 and 4.7, the dependent variable is the first difference of the log poverty measure against the first difference of log mean consumption. All the regressions of equations (4.5), (4.6) and (4.7) fitted well and passed various standard statistical tests.

Table 4A2.1   Change in head count poverty FGT(0); 7 regions, 1984–2002

Variable or statistic	Change in national poverty		Components of change in national poverty			
			Urban		Rural*	
	OLS	IV	OLS	IV	OLS	IV
Urban growth π_1	−0.945	−1.094	−0.769	−0.878	−0.143	−0.151
	(−4.21)	(−2.89)	(−4.53)	(−3.31)	(1.16)	(−1.01)
Rural growth π_2	−2.799	−6.775	−0.587	−2.110	−2.430	−4.237
	(−2.61)	(−2.50)	(−0.68)	(−1.11)	(−2.91)	(−2.74)
Population	0.038	−0.464	−0.326	−0.168	0.423	0.363
shift π_3	(0.05)	(−0.36)	(−0.59)	(−0.19)	(2.71)	(0.84)
Adjusted R^2	0.3243	0.184	0.2837	0.2054	0.4019	0.1689
Durbin–Wu–		7.367		1.30		2.29
Hausman $\chi^2(3)$		[0.061]		[0.284]		[0.092]
Sargan test $\chi^2(8)$		11.238		13.43		14.156
		[0.189]		[0.098]		[0.08]
Heteroscedasticity	4.56		3.81		26.1	
$\chi^2(9)$	[0.871]		[0.923]		[0.002]	
Wald $\pi1 = \pi2 = \pi3$	2.22	1.44				
$F(2, 45)$	[0.120]	[0.250]				
Wald $\pi1 = \pi2$	2.98	2.15				
$F(2, 45)$	[0.091]	[0.151]				

Note: t-statistics in parentheses, p-value in square brackets. * For rural, we estimated robust standard errors due to heteroscedasticity. The DWH test for endogeneity for IV estimates showed that for total poverty (first two columns) IV is indicated. For urban poverty (third and fourth columns) OLS would give consistent estimates, whereas for rural poverty (fifth and sixth columns) OLS consistency is not rejected at the 95% confidence level, but is rejected at the 90% confidence level (p-value of the DWH test was 0.092). For rural poverty, the story that each column (OLS or IV) tells is similar, although the coefficient for rural growth is higher in the IV estimates. The Sargan test for overidentifying restrictions shows that for total poverty the instruments used are valid (p-value of 0.189), and for urban and rural poverty this hypothesis cannot be rejected at 95% (p-values of 0.098 and 0.08, respectively).

Source: Own estimates.

Table 4A2.2   Change in poverty gap FGT(1); 7 regions, 1984–2002

Variable or statistic	Change in national poverty		Components of change in national poverty			
			Urban		Rural*	
	OLS	IV	OLS	IV	OLS	IV
Urban growth π_1	−1.182	−1.259	−0.838	−0.921	−0.292	−0.267
	(−4.02)	(−2.48)	(−4.69)	(−3.27)	(−1.52)	(−1.11)
Rural growth π_2	−3.189	−8.629	0.177	−1.485	−3.726	−6.503
	(−2.13)	(−2.38)	(0.20)	(−0.74)	(−3.32)	(−2.95)
Population shift π_3	−0.313	−1.247	−0.133	−0.560	0.603	0.524
	(0.33)	(−0.72)	(0.23)	(−0.50)	(2.09)	(0.78)
Adjusted R^2	0.2842	0.097	0.2863	0.196	0.3732	0.1694
Durbin–Wu–		2.425		1.480		1.673
Hausman $\chi^2(3)$		[0.079]		[0.25]		[0.187]
Sargan test		13.721		13.57		18.76
$\chi^2(8)$		[0.089]		[0.094]		[0.02]
Heteroscedasticity	4.96		6.63		16.9	
$\chi^2(9)$	[0.837]		[0.675]		[0.049]	
Wald $\pi1 = \pi2 = \pi3$	1.17					
$F(2, 45)$	[0.319]					
Wald $\pi1 = \pi2$	1.69					
$F(2, 45)$	[0.200]					

Notes: *t*-statistics in parentheses, *p*-value in square brackets. * Robust standard errors were estimated due to heteroscedasticity.

DWH test for endogeneity for IV estimates showed that for total poverty (first two columns) IV is indicated. For urban poverty (third and fourth columns) OLS would give consistent estimates, whereas for rural poverty (fifth and sixth columns) OLS consistency is not rejected even at the 95% confidence level. The Sargan test for overidentifying restrictions shows that for total and for urban this hypothesis cannot be rejected at 95% (*p*-values of 0.089 and 0.09, respectively). For rural poverty, the instruments were not statistically appropriate (*p*-value for the Sargan test of 0.02).

Source: Own estimates.

Country case studies

Table 4A2.3   Change in squared poverty gap FGT(2); 7 regions, 1984–2002

Variable or statistic	Change in national poverty		Components of change in national poverty			
			Urban		Rural	
	OLS	IV	OLS	IV	OLS	IV
Urban growth π_1	−1.285	−1.289	−0.801	−0.874	−0.392	−0.304
	(−3.55)	(−2.06)	(−4.00)	(−3.07)	(−1.91)	(−0.93)
Rural growth π_2	−4.142	−10.934	0.327	−1.10	−5.010	−8.720
	(−2.25)	(−2.44)	(0.27)	(−0.64)	(−4.79)	(−3.01)
Population shift π_3	−0.328	−1.545	0.169	−0.583	0.810	0.721
	(0.28)	(−0.72)	(0.30)	(−0.55)	(1.21)	(0.73)
Adjusted R^2	0.2499	0.046	0.286	0.217	0.386	0.210
Durbin–Wu–		2.181		1.471		1.34
Hausman $\chi^2(3)$		[0.104]		[0.2360]		[0.22]
Sargan test $\chi^2(8)$		14.072		14.343		20.16
		[0.080]		[0.073]		[0.01]
Heteroscedasticity	4.50		13.83		9.5	
$\chi^2(9)$	[0.875]		[0.1284]		[0.4325]	
Wald $\pi1 = \pi2 = \pi3$	1.38					
$F(2, 5)$	[0.261]					
Wald $\pi1 = \pi2$	2.27					
$F(2, 5)$	[0.138]					

Note: t-statistics in parentheses, p-value in square brackets.
  The DWH test for endogeneity for IV estimates showed that for all three poverty areas (total, urban and rural) the consistency of OLS could not be rejected. Nonetheless (at least marginally) for total poverty this hypothesis was marginally rejected at the 90% level (p-value of 0.104). The Sargan test for overidentifying restrictions shows that for total poverty the instruments used are valid for total and for urban poverty at the 95% confidence level. For rural poverty this hypothesis was rejected with a 99% confidence (p-values of 0.001).

Source: Own estimates.

5. India

Manoj Panda

5.1   INTRODUCTION

India is the second largest populated country in the world. The total population of India exceeded one billion at the beginning of the twenty-first century. According to the official government estimates, about a quarter of the country's total population remains below the poverty line at present. The total number of poor was about 260 million in 1999–2000, making it home to the largest number of poor in the world. About three-quarters of India's poor live in rural areas and depend mostly on agriculture for their livelihood.

The 'green revolution' with the associated technological innovations has been instrumental in improving the livelihood opportunities in rural India since the early 1970s. Hence, it is only natural that the relationship between agricultural growth and poverty reduction has been extensively studied in India over the last three decades. Several authors have emphasised the important role of agriculture in determining changes in magnitude of poverty through channels such as income rise, productivity growth, food prices and wage rate.

Against this background, this chapter aims to reassess the role of agriculture on the poverty-reduction process in India using both cross-section and time-series data for major Indian states. The following section deals with the definition of poverty line, different measures of poverty used in this chapter and the Indian database. Section 3 briefly discusses the recent trends in poverty in India and its variations across states. Sections 4–6 constitute the core of the chapter. Section 4 discusses the various dimensions of linkages between poverty and agriculture in the context of the Indian literature. Section 5 analyses profiles of poverty in India and examines cross-section variations in poverty using the latest available consumption distribution data for 1999–2000. Section 6 examines various channels through which agricultural growth influences rural poverty for low- and high-poverty states with the help of time-series panel data at the state level. Section 7 makes some concluding remarks.

5.2   POVERTY LINE AND POVERTY MEASURES

To measure magnitude of poverty, alternative indices are used based on income or consumption size distribution data and the poverty line. In what follows, we shall use three indices of poverty derived by Foster, Greer and Thorbecke (1984): the head count ratio (HCR), the poverty gap (PG), and the squared poverty gap (SPG). See the technical appendix for the definition of these indices.

Poverty is commonly measured with reference to a poverty line (PL) defined in terms of an absolute income or consumption level used as a benchmark to distinguish the poor and the non-poor. The Planning Commission, which has been in charge of making the official estimates of poverty in India since the early 1980s, has followed a methodology recommended by the Task Force on Projection of Minimum Needs and Effective Consumption Demand (Planning Commission, 1979). The Task Force had estimated the poverty line for 1973–74 as per capita per month consumption expenditure of Rs. 49 for rural areas and Rs. 57 for urban areas at that year's prices.[1] These lines met the recommended per capita daily intake of 2400 calories for rural areas and 2100 calories for urban areas as per observed NSSO[2] consumption patterns for 1973–74. An 'Expert Group' reviewed the methodology of poverty estimation in 1993 and endorsed continuation of the base PL for 1973–74 (Planning Commission, 1993). The updating of the PL is carried out using the consumer price index for agricultural labourers (CPIAL) for rural PL and the consumer price index for industrial workers (CPIIW) for urban PL.[3] The Group recommended that, given the diversity in a large country like India, poverty should be estimated at the state level using state-level data and the national-level estimates be then derived on the basis of state-level poverty estimates. Moreover, the official estimates of poverty are now based on only the NSSO data; the adjustment followed earlier in NSSO consumer expenditure to match with total consumption expenditure from the National Accounts Statistics (NAS) has been abandoned.

Income distribution data in India are few and far between. But a systematic database on household consumption expenditure is available from household surveys conducted by the National Sample Survey Organization from the early 1950s. The NSSO data have attracted a lot of interest from both researchers and policy makers within and outside India for the study of changes in inequality and poverty in the context of a large developing country. Our discussion below on poverty and inequality in India is based on the NSSO expenditure data.

The NSSO collects consumption expenditure and other socio-economic information of sample households through the interview method during successive, 'rounds'. The sample design is stratified and two stage for rural and urban sectors. Households are selected by simple random sampling. The data during the initial rounds were experimental in nature and were not comparable over time with regard to design and coverage of the survey, period of reference in the interview and concepts. Hence, we have used data from 1960 onwards. NSSO budget surveys were conducted more or less on an annual basis until 1972–73, and on a quinquennial basis after that. While continuing the practice of large-scale quinquennial surveys at present, the NSSO has also conducted annual surveys since 1986–87 for a small sample of households.

Household consumption in the NSSO data consists of consumption of goods and services from monetary purchases, receipts in exchange for goods and services, home-grown stocks and free receipts. Consumption of homegrown produce, which could be substantial for many rural households, is valued at ex-farm prices. Some researchers prefer to use consumption rather than income data for poverty analysis because consumption is less influenced by transient factors and so it is more closely related to permanent income. But the disadvantage of using consumption data is that the savings and, more importantly, the dissavings position of the household are ignored. Thus, if the poor make distressed borrowings to meet minimum essential consumption, such vulnerability would not be reflected in the consumption data.

5.3   TRENDS IN POVERTY

We start with the official poverty estimates made by the Planning Commission, Government of India based on the methodology recommended by the Expert Group using the NSSO consumption distribution data and the poverty lines mentioned earlier. Estimates of number and percentage of poor using the quinquennial NSSO surveys are given in Figure 5.1. The HCR has declined by about half from 56 percent in 1973–74 to 27 percent in 1999–2000 in rural areas and from 49 percent to 24 percent in urban areas over the same period. At the all-India level (that is, rural and urban combined), the HCR has fallen from 55 percent in 1973–74 to 26 percent in 1999–2000. The large drop in the HCR of this order has, however, not led to similar change in the absolute number of poor due to population growth. It remained virtually unchanged at about 320 million until 1993–94, though it dropped to about 260 million in 1999–2000.

The long-term trends in poverty in India as estimated by the World Bank are given in Table 5.1. These estimates are based on the above official

Country case studies

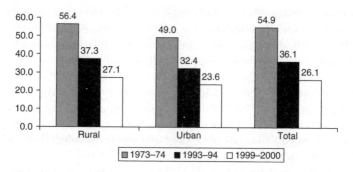

Figure 5.1   Head count ratio of poverty in India (official estimates)

Table 5.1   Incidence of poverty in India: 1960–2000

Year	Rural			Urban		
	HCR	PG	SPG	HCR	PG	SPG
1960–61	45.40	13.60	5.53	44.65	13.84	5.83
1961–62	47.20	13.60	5.31	43.55	13.79	6.05
1963–64	48.53	13.88	5.49	44.83	13.29	5.17
1964–65	53.66	16.08	6.60	48.78	15.24	6.38
1965–66	57.60	17.97	7.60	52.90	16.82	6.98
1966–67	64.30	22.01	10.01	52.24	16.81	7.19
1967–68	63.67	21.80	9.85	52.91	16.93	7.22
1968–69	59.00	18.96	8.17	49.29	15.54	6.54
1969–70	57.61	18.24	7.73	47.16	14.32	5.86
1970–71	54.84	16.55	6.80	44.98	13.35	5.35
1972–73	55.36	17.35	7.33	45.67	13.46	5.26
1973–74	55.72	17.18	7.13	47.96	13.60	5.22
1977–78	50.60	15.03	6.06	40.50	11.69	4.53
1983	45.31	12.65	4.84	35.65	9.52	3.56
1986–87	38.81	10.01	3.70	34.29	9.10	3.40
1987–88	39.60	9.70	3.40	35.65	9.31	3.25
1988–89	39.06	9.50	3.29	36.60	9.54	3.29
1989–90	34.30	7.80	2.58	33.40	8.51	3.04
1990–91	36.43	8.64	2.93	32.76	8.51	3.12
1991	37.42	8.29	2.68	33.23	8.24	2.90
1992	43.47	10.88	3.81	33.73	8.82	3.19
1993–94	37.30	8.52	2.78	32.40	8.07	2.83
1999–2000	27.20	5.27	1.48	23.70	5.17	1.58

Source: World Bank. Own estimates for the last two years.

benchmark poverty lines of Rs. 49 and Rs. 57 at 1973–74 prices for rural and urban areas, respectively, though the deflators used to estimate the poverty lines for other years are slightly different from the official ones.[4] The following major conclusions[5] could be derived from Table 5.1:

1. Poverty in India was marked by sharp year-to-year fluctuations without a long-term trend in either direction until 1973. There were, however, upward or downward movements for short periods of 3–4 years. The percentage of poor increased sharply through the mid-1960s to reach a peak of about 64 percent in 1966–67 and then fell with marginal upward movements in between. While the declining trend continued beyond 1973, the incidence of poverty did not fall below that in the early 1960s until 1983 in the rural sector and 1977 in the urban sector.

2. Poverty estimates from 1973–74 to 1989–90 clearly showed a declining trend in both rural and urban areas. During this period, the HCR fell from 56 to 34 percent in rural India and from 48 to 33 percent in urban India. The decline was particularly sharp until 1986–87. The severity index of poverty indicated by the SPG index fell even more by about half during this period.

3. India witnessed a macroeconomic crisis during 1990–91 and poverty increased during the period of the crisis and initial years of the reforms adopted in 1991. The HCR began to fall again in 1993–94.

4. The benefits of reform measures were, however, visible by 1999–2000. The poverty ratio in both rural and urban India had fallen considerably by then, compared to the pre-reform period. All three measures of poverty reflect this result. The fall in poverty seems to have been driven exclusively by the growth factor in the 1990s since there is some evidence of an increase in inequality in consumption expenditure distribution after the post–reform period in India, especially in the urban segment coupled with an increase in urban–rural differences (Deaton and Drèze, 2002).

Given the large size of India, it is important to have a look at the state-level experiences. Table 5.2 shows the growth rates in rural poverty indices and related variables for 14 major states (which account for more than 90 percent of the all-India population). The falling trend in poverty has been a general feature in almost all the states, but the rates of fall differ substantially across states, ranging from 0.23 percent per annum in Bihar in the north to 3.30 percent in Kerala in the south for the HCR. Other indices of poverty such as the PG and the SPG also indicate a falling trend, though at a faster rate. The only exception is the state of Assam in the northeast,

Table 5.2   *Average annual growth rates in poverty and related variables:*
              1960–2000

State	Average annual growth rates (%)					
	HCR	PG	SPG	MPCE	Gini	PCY
Andhra	−2.43	−3.91	−4.97	1.13	−0.30	2.72
Assam	0.14	0.15	0.17	−0.09	−0.18	2.30
Bihar	−0.23	−1.29	−2.19	0.06	−1.08	1.31
Gujarat	−1.98	−3.36	−4.36	0.91	−0.48	2.59
Karnataka	−1.27	−2.13	−2.79	0.57	−0.46	2.33
Kerala	−3.30	−5.27	−6.68	1.93	−0.20	2.51
Madhya Pradesh	−0.62	−1.51	−2.26	0.39	−0.39	1.94
Maharashtra	−1.31	−2.06	−2.59	0.92	0.17	2.98
Orissa	−1.63	−2.88	−4.01	0.83	−0.34	1.88
Punjab	−2.65	−3.86	−4.67	0.57	−0.56	2.91
Rajasthan	−1.27	−2.25	−3.03	0.50	−0.72	1.52
Tamil Nadu	−1.71	−2.83	−3.72	0.98	−0.21	2.96
Uttar Pradesh	−1.07	−1.88	−2.56	0.47	−0.25	1.66
West Bengal	−2.46	−3.79	−4.91	1.07	−0.11	1.95

Note: MPCE = Monthly Per Capita Consumption Expenditure, PCY = Per Capita
Income, other abbreviations as explained in the text.

Source: Own estimates.

where poverty has not fallen over the years by any of the three measures; instead, it has marginally increased.[6]

5.4   ISSUES AND LITERATURE

Promotion of growth and removal of poverty have been well-recognised objectives of India's economic policy for more than half a century. But whether the poor actually benefited from the growth process has been one of the most debated topics in India as elsewhere. Following Simon Kuznets's finding of an inverted 'U' curve type relationship between income inequality and per capita income growth, some authors thought that distribution would worsen in the initial stages of development before it gets better in developing countries. This line of thought, dominant in the 1960s, implied that the benefits to the poor from economic growth would be at best small, or even negative. Empirical works based mostly on the NSSO data have generated a lively debate since the early 1970s.[7]

In an oft-quoted paper, Ahluwalia (1978) investigated the trickle-down question by examining whether year-to-year changes in incidence of rural poverty in India could be explained by agricultural growth performance. He found an inverse relationship between agricultural output per head of rural population and percentage of population below the poverty line in rural India during 1956 to 1973 for most of the Indian states. This meant that there were 'trickle-down' effects of agricultural growth.

Another factor that has attracted a lot of attention is the role of prices, in particular food price. Saith (1981) took this into account and questioned the Ahluwalia hypothesis. Since real income change is based on factor price movements, it might not adequately reflect the purchasing power of the people to meet their consumption needs. The poor spend a large part, often most, of their income on foodgrains, a staple food that helps to meet the energy need. The real purchasing power of the poor would then depend on the price of food relative to their earnings. Hence, it is natural to consider relative food price as an important determinant of poverty.[8]

Datt and Ravallion (1998) jointly estimate three equations for poverty, agricultural wages and relative price of food to examine the effects of farm yield on rural poverty during 1958–94. They found that higher farm productivity led to both absolute and relative gains for the rural poor and that such gains were not confined to those near the poverty line. Real wages and relative prices were the main channels for the poor to benefit from the growth process. The poor benefited mostly from a higher average living standard as such and not so much from improved distribution.

Ravallion and Datt (1996) estimate the relative importance of sectoral composition of economic growth to poverty reduction. They find that primary and tertiary sector growth reduced poverty in both rural and urban areas. But secondary sector growth did not reduce poverty in either segment. In fact, it is growth in the tertiary sector – possibly in the informal component – that had the largest quantitative impact on the rural and urban poor. This finding thus questions the capital-intensive industrialisation strategy followed by India in the post-independence era in so far as it produced negligible gains to the poor.

Income distribution seems to have changed very little on a long-term basis. The Gini coefficient in consumption distribution for rural India fell marginally after the 1970s. There is no detectable trend in the Gini coefficient in urban areas. The near invariance of the distribution parameter over the decades is not unexpected in the liberal democratic mixed-economy framework that India adopted after independence. In such an environment, one would expect a steady growth in income to be a necessary but not sufficient condition for poverty reduction (Panda, 1999). It might not be sufficient if the growth rate is so small that its effects are offset by a minor deterioration in the distribution parameter. Hence, it is not surprising that a small per capita income growth until the mid-1970s did not lead to a declining trend in poverty. Poverty started to decline after the mid-1970s when per capita income growth picked up to about 3 percent per annum. Thus, the important role of a critical minimum growth is evident in the Indian context.

Srinivasan (1986) possibly had such logic in mind when he commented that, if the percolation hypothesis did not hold strongly earlier, it was because there was very little to percolate. Further studies confirmed the existence of the percolation mechanism as growth picked up in later years.

How do the poor benefit from the growth process? Poor households are generally landless labourers or farmers with marginal landholdings or village artisans with traditional crafts. Manual labour service is their major means of earning. They earn wages from hired-out labour service or imputed wages from self-employment. Agricultural growth, especially when brought about by area increase or multiple cropping, would typically expand the employment opportunities for the poor. A second channel is through the real wage rate increase as demand for employment grows from various sectors of the economy. Employment expansion and wage rate rise are certainly the most direct channels through which the poor benefit. Once these two effects operate, other effects start flowing in. As opportunities for gainful earnings expand, they might acquire small productive assets or invest in skill formation and human capital. These effects could be substantial for the poor after a particular stage of improvement.

What has been the quantitative response of poverty to growth in mean income or consumption? Ravallion and Datt (1996) provide estimates of change in poverty measures due to growth in (a) per capita consumption (for all households) as estimated from NSSO data; (b) per capita consumption from NAS; and (c) per capita net domestic product from NAS. Their results can be summarised as follows:

- The implied elasticities are in the range of –0.8 to –1.3 for the head count ratio of poverty, –1.15 to –1.9 for the poverty gap and –1.45 to –2.3 for the squared poverty gap.
- The higher elasticity for the SPG index, which is affected not only by the proportion of the poor but also by severity of poverty, means that effects of growth and contraction in the economy were not confined to those near the poverty line.
- The response of poverty is larger for consumption than for income, which might be explained in terms of consumption-smoothing behaviour of households to temporary changes in income.

The observed changes in poverty indices could be decomposed to growth and redistribution effects. The growth component is the change in poverty measure that would have occurred had the inequality parameter remained constant, whereas the redistribution component is the change in poverty measure when the mean consumption remains constant. Datt (1998) reports that the growth factor has accounted for as much as 87 percent of the cumulative fall in the HCR. The redistribution factor, however, accounted for about a third of the cumulative fall in the PG index and two-fifths of the SPG index. Most of the pro-poor effects of redistribution were realised by the mid-1960s and the poor have benefited almost entirely due to growth after the 1970s.

Both the central and state governments undertake several welfare-oriented programmes including health, education and public works. Such expenditures are classified under the category 'development expenditure' which excludes expenditure on public administration and defence, and interest payments but includes government's own capital expenditure.[9] In a persuasive paper, Sen (1996) argued for inclusion of government development expenditures as a determinant of poverty, and empirically verified that it had important effects in the Indian context. Fan et al. (2000) estimate the direct and indirect effects of different types of government expenditures on rural poverty. They found that additional investments in rural roads, agricultural research and education had the highest effects on poverty reduction as well as agricultural productivity growth.

5.5   PROFILE OF POVERTY

In this section, we build up profiles of poverty in India using unit-level cross-section data for the latest NSSO quinquennial round for 1999–2000 and examine the relationship of poverty with various agriculture related variables. The total number of sample households covered in the 55th round survey is about 120 thousand consisting of 71 thousand rural and 49 thousand urban households. The NSSO survey data on consumption expenditure provide information by several characteristics of households. The analysis is carried out at the all-India national level as well as separately at the state level for 15 major states that account for more than 90 percent of India's population.[10]

5.5.1   Regional Concentration

To begin with, we present the HCR for 1999–2000 for the major states in Table 5.3. Several key features about regional concentration of India's poor can be seen from this table:

*Table 5.3   Head count ratio of poverty for major states in India:
1999–2000*

State	HCR	Est. number of poor	Percentage contribution	Mean consumption expenditure
Andhra Pradesh	15.37	11.27	4.67	546.16
Assam	36.79	8.29	3.44	465.44
Bihar	42.70	39.02	16.18	412.90
Gujarat	13.13	5.67	2.35	659.66
Haryana	8.12	1.54	0.64	768.26
Karnataka	19.02	9.12	3.78	614.79
Kerala	12.12	3.32	1.38	809.37
Madhya Pradesh	37.52	28.79	11.94	466.01
Maharashtra	24.58	22.00	9.12	680.24
Orissa	47.38	16.64	6.90	413.16
Punjab	5.83	1.28	0.53	791.14
Rajasthan	14.78	6.89	2.86	602.95
Tamil Nadu	20.88	12.11	5.02	673.30
Uttar Pradesh	30.99	49.92	20.70	511.44
West Bengal	28.03	20.47	8.49	542.30
Total	26.10	241.21	100.00	578.62

Source: Own estimates.

- First, the estimates show that 26 percent of India's population remained below the official poverty line. All the states, however, are not equally poor and the average hides the large variations across states that range from as low as 6–8 percent for Punjab and Haryana in the north-west part of the country to as high as 47 percent for Orissa and 43 percent for Bihar in the east.
- Second, of the 15 major states, six have an incidence of poverty higher than the national level: Orissa, Bihar, Madhya Pradesh, Assam, Uttar Pradesh and West Bengal. These states together account for two-thirds of the total number of poor in the country. The PG and SPG measures indicating the depth and incidence of poverty also support this conclusion (Table 5.4).
- Third, another major state, Maharashtra has an HCR which is very close to the national level. The seven states – the above six and Maharashtra – taken together account for three-quarters of India's poor (see Table 5.3).

Table 5.4   Poverty indices for rural and urban areas by state: 1999–2000

State	Rural			Urban		
	HCR	PG	SPG	HCR	PG	SPG
Andhra Pradesh	10.53	1.80	0.54	27.23	5.56	1.70
Assam	40.15	8.44	2.69	7.22	1.48	0.41
Bihar	44.09	8.76	2.54	33.48	6.73	2.08
Gujarat	12.36	2.22	0.60	14.78	2.41	0.65
Haryana	7.41	1.26	0.36	10.02	2.04	0.76
Karnataka	16.84	2.72	0.69	24.61	5.59	1.84
Kerala	9.37	1.46	0.37	19.84	3.91	1.14
Madhya Pradesh	37.25	7.69	2.33	38.48	9.52	3.31
Maharashtra	23.22	4.36	1.28	26.75	6.72	2.40
Orissa	48.14	11.74	4.01	43.51	11.05	3.90
Punjab	5.99	0.80	0.18	5.47	0.63	0.13
Rajasthan	13.47	2.05	0.50	19.43	3.44	0.91
Tamil Nadu	20.02	3.81	1.13	22.50	4.79	1.54
Uttar Pradesh	31.06	5.80	1.61	30.74	6.58	2.00
West Bengal	31.66	6.49	1.95	14.70	2.54	0.70
All India	26.78	5.26	1.55	23.44	5.15	1.65

Source: Own estimates.

5.5.2   Poverty by Social Groups

Next, we estimate the poverty ratios by different social groups like scheduled tribe (ST), scheduled caste (SC) and other backward classes (OBC) in the Indian social hierarchy. The estimates given in Table 5.5 show that incidence of poverty varies widely across social groups. High incidence of poverty prevails among the ST and SC populations, which have suffered from social and/or economic exclusion for centuries.[11] More than 45 percent of households among the ST group are poor while the corresponding number is only 15 percent among the non-backward households classified under the 'others' category in Table 5.5. The differences across social groups turn out to be sharper if we use the PG or SPG measures.

5.5.3   Poverty by Activity Type

Table 5.6 gives magnitude of poverty by activity of the head of the household. Poverty level is the highest among households engaged as agricultural labourers followed by non-agricultural labourers in all the states.

Table 5.5 Poverty by social groups in major states in India: 1999–2000

State	HCR				PG				SPG			
	ST	SC	OBC	Others	ST	SC	OBC	Others	ST	SC	OBC	Others
Andhra Pradesh	23.07	16.47	9.59	3.40	4.34	3.03	1.46	0.60	1.30	1.05	0.38	0.17
Assam	39.16	44.97	40.40	39.36	7.15	8.25	8.52	8.83	1.84	2.43	2.65	3.00
Bihar	59.37	59.30	42.83	26.28	13.24	13.30	7.94	4.56	4.21	4.16	2.14	1.28
Gujarat	27.50	15.57	11.15	4.58	5.41	2.61	2.08	0.58	1.55	0.68	0.56	0.12
Haryana	0.00	17.02	10.82	1.13	0.00	2.98	1.64	0.26	0.00	0.85	0.42	0.10
Karnataka	24.86	25.67	15.74	11.05	3.78	4.32	2.64	1.64	0.87	1.20	0.62	0.44
Kerala	25.04	15.61	10.88	4.96	3.89	2.41	1.66	0.82	1.02	0.70	0.40	0.22
Madhya Pradesh	57.14	41.21	32.32	11.70	12.53	8.45	6.40	1.90	4.02	2.50	1.87	0.46
Maharashtra	44.20	31.64	21.89	12.78	9.97	5.86	3.86	1.93	3.34	1.64	1.10	0.45
Orissa	73.10	52.30	39.70	24.01	21.00	11.68	8.77	4.19	7.71	3.65	2.90	1.19
Punjab	16.64	11.88	6.97	0.56	2.11	1.62	0.86	0.07	0.34	0.39	0.17	0.01
Rajasthan	24.83	19.52	10.21	6.03	4.52	3.09	1.24	0.74	1.19	0.86	0.24	0.15
Tamil Nadu	44.58	31.73	14.64	10.64	11.31	6.04	2.69	2.63	3.95	1.67	0.82	0.93
Uttar Pradesh	34.68	43.38	32.96	17.62	8.00	8.63	5.99	3.03	2.80	2.50	1.62	0.79
West Bengal	50.05	34.91	20.00	29.42	10.31	7.15	4.57	5.97	2.92	2.23	1.63	1.75
All India	45.82	35.89	26.96	14.98	10.59	7.22	4.93	2.60	3.49	2.15	1.38	0.71

Source: Own estimates.

Table 5.6   Head count ratio of poverty in rural areas by household type

State	Self-employed		Labour		Others	All
	Agri	Non-Agri	Agri	Non-Agri		
Andra Pradesh	6.91	8.42	14.83	8.30	3.57	10.53
Assam	30.13	37.77	67.06	58.65	20.95	40.15
Bihar	31.30	39.38	59.17	64.36	36.90	44.09
Gujarat	6.42	8.18	19.91	18.91	5.46	12.36
Haryana	1.20	9.31	19.22	16.14	1.74	7.41
Karnataka	11.03	14.25	25.09	15.21	6.20	16.84
Kerala	3.69	7.20	19.37	9.45	3.89	9.37
Madhya Pradesh	27.11	30.18	53.58	56.54	15.22	37.25
Maharashtra	15.98	14.44	36.30	12.92	6.78	23.22
Orissa	40.39	35.06	63.78	55.18	22.35	48.14
Punjab	0.91	4.55	14.36	7.73	2.80	5.99
Rajasthan	11.25	9.41	27.51	21.24	8.40	13.47
Tamil Nadu	10.46	13.66	29.19	14.65	12.00	20.02
Uttar Pradesh	24.20	33.65	50.91	36.92	21.52	31.06
West Bengal	20.79	27.96	45.10	31.75	13.14	31.66
Total	20.09	23.82	39.83	27.52	15.07	26.78

Source: Own estimates.

The 'others' category comprising mostly salaried class generally have the least poverty in most states. The self-employed in agricultural households have relatively less poverty compared to the self-employed in non-agricultural operations in a majority of states (except in Maharashtra, Orissa and Rajasthan). Thus, the chances that a self-employed household in agriculture remains above the poverty line are higher than that for a self-employed in non-agriculture. This possibly explains why a typical rural household normally tends to hold land, which is not only a matter of social status but also a kind of insurance mechanism to move out of poverty, next only to a secured salary job.

5.5.4   Effect of Land Size

Table 5.7 shows poverty by size of land cultivated for rural India. Land is the most important asset among rural households. As such, the landless and marginal farmers happen to be among the poorest families in different states. More specifically, households with less than 1 hectare have more than the average poverty level.

Table 5.7   Head count ratio by land size

State	<1.01ha	1.01–2.00ha	2.01–4.00ha	>4.00ha	All
Andhra Pradesh	11.59	6.94	8.67	5.61	10.53
Assam	45.56	28.71	18.26	33.66	40.15
Bihar	47.68	32.48	20.16	18.10	44.09
Gujarat	16.11	7.84	2.86	1.82	12.36
Haryana	10.97	2.52	0.00	0.00	7.41
Karnataka	18.95	16.09	13.90	10.00	16.84
Kerala	10.02	0.99	0.00	0.00	9.37
Madhya Pradesh	45.29	34.91	30.28	18.66	37.25
Maharashtra	25.50	21.24	21.06	12.01	23.22
Orissa	50.66	41.50	37.37	38.06	48.14
Punjab	8.15	1.01	0.00	2.20	5.99
Rajasthan	17.58	13.38	10.02	7.98	13.47
Tamil Nadu	21.09	16.32	6.32	1.06	20.02
Uttar Pradesh	35.58	23.97	13.68	7.07	31.06
West Bengal	32.24	25.57	31.74	24.18	31.66
Total	30.03	22.59	17.32	10.62	26.78

Source: Own estimates.

5.5.5   Effect of Irrigation

The role of irrigation in the introduction of high-yielding varieties of new technology in agriculture has been well recognised. Table 5.8 examines the role of irrigation in poverty reduction of a rural household. It is clear that in most states households with access to irrigation have only about half the poverty incidence compared to households without such access. The effect of irrigation facility even among the ST households is evident from the fact that the HCR reduces dramatically from 51 percent for ST households without irrigation to 29 percent for ST households with irrigation.

5.6   CHANNELS

We now turn to an examination of various factors influencing the movement of poverty over time so as to identify the channels through which agricultural growth has brought about changes in the incidence of poverty in India. The analysis is based on econometric estimation using time-series data for 14 major states for 20 rounds of NSSO survey over the period 1960–61 to 1999–2000.[12] We have divided the states into two groups –

Table 5.8   Head count ratio by irrigated and non-irrigated land for social groups

State	Irrigated					Non-irrigated				
	ST	SC	OBC	Others	All	ST	SC	OBC	Others	All
Andhra Pradesh	15.98	9.51	5.26	2.03	5.38	25.30	18.15	11.28	4.33	12.63
Assam	48.04	0.00	18.17	23.00	24.75	38.92	45.69	40.92	39.86	40.57
Bihar	49.44	43.61	31.17	15.73	28.59	63.03	61.70	51.16	37.87	53.13
Gujarat	19.78	2.88	9.98	3.20	7.72	30.68	17.93	11.71	5.96	15.01
Haryana	0.00	16.68	2.91	0.72	1.79	0.00	17.05	15.32	2.19	12.44
Karnataka	14.79	12.50	8.14	4.27	7.43	27.57	27.52	19.35	14.20	20.37
Kerala	15.62	0.00	5.35	0.00	2.82	26.99	16.25	11.45	5.76	10.15
Madhya Pradesh	41.97	28.80	20.47	8.78	22.08	61.10	46.38	42.43	15.00	46.42
Maharashtra	27.35	16.32	15.07	9.66	12.99	46.42	32.81	24.06	14.42	26.44
Orissa	42.35	28.31	23.95	15.84	25.24	76.04	56.22	43.27	26.27	52.36
Punjab	0.00	0.66	5.91	0.43	1.04	18.82	12.54	7.42	0.90	9.36
Rajasthan	18.51	18.97	10.48	5.90	12.26	34.94	19.79	9.91	6.13	14.65
Tamil Nadu	83.91	31.36	12.22	2.18	15.25	30.60	31.78	15.67	13.53	21.51
Uttar Pradesh	20.42	39.83	31.37	15.90	28.26	55.48	47.56	37.27	21.45	36.73
West Bengal	34.58	23.88	10.36	17.72	19.42	53.12	39.35	24.56	34.81	36.85
All-India	29.11	31.24	22.66	10.41	19.79	51.37	37.02	27.76	20.12	30.71

Source: Own estimates.

low-poverty states and high-poverty states – on the basis of the extent of poverty in 1999–2000 discussed in the earlier section. The 'low-poverty' group includes: Andhra Pradesh, Gujarat, Karnataka, Kerala, Punjab-Haryana,[13] Rajasthan and Tamil Nadu. These states have been relatively successful in reducing poverty and their head count ratios ranged between 6 and 21 percent compared to the national average of 26 percent in 1999–2000. The 'high-poverty' group consists of seven states: Orissa, Bihar, Madhya Pradesh, Assam, Uttar Pradesh, West Bengal and Maharashtra. These states have head count ratios higher than or close to the national average of 26 percent (see Table 5.3) and together account for about three-quarters of the total number of rural poor in the country at present. These states have not been so successful in reducing poverty during the past decades. Such a grouping helps us to examine the differential effects of agricultural growth process on poverty for these two groups of states.

While reviewing the literature in Section 4, we discussed several channels through which agricultural developments might affect rural poverty; namely, income growth as reflected by income per head of rural population or yield per hectare, relative price of foodgrains and real wage rate of

Table 5.9(a)   *Regression results for low-poverty states (dependent variable: head count ratio)*

Explanatory variable	Equation no.			
	(1)	(2)	(3)	(4)
Per capita agricultural income	−0.2222 (2.48)*			−0.1268 (1.64)
Yield per hectare		−0.3001 (4.99)**	−0.1168 (1.52)	
Per capita net sown area			−0.3958 (2.07)*	
Relative food prices	1.6567 (4.61)**	1.1895 (3.38)**	0.5861 (1.73)+	0.6231 (1.83)+
Real agricultural wage	−0.7092 (10.03)**	−0.5449 (7.13)**	−0.3691 (4.80)**	−0.377 (4.89)**
Per capita development expenditure			−0.2947 (4.70)**	−0.2109 (6.82)**
Constant	6.5626 (11.38)**	7.0006 (18.13)**	6.0613 (12.35)**	6.045 (12.25)**
Observations	124	124	124	124
R-squared	0.85	0.87	0.90	0.89

Notes: Absolute value of *t*-statistics in parentheses.
+ significant at 10%; * significant at 5%; ** significant at 1%.
All regressions in double log form with state dummies for intercepts.

agricultural labour. We also drew attention to the role of government development expenditure stressed by some authors in this context. Tables 5.9(a)–5.9(c) and 5.10(a)–5.10(c) present regression results from the panel data[14] with about 125 observations in each group estimated using the ordinary least squares (OLS) method. The variables are in double log form and the coefficients thus indicate elasticities of the poverty indices with respect to the corresponding explanatory variables. We have also used state dummies in order to separate out the state-specific effects.

Let us first discuss results for the low-poverty states. Tables 5.9(a)–5.9(c) present regression results using poverty indices HCR, PG and SPG as dependent variables, respectively. There are four sets of equations in the tables. The explanatory variables used in equation (1) are per capita agricultural income (per head of rural population), relative food price (price index of foodgrains relative to that of all commodities) and real agricultural wage rate. All these variables have significant effects with the right signs on the three indices of poverty. Growth in agricultural income and rise in real wage rate have poverty-reducing effects. Potentially, these are the direct

Table 5.9(b)   *Regression results for low-poverty states (dependent variable: poverty gap index)*

Explanatory variable	Equation no.			
	(1)	(2)	(3)	(4)
Per capita agricultural income	−0.3915 (2.82)**			−0.2341 (2.01)*
Yield per hectare		−0.5174 (5.65)**	−0.2208 (1.90)+	
Per capita net sown area			−0.5935 (2.05)*	
Relative food prices	2.2992 (4.12)**	1.4988 (2.79)**	0.5437 (1.06)	0.5932 (1.16)
Real agricultural wage	−1.1696 (10.67)**	−0.8887 (7.63)**	−0.6107 (5.26)**	−0.6212 (5.35)**
Per capita development expenditure			−0.4601 (4.85)**	−0.3481 (7.47)**
Constant	7.3114 (8.18)**	8.0129 (13.62)**	6.4789 (8.74)**	6.4571 (8.68)**
Observations	124	124	124	124
R-squared	0.84	0.87	0.9	0.9

Note: As in Table 5.9(a).

channels for the poor to benefit from agriculture by way of employment and income and the results confirm the existence of these channels. Given that the incidence of poverty is high among agricultural labourers, elasticity of poverty with respect to real wage is larger than that with respect to overall agricultural income per capita. This means that a 1 percent increase in agricultural real wage reduces poverty to a greater extent than a 1 percent rise in overall agricultural income. Real wage increase appears to be the most effective channel through which agricultural growth reduces poverty.

Relative food price is another variable that has a very strong effect on movements of poverty. A rise in food price relative to overall price has a poverty-increasing effect. As a net seller of foodgrains, a farmer might gain from an increase in the relative price of foodgrains. But most of the poor in rural India are net purchasers of food grains. In fact, they spend most of their income on food items. Hence, a rise in food price has an adverse effect on their welfare. An expansion in agricultural supply reduces the relative price of food and enhances the real purchasing power of the poor, given the nominal income. Thus, terms of trade is an important indirect channel through which the agricultural sector contributes to poverty reduction.

Table 5.9(c)   Regression results for low-poverty states (dependent
variable: squared poverty gap)

Explanatory variable	Equation no.			
	(1)	(2)	(3)	(4)
Per capita agricultural	−0.5288			−0.3235
income	(2.86)**			(2.07)*
Yield per hectare		−0.6864	−0.3066	
		(5.62)**	(1.96)+	
Per capita net sown area			−0.7788	
			(2.00)*	
Relative food prices	2.7895	1.7334	0.5018	0.5646
	(3.76)**	(2.43)*	(0.73)	(0.82)
Real agricultural wage	−1.5054	−1.1354	−0.7768	−0.7902
	(10.33)**	(7.32)**	(4.98)**	(5.07)**
Per capita development			−0.5958	−0.454
expenditure			(4.68)**	(7.26)**
Constant	7.9234	8.7952	6.8368	6.8091
	(6.66)**	(11.22)**	(6.87)**	(6.82)**
Observations	124	124	124	124
R-squared	0.83	0.86	0.88	0.88

Note: As in Table 5.9(a).

Equation (2) uses yield per hectare as an indicator of agricultural growth rather than per capita income along with all other variables as in the first equation. The results turn out to be similar to those noted above. Agricultural yield increase has a significant poverty-reducing effect even after controlling for the real wage rate effect. It indicates that the growth process percolates down to the poor through other channels, such as the multiplier effects operating through the farmers' expenditure chain. In order to probe this aspect further and check the sensitivity of the results, we carried out the regressions with some more variations.[15]

In equation (3), two new variables are introduced over and above the variables in equation (2). One of them is per capita net sown area and indicates the land–man ratio reflecting land resource position in rural areas. Note that the variable per capita income could actually be decomposed as yield per unit land and land–man ratio. The new variable land–man ratio has a significant effect on all the three measures of poverty. Moreover, once we control for the land–man ratio, the effect of yield factor gets reduced. Yield effect is negative but insignificant in explaining HCR, though it continues to be significant in the case of the poverty gap and squared poverty gap (Tables 5.9(b) and 5.9(c)). One explanation for such an effect could be that agricultural area expansion creates more demand for farm employment and directly helps the poor, while effects of yield increases directly help only a section of the poor, namely, the owner cultivators.

The second new variable added in equation (3) is per capita development expenditure. This includes the expenditure on direct poverty alleviation programmes carried out by the government to create wage and self-employment for the poor households. Such programmes have been a major source of non-farm income for the rural poor and not surprisingly per capita development expenditure has a significant income poverty-reducing effect.[16]

Equation (4) repeats equation (1) with the inclusion of per capita development expenditure whose coefficient remains negative and significant. But, more surprisingly, the coefficient of per capita agricultural income turns out to be insignificant for explaining HCR (Table 5.9(a)), though it remains significant in the equations for poverty gap and squared poverty gap in Tables 5.9(b) and 5.9(c). Controlling for other effects in equation (4), agricultural income growth thus seems to affect the very poor more strongly than the moderately poor.

Comparing the results across Tables 5.9(a)–5.9(c), we find that the effects of most variables generally become stronger as we move from the HCR to the PG and then to the SPG measure. Thus, the effects noticed through various channels are not confined to people around the poverty line, but run across the poor as well as the very poor.

Let us now consider the states which have been less successful in reducing poverty and where a high incidence of poverty still prevails. The regression results for this group of states are presented in Tables 5.10(a)–5.10(c). Real wage has a poverty-reducing effect in the high-poverty states. Similarly, relative price of food has a positive relationship with poverty. The contrast that seems to operate in the high-poverty states is that agricultural income variables – per capita income or yield – do not seem to exert a significant impact on variations in poverty incidence in all the equations in the table. Per capita development expenditure too does not have any significant impact on poverty in the high-poverty states group (equations (3–4)).

How do we interpret these results? As we have noted earlier, the high-poverty states lie in the central and eastern part of India. The green revolution that started in the northwest did not spread to the central and eastern area in an effective way. Some local agricultural growth effects could be seen in the high-poverty states only in the second half of the period considered in the dataset. Thus, one interpretation could be that there was not much growth in the high-poverty states (taken together) for

Table 5.10(a)   Regression results for high-poverty states (dependent variable: head count ratio)

Explanatory variable	Equation no.			
	(1)	(2)	(3)	(4)
Per capita agricultural income	−0.1329 (1.28)			−0.1458 (1.38)
Yield per hectare		−0.0036 (0.05)	−0.1063 (0.98)	
Per capita net sown area			−0.4501 (2.00)*	
Relative food prices	0.54 (1.65)	0.5952 (1.80)+	0.5266 (1.56)	0.596 (1.77)+
Real agricultural wage	−0.5152 (8.03)**	−0.553 (6.05)**	−0.5938 (5.83)**	−0.5733 (5.65)**
Per capita development expenditure			−0.073 (0.88)	0.0333 (0.74)
Constant	5.4374 (8.87)**	4.7776 (10.31)**	5.726 (9.53)**	5.7126 (10.22)**
Observations	125	125	125	125
R-squared	0.66	0.65	0.67	0.66

Note: As in Table 5.9(a).

it to make a significant impact on poverty. The wage and price variables could have only limited impact in the absence of high growth. As a result, poverty levels still remain high in these states. The policy conclusion that then emerges is that agricultural growth in these states should be enhanced in order to make an impact on poverty. The significant poverty-reducing effects of agricultural growth or yield noticed in low-poverty states supports such a conclusion.

Agricultural developments thus have a very dominant influence on poverty in India. Agricultural growth directly affects the welfare of the farmers and agricultural labourers. At the same time, it is important to share the benefits of growth through the wage channel to reduce the incidence of poverty. Terms-of-trade movement is also an important channel that has strong effects on poverty.

Finally, we might mention that the yield channel would most likely operate through irrigation. The effect of irrigation could not be directly measured in the equations using panel data due to various implementation difficulties including consistent time-series data problems at the state level. The cross-section analysis in the previous section did reveal the importance

Table 5.10(b)   Regression results for high-poverty states (dependent variable: poverty gap index)

Explanatory variable	Equation no.			
	(1)	(2)	(3)	(4)
Per capita agri. income	−0.2595			−0.2581
	(1.65)			(1.62)
Yield per hectare		−0.1133	−0.2195	
		(0.94)	(1.33)	
Per capita net sown area			−0.5552	
			(1.62)	
Relative food prices	0.8225	0.8499	0.7486	0.8164
	(1.66)+	(1.69)+	(1.45)	(1.60)
Real agricultural wage	−0.8982	−0.8753	−0.9118	−0.8919
	(9.25)**	(6.32)**	(5.87)**	(5.79)**
Per capita development			−0.1074	−0.0036
expenditure			(0.85)	(0.05)
Constant	5.4984	4.7752	5.866	5.7926
	(5.93)**	(6.80)**	(6.40)**	(6.83)**
Observations	125	125	125	125
R-squared	0.72	0.72	0.72	0.72

Note: As in Table 5.9(a).

of irrigation on income and livelihood of the poor (see Table 5.8). It has been found to be a major factor in poverty reduction, measured by any of the three indicators, across all states considered and all social groups.

5.7   CONCLUSIONS

India is home to the largest number of poor in the world. About three-quarters of about 260 million poor in India live in rural areas where agriculture is the main source of livelihood. Enhancement of the ability of the poor to earn their living is the most sustainable way of poverty reduction. By now, it is acknowledged that agricultural growth over and above the population growth has a poverty-reducing effect in India. Land is the primary asset in rural areas and increasing agricultural yield per hectare reduces rural poverty. Irrigation is the most critical input for land productivity gains and its effects on poverty reduction are clearly seen from cross-section data across all social groups and in all states. The poor do benefit from growth by income and employment expansion that accompanies the

Country case studies

Table 5.10(c)   Regression results for high-poverty states (dependent variable: squared poverty gap)

Explanatory variable	Equation no.			
	(1)	(2)	(3)	(4)
Per capita agri. Income	−0.2699			−0.2482
	(1.29)			(1.17)
Yield per hectare		−0.1715	−0.212	
		(1.08)	(0.97)	
Per capita net sown area			−0.5268	
			(1.15)	
Relative food prices	1.1347	1.1227	0.9775	1.041
	(1.72)+	(1.69)+	(1.43)	(1.54)
Real agricultural wage	−1.2359	−1.1633	−1.1573	−1.1386
	(9.55)**	(6.35)**	(5.59)**	(5.56)**
Per capita development expenditure			−0.153	−0.0557
			(0.91)	(0.61)
Constant	5.0714	4.6607	5.48	5.4141
	(4.11)**	(5.01)**	(4.49)**	(4.80)**
Observations	125	125	125	125
R-squared	0.73	0.73	0.73	0.73

Note: As in Table 5.9(a).

growth process (say, multiple cropping). However, the real wage effect and relative food price effects have been found to be strong and robust and their quantitative effects dominate the direct growth effect.

Three-quarters of India's poor could be found in the seven states – Uttar Pradesh, Bihar, Assam, West Bengal, Orissa, Madhya Pradesh and Maharashtra – in the northern, eastern and central parts of India where the green revolution has had only a marginal effect, except in western Uttar Pradesh. Green revolution type productivity increases must be extended to these regions with a suitable cropping pattern put in place. In addition, poverty is highly prevalent among the social groups known as the scheduled tribes and the scheduled castes, which have remained socially excluded for centuries. Efforts must be made to integrate them into the mainstream of economic activities and strengthen the linkage effects of agricultural growth and their livelihood. It can be observed that while the SC groups are spread all over India, the STs are concentrated in the above regions (except in Uttar Pradesh). Regional and social group focus is thus needed in the near future in the poverty-reduction strategy in India.

NOTES

1. Several studies had already used other estimates of PL. See, for example, Dandekar and Rath (1971) and Srinivasan and Bardhan (1974).
2. National Sample Survey Organization See below for further discussion on the NSSO data.
3. Note that the poverty line meets the nutritional norms *only* in the base year (1973–74), given the food behavioural pattern of the population. The price updating procedure does not ensure that calorie norms are met in other years and in fact could be very different (see Panda and Rath, 2004).
4. World Bank dataset adjusts the CPIAL to correct for the constant price of firewood.
5. We might note other alternative estimates (say, those made by Tendulkar and Jain, 1995) to support the broad trends over the years, though absolute magnitudes differ.
6. Datt (1998) also notes this.
7. See, for example, two edited volumes: Srinivasan and Bardhan (1974) and Mellor and Desai (1986).
8. See Mellor and Desai (1986) for an interesting debate on this issue.
9. It excludes capital expenditure undertaken by public sector enterprises without budgetary support.
10. All tabulations in this section have been made using household-level data available on CD. Since we are using unit-level data, the results might differ slightly from those based on grouped data.
11. The ST and SC categories account for a little less than a quarter of the population.
12. As noted earlier, the NSSO rounds in 1980s and 1990s include large quinquennial samples as well as small samples.
13. The states of Punjab and Haryana formed parts of a larger state during the early part of the sample period and the World Bank dataset up to 1993–94 provides combined estimates for these two states. We have maintained this while updating the dataset.
14. The primary database is 'World Bank: A Database on Poverty and Growth in India', by Berk Özler, Gaurav Datt and Martin Ravallion available on the web. We have updated this database to include the NSSO 55th round for 1999–2000. This is supplemented by: (a) state income from the Economic and Political Weekly Research Foundation's 'Domestic Product of States of India 60–61 to 2000–01'; (b) nominal wages from the publication 'Agricultural Wages in India'; (c) CPIAL (Food and General) from *Indian Labour Journal*; and (d) state development expenditure from the Reserve Bank of India's 'Report on Currency and Finance', and 'State Finances: A Study of Budgets of 2001–02'.
15. Although we have tried several other combinations of the explanatory variables, we report here four sets of equations which capture the essential points.
16. Note that Datt and Ravallion (1998) report that exogeneity for current values of mean income, yield and development expenditure was acceptable for all poverty measures.

REFERENCES

Ahluwalia, Montek S. (1978), 'Rural poverty and agricultural performance in India', *Journal of Development Studies*, **14**(3): 298–323.

Dandekar, V.M. and N. Rath (1971), 'Poverty in India', Indian School of Political Economy, Pune.

Datt, Gaurav (1998), 'Poverty in India and Indian states: an update', *Indian Journal of Labour Economics*, **41**(2): 191–211.

Datt, Gaurav and Martin Ravallion (1998), 'Farm productivity and rural poverty in India', *Journal of Development Studies*, **34**(4): 64–85.

Deaton, Angus and Jean Drèze (2002), 'Poverty and inequality in India: a re-examination', *Economic and Political Weekly*, **37**(36): 3729–48.

Fan, Shenggen, Peter Hazell and Sukhadeo Thorat (2000), 'Government spending, growth and poverty in rural India', *American Journal of Agricultural Economics*, **82**(4): 1038–51.

Foster, J., J. Greer and E. Thorbecke (1984), 'A class of decomposable poverty measures', *Econometrica*, **52**(3): 761–5.

Mellor, J.W. and G.M. Desai (eds) (1986), *Agricultural Change and Rural Poverty*, Oxford and Delhi: Oxford University Press.

Panda, Manoj (1999), 'Growth with equity: policy lessons from the experience of India', in *Growth with Equity: Policy Lessons from the Experiences of Selected Asian Countries*, United Nations, New York (ST/ESCAP/2007), pp. 59–115.

Panda, Manoj and Kali Rath (2004), 'Price changes and some underlying aspects of measurement of poverty', *Journal of Quantitative Economics*, **2**(1): 25–43.

Planning Commission (1979), 'Report of the Task Force on Projection of Minimum Needs and Effective Consumption Demand', Government of India, New Delhi.

Planning Commission (1993), 'Report of the Expert Group on Estimation of Proportion and Number of Poor', Government of India, New Delhi.

Ravallion, Martin and Gaurav Datt (1996), 'How important to India's poor is the sectoral composition of economic growth?', *World Bank Economic Review*, **10**(1): 1–25.

Saith, Ashwani (1981), 'Production, prices and poverty in rural India', *Journal of Development Studies*, **17**(2): 196–213.

Sen, Abhijit (1996), 'Economic reforms, employment and poverty', *Economic and Political Weekly*, **31**, Special Issue: 2459–77.

Srinivasan, T.N. (1986), 'Agricultural production, relative prices, entitlements and poverty', in Mellor and Desai (eds), pp. 41–53.

Srinivasan, T.N. and P.K. Bardhan (eds) (1974), *Poverty and Income Distribution in India*, Calcutta: Statistical Publishing Society.

Tendulkar, S.D. and L.R. Jain (1995), 'Economic reforms and poverty', *Economic and Political Weekly*, **30**(23): 1373–77.

6. Indonesia

Sudarno Sumarto and Asep Suryahadi

6.1 INTRODUCTION

Before being hit by the recent economic crisis starting in mid-1997, Indonesia was considered as one of the most successful countries in the world in the endeavor to reduce poverty. The proportion of the population living below the 'official' poverty line dropped from about 40 percent in 1976 to about 11 percent in 1996. In absolute numbers, even though the total population increased from 135 million in 1976 to 200 million in 1996, the officially poor population decreased markedly from 54 million to 22.5 million during the same period (see BPS, 2002).

There are methodological questions as to whether BPS poverty rates are comparable over time as well as across urban–rural populations. Nevertheless, this clearly points out that Indonesia has experienced a rapid reduction in poverty during the pre-crisis period. This rapid reduction has generally been attributed to the pre-crisis high economic growth experienced by the country, prior to the which, Indonesia was one of the most rapidly growing economies in the world. Between 1986 and 1996, the real GDP growth was more than 7 percent per year.

However, beginning in mid-1997, Indonesia was struck by economic and political crises, exacerbated by the El Niño drought. During this crisis period, the Indonesian people witnessed the value of their currency fall to as low as 15 percent of its pre-crisis value in less than one year, an economic contraction by an unprecedented magnitude of 13.7 percent in 1998, and a high inflation rate of 78 percent in 1998, which led to riots in several cities and culminated in the fall of the New Order government – which had been in power since the mid-1960s – in May 1998.

The social impact of the crisis was substantial. An estimate indicates that the national poverty rate increased from about 16 percent in February 1996 to 27 percent in February 1999 (see Pradhan et al., 2001). During the period, the number of urban poor doubled, while the rural poor increased by 75 percent. Another study which tracks down poverty rates over the course of the crisis shows that the poverty rate increased by 164 percent from the onset of the crisis in mid-1997 to the peak of the crisis around the end of 1998 (see Suryahadi et al., 2000).

This has raised a question on the sustainability of poverty reduction achieved during the pre-crisis high economic growth era. In particular, the emphasis of development on industrialization has been questioned. During the crisis period, the agriculture sector fared much better than other sectors. In 1998, when real output shrank from the level in the previous year by unprecedented magnitudes of 9.2 percent in the industrial sector, 18 percent in the trade sector and 19.6 percent in the services sector, respectively, the output of the agricultural sector fell only slightly by 0.7 percent. In the following year, the agricultural sector led the recovery by growing positively at 2.1 percent, helped by the industrial sector which grew by 1.4 percent, while the trade and services sectors were still in negative growth territory of 0.4 and 1.5 percent, respectively.

This has led some to hypothesize that had Indonesia not industrialized 'too quickly' and instead focused on strengthening its basis in the agricultural sector, the country would not have been hurt so much by the economic crisis. Furthermore, had the country based its development strategy through developing the agricultural sector, the poverty reduction achieved would have been greater and more sustainable than what has occurred.

This line of thinking is based on the notion that it is not only the rate of economic growth itself which is important, but also the 'quality of growth' is equally important (see Thomas et al., 2000). One criterion for determining the quality of growth, though certainly not the only one, is its effects on the poor (see Warr, 2002). What kinds of growth are most beneficial for the poor and hence most effective in reducing poverty? In seeking an answer to this question, some researchers have focused on the composition of economic growth (see, for example, Ravallion and Datt, 1996; Warr and Wang, 1999; Warr, 2002). Since in most poor countries the majority of the poor live in rural areas and are employed in agriculture, it is logical that growth of agriculture is more important for poverty reduction than growth of industry or services.

Therefore, this chapter aims to assess the role of agricultural growth on poverty reduction as has been experienced by Indonesia. Specifically, it estimates the elasticity of poverty reduction with respect to agricultural versus non-agricultural growth. In addition, it also estimates the marginal contribution of being employed in agriculture to the probability of being poor, net of other relevant socio-economic factors.

The rest of this chapter is organized as follows. Section 2 describes the sources of data analyzed in this study. Section 3 discusses the role of agriculture in the rural economy. Section 4 calculates the trends in poverty in Indonesia based on a consistently set standard of living and taking into account variations in prices both across regions and over time, and also estimates the marginal contribution of being employed in agriculture to the probability of being poor. Section 5 evaluates the impact of agricultural growth on poverty reduction in comparison with that of non-agricultural sectors. Section 6 makes some empirical estimations. Section 7 provides an account of agriculture's contribution to poverty reduction in Indonesia. Finally, section 8 provides the conclusion and policy implications from the findings of this study.

6.2 DATA

The main data source for the calculations of poverty in Indonesia is the Consumption Module of SUSENAS (the National Socio-Economic Survey) collected by Statistics Indonesia (*Badan Pusat Statistik* or BPS). SUSENAS is a nationally representative household survey, covering all areas of the country. The Consumption Module of SUSENAS is conducted every three years, specifically collecting information on very detailed consumption expenditures from around 65,000 households. This study uses the data collected in the 1984, 1987, 1990, 1993, 1996 and 1999 surveys. It also utilizes the data from Core SUSENAS, which is conducted every year in the month of February, collecting information on the characteristics of over 200,000 households and over 800,000 individuals.

In addition, this study also uses the data of regional gross domestic product (RGDP) and regional consumer price index (RCPI), both published by BPS. In line with the SUSENAS data, the RGDP data used are from 1984 until 1999. For real RGDP, starting from the 1993 data BPS uses new 1993 prices, while for the earlier series they used the 1983 prices. To get a consistent series of real RGDP, the earlier series are converted to the 1993 prices. The RCPI data are based on urban prices only.

6.3 THE ROLE OF AGRICULTURE IN THE RURAL ECONOMY

Industrialization was at the heart of the economic development strategy adopted by the Indonesian New Order government during its tenure in power from the late 1960s to the late 1990s. As a consequence, the role of the agricultural sector in the national economy has continuously declined during the whole period. Nevertheless, agriculture remains an important source of livelihood for a large number of households, in particular in rural areas.

6.3.1   The Macro Picture

The economic development of the New Order can be divided into three phases. The first is from the late 1960s to the mid-1970s, when the New Order regime embraced trade and investment policies which were remarkably open. In 1967, a foreign investment law that guaranteed foreign investors the right to repatriate capital and profits was passed. In 1970, reforms were introduced that reduced the existing barriers to goods trade and foreign borrowing by unifying the multiple exchange rate system and abolishing most of the exchange controls on capital and current account transactions.

In the second phase, from the mid-1970s to the mid-1980s, Indonesia adopted an inward-looking import-substitution strategy. Awash with revenue from oil exports, the government was eager to build capital-intensive industries to replace imports. In addition, it spent a large sum of money on building infrastructure. Not surprisingly, the role of the public sector in the economy's growth was dominant during this period.

The third phase started in the mid-1980s, when the Indonesian economy started to open again. This was an indirect result of the large drop in oil prices that began in the early 1980s (see Hill, 1996). Because the oil revenue shrank quickly, the government faced a sudden external imbalance. The import-substitution strategy had left industries inefficient and unable to compete in the world market at the maintained exchange rate. A combination of this and a general decline in primary commodity prices raised the premium on foreign exchange. In 1986, the import-substitution strategy was therefore discarded and replaced with export orientation, followed by a devaluation of the exchange rate and combined with deregulation in the domestic economy.

During three decades of economic development starting in the early 1970s, the economy underwent substantial structural change, notably a reduction in the importance of the agricultural sector in the economy. Table 6.1 compares the share of agriculture in gross domestic product (GDP) and its share

Table 6.1   GDP and employment shares of agriculture in Indonesia, 1971–2000 (%)

	1971	1980	1990	2000
GDP	45	25	22	17
Employment	67	55	50	45
Ratio of GDP to employment share	0.67	0.45	0.44	0.38

Source: BPS (various years).

in employment from 1971 to 2000. The shares of the agricultural sector in both GDP and employment have declined throughout the period. However, it appears that the reduction in agricultural GDP share has been much faster than its employment share. This is apparent from the declining ratio of GDP to employment share from 0.67 in 1971 to 0.38 in 2000.

6.3.2 Agriculture and Household Livelihood

The macroeconomic picture discussed in the previous subsection clearly indicates that the role of the agricultural sector in the national economy has declined along with the industrialization of the economy. This is also reflected at the household level. Figure 6.1 shows the proportion of agri-cultural households – defined as households which derive most of their income from the agricultural sector – from the total households in both rural and urban areas. The data used in this figure are calculated from SUSENAS.

Consistent with the national employment data in Table 6.1, Figure 6.1 shows that nationally the proportion of agricultural households declined from about 55 percent in 1984 to 39 percent in 1999. Interestingly, most of the decline was driven by the decline in rural areas, while the proportion of agricultural households in urban areas was relatively stable between 8 and 10 percent. Nevertheless, in 1999 about 59 percent of rural households still derived most of their income from the agricultural sector. This indicates that agriculture still constitutes the most important source of livelihood for the majority of rural Indonesians.

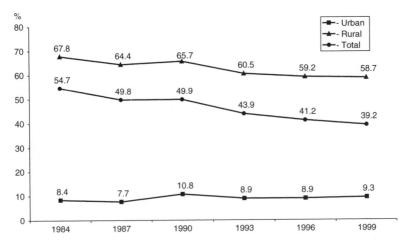

Figure 6.1   Proportion of agricultural households in Indonesia, 1984–1999

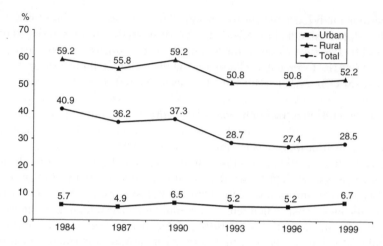

Figure 6.2   Share of agricultural household income from total household income

Figure 6.2 shows the total income of all agricultural households as a pro-portion of total income of all households.[1] The data used are also calculated from SUSENAS. Even though they are declining, the numbers indicate that the role of agricultural income at the household level, particularly in rural areas, is much greater than those suggested by the GDP share of the agri-cultural sector shown in Table 6.1. While in urban areas the income of agri-cultural households make up only between 5 and 7 percent of the income of total households, in rural areas the proportion is still more than 50 percent.

6.4   POVERTY TRENDS AND SECTORAL PROFILE OF POVERTY

The method for measuring poverty has always been subject to controversy (see Sen, 1981; Ravallion, 1994). The definition of poverty has evolved over time from the narrow definition of inability to fulfill the basic needs to incorporate broader aspects of life such as health and education, and more recently to include socio-political dimensions that affect one's life (see Narayan, 2000; Narayan et al., 2000; and World Bank, 2000). Despite acknowledging that there is more to poverty than simply the inability to fulfill the basic needs, this study uses the most widely used measure of poverty, which is the current consumption expenditure deficit. In this measure, a household is categorized as poor if its per capita consumption expenditure is less than a specified threshold, the 'poverty line'. The poverty measures analyzed here are the Foster–Greer–Thorbecke (FGT) poverty indices (see Foster et al., 1984). This class of poverty measures meets all the desirable axioms in consumption-based poverty measures. Readers are referred to the technical appendix for the definition of these indices.

Statistics Indonesia (BPS) is the government body which calculates the official poverty figures in Indonesia. They base their calculations on the data collected through the three-yearly Consumption Module of SUSENAS. The BPS poverty line consists of two parts: the food poverty line and the non-food poverty line (see BPS, 2002).

The food poverty line is set to achieve a caloric intake of 2100 calories per person per day. The value of this caloric intake is calculated based on the actual consumption of a food basket, which consists of 52 food commodities, by a pre-specified reference population. The reference population comprises all households within a subjectively determined range of nominal per capita expenditure. The food poverty line is calculated by multiplying the actual value of the food poverty basket consumption of the reference population by the ratio of 2100 to the actual caloric intake.

Meanwhile, the non-food poverty line is obtained by first calculating the mean of actual consumption of a non-food basket, which consists of 27 commodities, by the reference population. Then, for each commodity a scaling factor between 0 and 1 is independently determined to indicate the portion of the commodity consumption which is deemed essential.[2] The non-food poverty line is the sum of these scaled values across the 27 commodities. Finally, the poverty line is obtained by summing up the food and the non-food poverty lines.

Although BPS has published the results of their calculations on the number of the poor since 1976, these numbers cannot be used as the basis for the analysis in this study for two reasons. First, BPS applies its poverty calculation method separately for urban and rural areas, which means that the resulting poverty lines for urban and rural areas represent different and not comparable welfare levels. Second, each poverty calculation is made entirely independently of the BPS calculations in previous years. This means that the poverty lines obtained each year again represent different and not comparable welfare levels. Because of these two drawbacks, the BPS poverty numbers are not comparable across regions and over time. Therefore, for the purpose of this study, an alternative source of poverty calculations that provide a consistent and comparable welfare level has to be found.

6.4.1 Consistent Poverty Estimates

To overcome the regional comparability problem, alternative sources can be found in Bidani and Ravallion (1993), Chesher (1998) and Pradhan et al.

(2001). These three studies provide provincial poverty figures for Indonesia which are based on a single poverty basket and, hence, represent comparable poverty measures across regions. Since Pradhan et al. (2001) provide the poverty figures for the latest year available, 1999, this study is selected as the basis for calculating poverty figures used in the present chapter.[3]

In terms of comparability over time, however, there is no alternative source readily available. This means that a consistent time series of poverty figures has to be calculated, using the 1999 provincial poverty figures from Pradhan et al. as the basis. To calculate the poverty figures in the previous years, first it is necessary to construct a deflator which will be used to deflate the 1999 poverty lines to the previous years. Following Suryahadi et al. (2000), this deflator is a re-weighted consumer price index (CPI) to reflect the share of food in the poverty basket. While the CPI has a 40 percent food share, this poverty line deflator has an 80 percent food share.

Pradhan et al. (2001) calculate nominal poverty lines separately for urban and rural areas within each province. However, since the CPI in Indonesia is available only for urban areas, there is only one poverty line deflator available for each province. Therefore, both urban and rural poverty lines within one province are deflated using the same urban-based provincial poverty line deflator. The regional poverty lines obtained through this method are then applied to the Consumption Module SUSENAS data to calculate the poverty figures in the pre-1999 years.

The results of the calculations for poverty head count, aggregated at the national level, are shown in Figure 6.3. There was clearly a sharp reduction in both urban and rural poverty between 1984 and 1996. Despite a continuously growing population, total poverty head count dropped from 56.7 percent in 1984 to 17.4 percent in 1996, a reduction by 39.3 percentage points in a 12-year period. During the same period, urban poverty fell by 22.2 percentage points from 29.3 to 7.1 percent, while rural poverty fell by 41.8 percentage points from 65.1 to 23.3 percent.

However, the crisis has evidently reversed the course of poverty reduction of the previous decade. Poverty in both urban and rural areas increased again between 1996 and 1999. The total poverty rate in 1999 was 27.0 percent, while urban and rural poverty rates were 16.3 and 33.9 percent, respectively. In fact, reflecting the severity of the crisis, these 1999 total, rural, and particularly urban poverty levels are even higher than their respective 1993 levels.

Other poverty measures calculated, the poverty gap index and the poverty severity index, are shown in Figures 6.4 and 6.5, respectively. Their trends show the same pattern as the poverty head count. In both urban and rural areas, both poverty indices fell significantly during the period between 1984 and 1996, but increased again between 1996 and 1999.

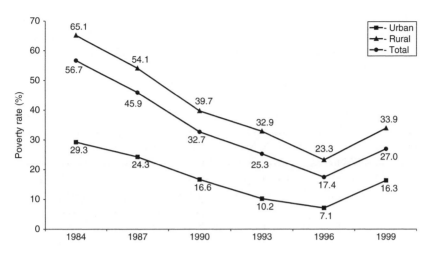

Figure 6.3   Head count poverty rate

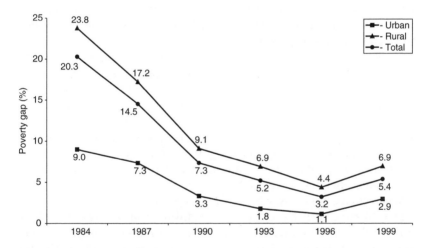

Figure 6.4   Poverty gap index

The poverty gap indicates the total expenditure deficit of the poor to the poverty line averaged over the whole population. The total poverty gap fell substantially by 17.1 percentage points from 20.3 percent in 1984 to only 3.2 percent in 1996. In urban areas, the gap fell by 7.9 percentage points from 9 to 1.1 percent and in rural areas fell by 19.4 percentage points from 23.8 to 4.4 percent during the same period. However, in 1999 the total, urban and rural poverty gaps increased again to reach 5.4, 2.9

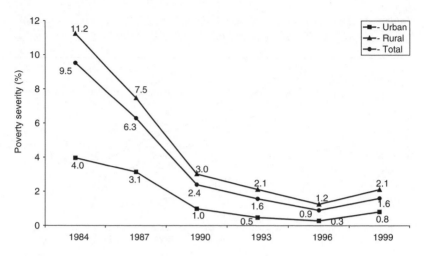

Figure 6.5   Poverty severity index

and 6.9 percent, respectively. Just like the poverty head count, the crisis has brought back the poverty gap levels in 1999 even higher than their 1993 levels, notably in urban areas.

Poverty severity gives more weight to the poorest among the poor by squaring the expenditure deficit to the poverty line. The total poverty severity index also fell substantially from 9.5 percent in 1984 to 0.9 percent in 1996, a fall of 8.6 percentage points. During the same period, the poverty severity in urban areas fell by 3.7 percentage points from 4 to 0.3 percent, while in rural areas it fell by 10 percentage points from 11.2 to 1.2 percent. Like the other two poverty measures, the poverty severity has increased again in 1999 due to the crisis. However, only in urban areas did it reach a level higher than that in 1993.

While Figure 6.3 shows that the reduction in poverty head count rate between 1984 and 1996 occurred at a relatively steady rate, Figure 6.4 and more so Figure 6.5 show that the reduction in higher dimension poverty measures occurred much faster during the 1980s than in the 1990s. This indicates that during the 1980s there was some progress in reducing more severe forms of poverty. This also indicates that there was a significant improvement in income distribution among the poor during this period.

6.4.2   Sectoral Profile of Poverty

It is well known that poverty in Indonesia is a phenomenon mainly found in rural areas, while in urban areas poverty is mainly found in the informal sector. Therefore, poverty in Indonesia is very much related to the agricultural

Table 6.2   *Poverty head count rate and contribution to total poor by main sector of occupation in Indonesia, 1987–1999 (%)*

Sector	Urban		Rural		Urban + rural	
	Poverty head count	Contribution to total poor	Poverty head count	Contribution to total poor	Poverty head count	Contribution to total poor
1987						
Agriculture	51.7	15.6	58.5	69.7	58.2	61.8
Industry	28.4	14.5	54.2	5.4	42.3	6.8
Services	21.2	69.9	44.6	24.9	32.9	31.4
Total	24.3	100.0	54.1	100.0	45.9	100.0
1996						
Agriculture	20.7	25.1	29.9	76.0	29.2	68.6
Industry	7.1	13.2	18.1	5.7	12.6	6.8
Services	5.6	61.7	12.7	18.3	8.7	24.6
Total	7.1	100.0	23.3	100.0	17.4	100.0
1999						
Agriculture	33.6	18.9	40.1	70.5	39.5	58.1
Industry	18.1	15.3	30.1	6.7	23.5	8.8
Services	14.1	65.9	23.5	22.7	17.8	33.1
Total	16.4	100.0	33.9	100.0	27.0	100.0

sector. Table 6.2 shows the poverty head count rate and contribution to total poverty by main sector of occupation of household heads in 1987, 1996 and 1999.[4] A comparison between the 1987 and 1996 sectoral profile of poverty will show how it is affected by growth, while the 1996 and 1999 comparison will show how it is affected by the crisis.

The table shows clearly that during the whole period between 1987 and 1999, in both urban and rural areas, the agricultural sector always has the highest poverty incidence compared to other sectors. In 1987, the poverty head count rate in the agricultural sector was 58 percent, much higher than the poverty rates of 42 and 33 percent in the industrial and services sectors, respectively. Disaggregation into urban and rural areas reveals a similar pattern.

In terms of contribution to total poverty, 62 percent of the poor have a livelihood in the agricultural sector. In rural areas, about 70 percent of all the poor were in the agricultural sector. In urban areas, however, because agricultural households made up only a small fraction of the total households, the poor in the agricultural sector made up only 16 percent of all the poor. In these areas, most of the poor were found in the services sector, that is, the sector where most urban informal workers are employed.

High economic growth between 1987 and 1996 obviously provided benefits for the poor. As a result, the poverty head count rate in the agricultural sector by 1996 was halved to 29 percent. However, it appears that poverty reduction in other sectors occurred even faster, so that the poverty rates in the industrial and services sectors in 1996 were only 13 and 9 percent, respectively. As a result, the contribution of the agricultural sector to total poverty increased to 69 percent. Similarly, in urban and rural areas the contribution of the agricultural sector to poverty increased to 25 and 76 percent, respectively.

The economic crisis reversed the declining trend in poverty and it occurred in all sectors, including agriculture. The poverty head count rate in the agricultural sector increased again to reach 40 percent in 1999. In accordance with the urban and modern sector nature of the origin of the crisis, the proportionate increase in poverty in the industrial and services sectors was higher and the poverty rates in these sectors in 1999 reached 24 and 18 percent, respectively. Consequently, the contribution of the agricultural sector to poverty declined to 58 percent for total poverty and, respectively, 19 and 71 percent for urban and rural poverty.

6.4.3 Agriculture and the Probability of Being Poor

Table 6.2 shows that most of the poor in Indonesia have a livelihood in the agricultural sector. This raises a question of whether people whose livelihood is in the agricultural sector indeed have a higher tendency to become poor compared to those whose livelihood is outside the agricultural sector. That is, controlling for other characteristics, what is the probability that a household whose livelihood is in the agricultural sector will be poor.

To answer this question, Table 6.3 shows the results of estimating a probit model where the dependent variable is a dummy variable of whether a household is poor or not and the independent variables are various characteristics of the household, including whether or not the household is an agricultural household. The estimations were implemented again using data from SUSENAS for 1987, 1996 and 1999.

Table 6.3 shows that in 1987, controlling for other household characteristics, agricultural households had a 16 percent higher probability of becoming poor compared to non-agricultural households. This is consistent with the higher incidence of poverty in the agricultural sector *vis-à-vis* other sectors shown in Table 6.2. More importantly, this shows that the higher incidence of poverty in the agricultural sector cannot entirely be explained by the observed characteristics of those who work in this sector relative to those who work in other sectors.

*Table 6.3   The probability of agricultural households being poor
(dependent variable: dummy variable of poor household)*

Variables	1987	1996	1999
Agricultural household	0.1609**	0.1064**	0.1249**
	(27.75)	(37.49)	(32.85)
Urban location	−0.1607**	−0.0631**	−0.0759**
	(−25.20)	(−22.72)	(−20.23)
Household size	0.1628**	0.0698**	0.1150**
	(39.81)	(28.18)	(33.21)
Household size square	−0.0076**	−0.0035**	−0.0056**
	(−23.26)	(−16.02)	(−17.62)
Household head characteristics:			
Female	0.0536**	0.0533**	0.1109**
	(4.67)	(7.96)	(11.71)
Age	−0.0139**	−0.0067**	−0.0125**
	(−13.68)	(−13.33)	(−17.75)
Age square	0.0001**	0.0001**	0.0001**
	(10.40)	(12.45)	(17.38)
Married	−0.0122	−0.0074	(−0.0180*
	(−1.22)	1.32)	(2.34)
Household head education level:			
Not completed primary	−0.1178**	−0.0266**	−0.0537**
school but literate	(−18.05)	(−4.74)	(−5.51)
Completed primary school	−0.1773**	−0.0494**	−0.0819**
	(−25.97)	(−9.03)	(−8.48)
Completed lower secondary	−0.2499**	−0.0645**	−0.1139**
school	(−30.92)	(−12.49)	(−12.39)
Completed upper secondary	−0.3332**	−0.0452**	−0.1191**
school or higher	(−43.49)	(−8.02)	(−12.39)
Province dummy variables	Yes	Yes	Yes
Pseudo *R*-squared	0.3186	0.2125	0.1809
Number of observations	50956	59852	60601

Notes:
The command use is DPROBIT in STATA.
The coefficients are in terms of probability of being poor.
Numbers in parentheses are *z*-values.
**   = significant at 1 percent level.
*   = significant at 5 percent level.

Growth between 1987 and 1996 has brought down this probability of being poor. In 1996, agricultural households had 11 percent higher probability of becoming poor compared to non-agricultural households. This fall in the probability of being poor is in line with the reduction in poverty incidence in this sector during the period.

However, the economic crisis has again slightly increased the probability to 12 percent in 1999. This probably has to do with the reversed migration that occurred during the first year of the crisis. Many of those who lost jobs in the modern sector in urban areas returned to the rural areas and rejoined the agricultural workforce. As a result, the agricultural sector had to cope with a sudden increase in its labor absorption, forcing down the marginal productivity of labor in this sector (see Feridhanusetyawan, 1999).

6.5   MEASURING THE IMPACT OF ECONOMIC GROWTH ON POVERTY

The previous section shows that Indonesia experienced a fast reduction in poverty during the pre-crisis period. This reduction in poverty is often attributed to the high economic growth experienced by the country. Figure 6.6 shows the indices of total and sectoral real GDP from 1984 to 1999. The figure shows that in the period between 1984 and 1996, the total real GDP doubled. In terms of sectoral growth, the figure clearly shows that the real GDP growth of the industrial sector was the fastest, so that by 1996 the real GDP of this sector was almost three times its size in 1984. Meanwhile, the real GDP of both the agricultural and services sectors grew more slowly than the total real GDP and much more slowly than that of the industrial sector. The real GDP of these two sectors in 1996 was about 1.75 times their size in 1984.

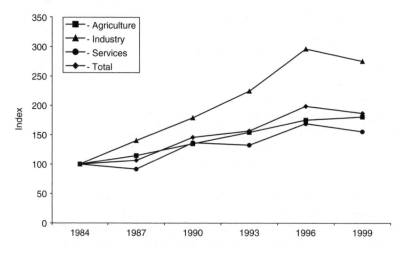

Figure 6.6   Index of real GDP (1984 = 100)

This section assesses how economic growth has affected the observed reduction in poverty. In particular, it examines whether sectoral composition of economic growth matters in determining the impact of growth on poverty.

6.5.1 Previous Approaches

The basic model to estimate the impact of economic growth on poverty can be defined as:

$$dP = \alpha + \beta \dot{y} + \varepsilon, \tag{6.1}$$

where P refers to the level of poverty rate and dP refers to the change in poverty rate, $\dot{y}$ represents the rate of economic growth (that is $\dot{y} = (dY/Y)$, where Y is the level of GDP and dY is its change), ε is the error term, while α and β, are parameters to be estimated. In particular, the parameter of interest is β which shows the percentage point change in poverty rate due to 1 percent GDP growth.

Using Indian national time-series data spanning from 1951 to 1991, Ravallion and Datt (1996) estimate various specifications and extensions of equation (6.1), but always forcing $\alpha = 0$ and the growth variable is measured in per capita terms. They find that, during the period of analysis, 85 percent of the reduction in poverty in India was due to agricultural growth.

This finding is contrary to the finding of Quizon and Binswanger (1986, 1989). Using a partial equilibrium multimarket model for India, they show that the agricultural growth effects of the green revolution did not benefit the rural poor. They show that the main way to help the poor is to raise non-agricultural incomes. Sarris (2001), however, criticizes their analysis since they consider only agricultural incomes and did not take into account spillover effects to non-agricultural incomes. It is quite plausible that initial rises in agricultural incomes help increase the non-agricultural incomes, which eventually help the poor.

A different finding from Ravallion and Datt (1996) is found by Warr and Wang (1999). Using national time-series data for Taiwan, they find that in this country it is the growth of the industrial sector which has the largest impact on poverty reduction. Different again, Warr (2002), by pooling the data from four Southeast Asian countries (Thailand, Indonesia, Malaysia and the Philippines), finds that it is the growth of the services sector which accounts for the largest reduction in poverty in these countries.

The findings that the impact of sectoral growth on poverty differs across countries is consistent with Timmer (1997), who finds that the impact of agricultural growth on poverty depends on income distribution and that income inequality affects the elasticity of poverty reduction with respect to different types of sectoral growth. In countries where the relative income inequality is large, the 'elasticities of connection' of per capita income of the bottom quintile with respect to both agricultural and non-agricultural labor productivity are very small and statistically insignificant. On the other hand, the elasticities for the top quintile are larger than one. In countries with small relative inequality, the elasticities are close to one for both bottom and top quintiles and slightly higher for agriculture. This implies that the contribution of agricultural growth to poverty reduction is a function of inequality, where more inequality leads to lower elasticity of connection.

6.5.2   A Regional Panel Data Approach

Ravallion and Datt (1996) and War and Wang (1999) obviously have the advantage of available time-series data spanning a sufficiently long period to conduct empirical estimations of equation (6.1). However, the availability of long time-series data in developing countries is not the norm. In most countries, sufficiently long period time-series data to perform meaningful statistical analysis is not available. This has forced Warr (2002) to pool the data from four Southeast Asian countries: Thailand, Indonesia, Malaysia and the Philippines. Such an approach, however, requires a strong assumption that the elasticities of poverty reduction to economic growth are the same across countries, which in many cases may be implausible.

   To circumvent the dual problems of the unavailability of sufficiently long time-series national-level data and the implausibility of pooling data across countries, this study employs a panel data with provinces as the unit of observations. However, this requires some adjustments in estimating the model to take into account the effect of migration across regions. This adjustment is necessary for the following reason. Suppose that a province experienced high economic growth for a long period, which caused it to attract a large number of poor people from other provinces to migrate to this province. On the other hand, suppose another province experienced recession for a long period, which forced many of its poor people to migrate out to other provinces in search of a better life. Without controlling for the effect of the inter-provincial migration, the data may suggest that economic growth has a positive correlation with poverty, implying that economic growth is associated with poverty increase.

   Now, suppose that a country has T number of provinces. Define N as the total population and N^P as the total number of poor people in the country, while N_j and N_j^P, respectively, refer to the total population and number of poor people in province j, so that $N = N_1 + N_2 + \ldots + N_T$ and $N^P = N_1^P + N_2^P + \ldots + N_T^P$.

Since the national poverty rate P is:

$$P = \frac{N^P}{N} = \frac{N_1^P + N_2^P + \ldots + N_T^P}{N}, \qquad (6.2)$$

then:

$$P = \frac{N_1}{N}\frac{N_1^P}{N_1} + \frac{N_2}{N}\frac{N_2^P}{N_2} + \ldots + \frac{N_T}{N}\frac{N_T^P}{N_T} = S_1 P_1 + S_2 P_2 + \ldots + S_T P_T, \qquad (6.3)$$

where S_j is the share of population and P_j is the poverty rate in province j. Equation (6.3) simply says that the national poverty rate is the average of provincial poverty rates weighted by the population share of each province.

Therefore, the change in national poverty rate can be decomposed by the changes in provincial poverty rates. Totally differentiating equation (6.3):

$$dP = (S_1 dP_1 + S_2 dP_2 + \ldots + S_T dP_T) + (P_1 dS_1 + P_2 dS_2 + \ldots + P_T dS_T). \qquad (6.4)$$

Equation (6.4) says that the change in the national poverty rate is due to the changes in provincial poverty rates weighted by each province's population share and the changes in provincial population share weighted by each province's initial poverty rate. The terms in the second bracket identify the change in national poverty rate due to differences in population growth across provinces – which may be due to differences in natural population growth as well as inter-provincial migration – and differences in each province's initial poverty rate.

Rearranging equation (6.4):

$$dP = (S_1 dP_1 + P_1 dS_1) + (S_2 dP_2 + P_2 dS_2) + \ldots + (S_T dP_T + P_T dS_T). \qquad (6.5)$$

Each bracket in equation (6.5) identifies the total contribution of each province to the change in national poverty rate. Equations (6.4) and (6.5) suggest that in estimating equation (6.1) using provincial panel data, it is necessary to control for each province's population growth and initial poverty rate.[5]

Therefore, the model to be estimated becomes:

$$dP_j = \alpha + \beta \dot{y}_j + \gamma \dot{n}_j + \delta P_j + \varepsilon, \qquad (6.6)$$

where $\dot{n}_j$ is the population growth in the province j.

To test the hypothesis that different sectoral growth affects poverty reduction differently, first decompose the total economic growth in each province into its sectoral components. Since $dY_j = dY_j^A + dY_j^I + dY_j^S$, then:

$$\dot{y}_j = \frac{dY_j}{Y_j} = \frac{Y_j^A}{Y_j}\frac{dY_j^A}{Y_j^A} + \frac{Y_j^I}{Y_j}\frac{dY_j^I}{Y_j^I} + \frac{Y_j^S}{Y_j}\frac{dY_j^S}{Y_j^S} = H_j^A\dot{y}_j^A + H_j^I\dot{y}_j^I + H_j^S\dot{y}_j^S, \quad (6.7)$$

where the superscript $k = \{A, I, S\}$ indexes the agricultural, industrial and services sectors, respectively, and H^k is the sectoral share of GDP.

Substituting equation (6.7) into equation (6.6) results in the model of sectoral growth impact on poverty reduction:

$$dP_j = \alpha + \beta^A(H_j^A\dot{y}_j^A) + \beta^I(H_j^I\dot{y}_j^I) + \beta^S(H_j^S\dot{y}_j^S) + \gamma\dot{n}_j + \delta P_j + \varepsilon. \quad (6.8)$$

If $\beta^A = \beta^I = \beta^S$, then equation (6.8) collapses to equation (6.6), suggesting that sectoral composition of economic growth does not matter to its impact on poverty. Otherwise, it does matter because the growth of each sector affects poverty differently. The advantage of this method is that the estimated elasticities encompass all direct and indirect effects of growth on poverty, including income distribution and general equilibrium effects.

6.6   EMPIRICAL ESTIMATIONS

The provincial-level poverty measures are merged with the RGDP database to create a panel with province as the unit of observation, which is used to estimate the models of economic growth impact on poverty discussed above. The dependent variable is change in poverty, while the independent variables are either total GDP growth (equation (6.6)) or share-weighted sectoral GDP growth (equation (6.8)), controlled by population growth and initial poverty level. The estimation method used is ordinary least squares (OLS). The inclusion of initial poverty level as a control variable removes the need to control for individual province fixed effects as this variable has the same value within a province across time period.

Table 6.4 presents the results of estimations using poverty head count as the measure of poverty. The column heading 'Total growth' shows the results of estimations of equation (6.6), while the column heading 'Sectoral growth' shows the results of estimations of equation (6.8). The coefficient of the total GDP growth shows the percentage point change in poverty due to 1 percent economic growth. However, the interpretation of the

Table 6.4   The impact of economic growth on poverty head count

Independent variables	Total growth		Sectoral growth	
	Coefficient	*t*-values	Coefficient	*t*-values
Total poverty head count				
Total GDP growth	−0.0254	−0.90		
Agricultural GDP growth			−1.8595	−3.62**
Industrial GDP growth			−0.0664	−1.63
Services GDP growth			0.0048	0.09
Total population growth	0.0653	2.37*	0.1193	3.93**
Initial poverty head count	−0.1316	−2.96**	−0.1085	−2.55**
Constant	0.0189	0.78	0.0524	2.16*
Number of observations	130		130	
F-test	5.43**		7.16**	
R-squared	0.1144		0.224	
Urban poverty head count				
Total GDP growth	−0.0095	−0.42		
Agricultural GDP growth			−1.1254	−2.84**
Industrial GDP growth			−0.0624	−1.90*
Services GDP growth			0.0268	0.58
Urban population growth	0.0062	0.17	0.0474	1.23
Initial poverty head count	−0.1497	−3.33**	−0.1356	−3.13**
Constant	0.0165	1.03	0.0352	2.16*
Number of observations	130		130	
F-test	3.81**		5.12**	
R-squared	0.0832		0.1711	
Rural poverty head count				
Total GDP growth	−0.0230	−0.72		
Agricultural GDP growth			−2.8789	−4.56**
Industrial GDP growth			−0.0598	−1.33
Services GDP growth			0.0315	0.50
Rural population growth	0.0479	2.23*	0.1046	4.45**
Initial poverty head count	−0.1373	−2.58**	−0.1393	−2.85**
Constant	0.0320	1.00	0.1066	3.22**
Number of observations	125		125	
F-test	4.2**		7.95**	
R-squared	0.0942		0.2505	

Notes:
** = significant at 1 percent level.
* = significant at 5 percent level.

coefficient of sectoral GDP growth is not so straightforward as the independent variables in equation (6.8) are sectoral economic growth weighted by their GDP share. If it is assumed that the whole economy consists of only one particular sector, then the weight of that sector is one and the weight of the other sectors is zero. In this case equation (6.8) will also collapse to equation (6.6). Hence, the coefficient of a particular sector GDP growth can be interpreted as the percentage point change in poverty due to 1 percent growth of that sector conditional on the whole economy consisting only of that particular sector.

The results of estimations in Table 6.4 indicate that the coefficient of total GDP growth is negative – indicating that economic growth is poverty reducing – but statistically insignificant. This is true for total, urban as well as rural poverty. The sectoral economic growth, however, conveys a more illuminating story. The coefficients of agricultural, industrial and services GDP growths are obviously significantly different from one another. This means that the sectoral composition of economic growth does matter in determining the impact of economic growth on poverty.

Agricultural growth has negative and statistically significant coefficients for total, urban and rural poverty and the magnitudes of the coefficients are much larger than those of the other sectors. Industrial growth also has negative coefficients, but these are only statistically significant for urban areas. Meanwhile, services growth has positive but relatively small and insignificant coefficients. These coefficients indicate that agricultural growth has the strongest impact on reducing total, urban and rural poverty. Industrial growth also tends to reduce poverty, but its impact is significant only in reducing urban poverty. Finally, it appears that services growth has no significant impact on poverty.

Using the poverty gap, Table 6.5 shows the results of estimations of the same models. Like the poverty head count, the impact of total GDP growth on the poverty gap is negative but statistically not significant. In terms of sectoral growth, agricultural growth again has the strongest, negative and statistically significant impact on the total, urban and rural poverty gap. Industrial growth also has a negative impact but none of its coefficients in reducing the total, urban and rural poverty gap is statistically significant. As in the poverty head count, services growth is of no significant consequence to the poverty gap.

Finally, Table 6.6 shows the results of estimations of the models using poverty severity as the measure of poverty. Like poverty head count and poverty gap, total GDP growth has a negative but statistically insignificant impact on poverty severity. Furthermore, sectoral growth does not have a statistically significant impact on poverty severity, except for agricultural growth in rural areas.

Table 6.5   The impact of economic growth on the poverty gap

Independent variables	Total growth		Sectoral growth	
	Coefficient	*t*-values	Coefficient	*t*-values
Total poverty gap				
Total GDP growth	−0.0068	−0.49		
Agricultural GDP growth			−0.6605	−2.54**
Industrial GDP growth			−0.0200	−0.97
Services GDP growth			0.0039	0.14
Total population growth	0.0332	2.46*	0.0524	3.41**
Initial poverty gap	−0.1690	−4.23**	−0.1535	−3.87**
Constant	0.0045	0.52	0.0177	1.84
Number of observations	130		130	
F-test	8.5**		7**	
R-squared	0.1683		0.2202	
Urban poverty gap				
Total GDP growth	−0.0030	−0.41		
Agricultural GDP growth			−0.2624	−2.01*
Industrial GDP growth			−0.0129	−1.19
Services GDP growth			0.0044	0.29
Urban population growth	0.0000	0.00	0.0097	0.77
Initial poverty gap	−0.1707	−4.44**	−0.1660	−4.37**
Constant	0.0035	0.76	0.0082	1.67
Number of observations	130		130	
F-test	6.64**		5.31**	
R-squared	0.1365		0.1764	
Rural poverty gap				
Total GDP growth	−0.0039	−0.25		
Agricultural GDP growth			−1.0244	−3.13**
Industrial GDP growth			−0.0191	−0.82
Services GDP growth			0.0185	0.57
Rural population growth	0.0274	2.59**	0.0476	3.91**
Initial poverty headcount	−0.1729	−3.92**	−0.1641	−3.84**
Constant	0.0082	0.78	0.0326	2.63**
Number of observations	125		125	
F-test	7.62**		7.24**	
R-squared	0.1589		0.2333	

Notes:
** = significant at 1 percent level.
* = significant at 5 percent level.

Table 6.6   The impact of economic growth on poverty severity

Independent variables	Total growth		Sectoral growth	
	Coefficient	*t*-values	Coefficient	*t*-values
Total poverty severity				
Total GDP growth	−0.0022	−0.26		
Agricultural GDP growth			−0.2079	−1.25
Industrial GDP growth			−0.0079	−0.60
Services GDP growth			−0.0028	−0.15
Total population growth	0.0169	2.01*	0.0229	2.34*
Initial poverty severity	−0.1820	−4.31**	−0.1730	−4.02**
Constant	0.0011	0.24	0.0060	1.06
Number of observations	130		130	
F-test	7.9**		5.21**	
R-squared	0.1582		0.1737	
Urban poverty severity				
Total GDP growth	−0.0013	−0.39		
Agricultural GDP growth			−0.1018	−1.69
Industrial GDP growth			−0.0044	−0.88
Services GDP growth			0.0009	0.12
Urban population growth	0.0008	0.16	0.0047	0.80
Initial poverty severity	−0.1807	−4.96**	−0.1782	−4.91**
Constant	0.0008	0.42	0.0027	1.23
Number of observations	130		130	
F-test	8.25**		5.82**	
R-squared	0.1642		0.1899	
Rural poverty severity				
Total GDP growth	−0.0012	−0.13		
Agricultural GDP growth			−0.4545	−2.30*
Industrial GDP growth			−0.0078	−0.56
Services GDP growth			0.0090	0.46
Rural population growth	0.0157	2.53**	0.0247	3.38**
Initial poverty severity	−0.1841	−4.32**	−0.1732	−4.09**
Constant	0.0025	0.47	0.0131	1.94*
Number of observations	125		125	
F-test	8.63**		6.6**	
R-squared	0.1762		0.2170	

Notes:
** = significant at 1 percent level.
* = significant at 5 percent level.

6.7 AGRICULTURE CONTRIBUTION TO POVERTY REDUCTION

The results of the estimations have shown that agricultural growth is the strongest factor in reducing poverty in Indonesia. But what is the contribution of the agricultural sector to poverty reduction? To answer this question, Table 6.7 calculates the contribution of agricultural growth to poverty reduction using the estimated coefficients and other empirical data. The calculation is made for the 1984–96 period only as this is the high growth period where the poverty reduction has occurred, while the 1996–99 period is a crisis period where poverty actually increased.

In Table 6.7, the 'Observed change in poverty' shows the actual reduction in poverty between 1984 and 1996 in terms of percentage point change. The numbers are obtained from Figures 6.3 to 6.5 for the respective measure of poverty. The 'Impact of agricultural growth' is calculated by multiplying the estimated coefficients in Tables 6.4 to 6.6 with the share of agricultural GDP from the total GDP and the growth of agricultural GDP. To take into account varying share and growth of agricultural GDP from period to period, the calculation is done sequentially for each three-year period. The numbers shown in the table are the cumulative results for the whole period between 1984 and 1996. To obtain consistent estimates of poverty change across regions, the calculations are done separately for urban and rural poverty, while the change in total poverty is obtained as the population-weighted average of the changes in urban and rural poverty. Finally, the 'Contribution of agricultural growth' is the ratio of the 'Impact

Table 6.7   The contribution of agricultural growth to poverty reduction, 1984–1996

	Urban	Rural	Total
Poverty head count			
Observed change in poverty (% point)	−22.14	−41.82	−39.24
Impact of agricultural growth (% point)	−12.16	−31.12	−25.74
Contribution of agricultural growth (%)	54.94	74.40	65.58
Poverty gap			
Observed change in poverty (% point)	−7.87	−19.38	−17.08
Impact of agricultural growth (% point)	−2.84	−11.07	−8.73
Contribution of agricultural growth (%)	36.05	57.15	51.13
Poverty severity			
Observed change in poverty (% point)	–	−9.98	–
Impact of agricultural growth (% point)	–	−4.91	–
Contribution of agricultural growth (%)	–	49.22	–

of agricultural growth' to the 'Observed change in poverty', which shows the contribution of agricultural GDP growth to poverty reduction.

The results show that agricultural growth has indeed been the most important factor contributing to rapid poverty reduction experienced by Indonesia during the high growth pre-crisis period. In terms of poverty head count, agricultural growth accounts for 66 percent of total poverty reduction, 55 percent of urban poverty reduction and 74 percent of rural poverty reduction. In terms of poverty gap, agricultural growth accounts for 51, 36 and 57 percent, respectively of total, urban and rural poverty gap reduction. Meanwhile, for poverty severity only the reduction in rural areas is calculated as only for these areas is the coefficient statistically significant. It appears that 49 percent of reduction in poverty severity in rural areas is due to agricultural growth.

6.8   CONCLUSION AND IMPLICATION

As in other developing countries, most of the poor in Indonesia are located in rural areas and their livelihood is in the agricultural sector. Despite the pace of development and industrialization in Indonesia during the last three decades, the majority of households in rural areas still derive most of their income from the agricultural sector. The findings of this study show that, after controlling for other characteristics, a person who's livelihood is in the agricultural sector does have a higher probability of being poor than those whose livelihood is in non-agricultural sectors.

Indonesia has adopted a development strategy emphasizing industrialization, with the purpose of developing a high productivity industrial sector. It was hoped that people would move from the low productivity agricultural sector to the high productivity industrial sector. The findings of this study indicate that this strategy has not worked well for two related reasons.

First, as the industrial sector expanded and the importance of the agricultural sector in the economy quickly diminished, the movement of people out of the agricultural sector into the industrial sector has not occurred as rapidly. This failure of the industrial sector to absorb a larger fraction of the workforce has left the agricultural sector with a sizeable fraction of the workforce while its relative importance in the economy was quickly diminishing.

Second, it turns out that agricultural growth is a much more potent factor in reducing poverty than industrial growth. Even in urban areas, where the industrial sector has a significant impact on poverty reduction, the impact of agricultural growth on reducing poverty is still much larger. As a result, during the pre-crisis high growth period of 1984–96, it is estimated that agricultural growth accounted for 66 percent of total poverty reduction, 55 percent of urban poverty reduction and 74 percent of rural poverty reduction.

These findings have important implications for policies aimed at eliminating poverty in Indonesia and other developing countries. First, it is clear that direct efforts to push agricultural growth are the most effective means to reduce poverty. Second, the strategy of industrialization should be directed at developing industries that have strong linkages with the agricultural sector, such as the agro-industries, so that industrial growth will have a bigger impact on reducing poverty.

At the very least, government should create an environment conducive to private sector participation in the agribusiness development. Hence, agricultural policies that harm agro-industries – including the imposition of high tariffs on imported inputs for agro-industries, export taxes on agricultural products, and restrictions of interregional trade of agricultural commodities – should be removed.

These findings also imply that the policy of industrialized countries to support their agricultural sector through subsidies and protectionist measures, which has hampered agricultural growth in developing countries, is detrimental to the efforts of reducing global poverty. Therefore, removal of subsidies and dismantling of protections in the agricultural sector of developed countries are crucial for poverty reduction in developing countries.

NOTES

1. This is a proxy for the proportion of agricultural income as agricultural households derive some of their income from non-agricultural sectors and vice versa non-agricultural households derive some of their income from agriculture.
2. This is based on a basic needs commodities survey (*Survei Paket Komoditi Kebutuhan Dasar* – SPKKD).
3. Pradhan et al. (2001) use the same 52 commodities in the food poverty basket as BPS, but use the food-share-based Engel curve method for calculating the non-food poverty basket.
4. While the access to Consumption Module SUSENAS can be obtained starting from the 1984 data, the access to Core SUSENAS – which provides household characteristics – can only be obtained starting from the 1987 data.
5. Ravallion and Datt (1999) find that initial conditions do not affect the elasticities of poverty to farm yields and development spending. However, the non-farm growth process is more pro-poor in Indian states with initially higher farm productivity, higher rural living standards relative to urban areas, and higher literacy.

REFERENCES

Bidani, Benu and Martin Ravallion (1993), 'A regional poverty profile for Indonesia', *Bulletin of Indonesian Economic Studies*, **29**, 37–68.

BPS (various years), *Statistik Indonesia* (Statistical Yearbook of Indonesia), Badan Pusat Statistik, Jakarta.

BPS (2002), *Dasar-dasar Analisis Kemiskinan* (The Basics of Poverty Analysis), Statistics Indonesia and World Bank Institute, Jakarta.

Chesher, Andrew (1998), 'Local Poverty Lines and Poverty Measures for Indonesia', Report prepared for the World Bank, Department of Economics, University of Bristol.

Feridhanusetyawan, Tubagus (1999), 'The Impact of the Crisis on the Labor Market in Indonesia', Report prepared for the Asian Development Bank, Centre for Strategic and International Studies, Jakarta.

Foster, J., J. Greer and E. Thorbecke (1984), 'A class of decomposable poverty measures', *Econometrica*, **52**, 761–6.

Hill, Hal (1996), *The Indonesian Economy Since 1996: Southeast Asia's Emerging Giant*, Cambridge University Press, Cambridge.

Narayan, Deepa (2000), *Voices of the Poor: Can Anyone Hear Us?*, Oxford University Press for the World Bank, Oxford.

Narayan, Deepa, Robert Chambers, Meera K. Shah and Patti Petesch (2000), *Voices of the Poor: Crying Out for Change*, Oxford University Press for the World Bank, Oxford.

Pradhan, Menno, Asep Suryahadi, Sudarno Sumarto and Lant Pritchett (2001), 'Eating like which "Joneses"? An iterative solution to the choice of poverty line reference group', *Review of Income and Wealth*, **47**(4), 473–87.

Quizon, J. and H. Binswanger (1986), 'Modeling the impact of agricultural growth and government policy on income distribution in India', *World Bank Economic Review*, **1**(1), 103–48.

Quizon, J. and H. Binswanger (1989), 'What can agriculture do for the poorest rural groups?', in I. Adelman and S. Lane (eds), *The Balance between Agriculture and Industry in Economic Development*, vol. 4 (Social Effects), St. Martin Press, New York.

Ravallion, Martin (1994), *Poverty Comparisons*, Fundamentals of Pure and Applied Economics Vol. 56, Harwood Academic Press, Chur, Switzerland.

Ravallion, Martin and Gaurav Datt (1996), 'How important to India's poor is the sectoral composition of economic growth?', *World Bank Economic Review*, **10**(1), 1–25.

Ravallion, Martin and Gaurav Datt (1999), 'When is growth pro-poor? Evidence from the diverse experiences of India's states', Policy Research Working Paper No. 2263, World Bank, Washington, DC.

Sarris, Alexander H. (2001), 'The role of agriculture in economic development and poverty reduction: an empirical and conceptual foundation', Paper prepared for the Rural Development Department of the World Bank, University of Athens, Athens.

Sen, Amartya (1981), *Poverty and Famines: An Essay on Entitlement and Deprivation*, Oxford University Press, Oxford.

Suryahadi, Asep, Sudarno Sumarto, Yusuf Suharso and Lant Pritchett (2000), 'The evolution of poverty during the crisis in Indonesia, 1996–99', Policy Research Working Paper No. 2435, September, World Bank, Washington, DC.

Thomas, Vinod, Mansoor Dailami, Ashok Dhareshwar, Daniel Kaufman, Nalin Kishor, Ramon López and Yan Wang (2000), *The Quality of Growth*, Oxford University Press for the World Bank, Oxford.

Timmer, C. Peter (1997), 'How well do the poor connect to the growth process', CAER Discussion Paper No. 178, Harvard Institute for International Development, Cambridge, MA.

Warr, Peter G. (2002), 'Poverty reduction and sectoral growth: evidence from Southeast Asia', mimeo, Australian National University, Canberra.

Warr, Peter G. and Wang Wen-Thuen (1999), 'Poverty, inequality and economic growth in Taiwan', in Gustav Ranis and Hu Sheng-Cheng (eds), *The Political Economy of Development in Taiwan: Essays in Memory of John C.H. Fei*, Edward Elgar, Cheltenham, UK and Northampton, MA, USA, pp. 133–65.

World Bank (2000), *World Development Report 2000/2001: Attacking Poverty*, Oxford University Press, Oxford and New York.

7. Ghana

Ramatu M. Al-Hassan and
John Baptist D. Jatoe

7.1 INTRODUCTION

Poverty reduction has been a principal developmental goal in Ghana since 1995. This was clearly spelt out in the Vision 2020 development plan (Republic of Ghana, 1995), which was implemented over the 1996–2000 period. There have been significant declines in poverty levels since the 1980s but the extent of these changes has varied across locations and socio-economic groups with the savanna zones and groups in agriculture-related employment showing the least improvement in poverty levels.

The country's economic fortunes have been tied to agriculture, whose average contributions to GDP were 60 percent in the 1970s, 54 percent in the 1980s and 36 percent in the last half of the 1990s. Agriculture employs about 60 percent of the economically active of the country's 18 million people (GSS, 2000a). The performance of the agricultural sector has lagged behind that of services and industry in the last 10 to 15 years. In the last half of the 1980s, performance in the sector dragged down growth in total GDP; in the 1990s, when growth in services and industry slackened, growth in agriculture was not sufficient to pull the economy's growth with it (Table 7.1). With population growing at 2.6 percent, per capita GDP declined from US$439 in 1993 to US$346 in 2001.

Given its contribution to GDP and the high prevalence of poverty in agriculture, much is expected from the sector in the fight to reduce poverty. Information on how agriculture can reduce poverty is necessary to guide the right policy choices. Ghana's Poverty Reduction Strategy Paper (Government of Ghana, 2003) recognises that poverty reduction in Ghana is limited by lack of growth in agriculture and agro-processing. This attempts to identify how the link between agricultural growth and poverty reduction can be realised.

Agricultural growth influences poverty through a number of channels, including effects of agricultural growth on food prices, effects on non-farm (and farm) wages, effects on smallholder incomes and multiplier effects

Table 7.1   Trends in sectoral growth rates

	Sector growth rates (%)			
	1984–85	1986–90	1991–95	1996–2001
Agriculture	5.2	1.8	2.8	4.1
Services	7.1	7.7	6.1	5.4
Industry	13.4	7.2	4.3	4.6
GDP	6.9	4.8	4.5	4.3

Source: Computed from the Statistical Newsletter, Ghana Statistical Service (various issues).

through rural growth linkages. See Chapter 2 for an in-depth analysis. Due to the lack of time-series data on informal and private sector wages, and farm incomes, we cannot test the hypotheses related to non-farm wages and smallholder incomes. We shall therefore focus our attention on the food price channel and on the role of growth multipliers. Before doing so, we shall first review the key features of Ghana's agricultural sector and the evolution of poverty in Ghana. We then decompose the changes in poverty that ocurred between 1991 and 1999 and provide an assessment of the responsiveness of poverty to sectoral growth. An analysis of the long-run determinants of food prices precedes the estimation of the growth multipliers.

7.2   OVERVIEW OF GHANA'S AGRICULTURAL SECTOR

The agricultural sector in Ghana is dominated by smallholders farming about 2–5 hectares and who produce 90 percent of total output. Large-scale production is currently prominent with plantation crops such as oil palm, rubber and pineapple. Smallholder agriculture is characterised by the use of simple hand tools for farm activities, limited use of agro-chemicals especially fertiliser, and shifting cultivation and fallow rotations – although the fallow periods are on the decline because of population pressure. Farmers prefer to select seed from their own production even when the seed variety is of the improved type (Delmini, 2000). The low adoption of improved or modern farm practices is largely attributed to limited liquidity of farmers, in the absence of well-functioning credit markets.

Farm labour is drawn from family sources but complemented more and more with hired labour. Land is acquired through various land tenure systems, most of which give only usufruct rights to farmers. As a result, the tenure systems do not provide the security in land ownership that is necessary for long-term investment in land improvements and planting of permanent crops.

The agro-processing industry is underdeveloped since much of the food produced is purchased in the raw form. Like farming, food processing is done on a small scale, using traditional technology. Marketing infrastructure is also undeveloped. Post-harvest losses are estimated at about 30 percent and are even higher for fruits and vegetables. Produce is transported in inappropriate haulage trucks, and sold on unpaved floors. Food packaging is also minimal. There are no quality standards, or standard weights and measures.

Policy interventions in the sector, since the implementation of structural adjustment in the mid-1980s, have included privatisation of input markets and of internal purchases of cocoa beans, removal of subsidies on inputs and guaranteed prices of cereals, and removal of mandatory 20 percent allocation of banks' credit portfolios to agriculture. Implementation of policies was supplemented with specific donor-funded projects and programmes.

The response of the private sector to the liberalisation policies in the agricultural sector was below expectation. The major limitations have been the large capital investments required in the face of limited capacity of the private sector, limited margins allowed for service providers, and high interest rates. Additional problems in the case of privatisation of input distribution were seasonality in trade, fear of loss of market share to subsidised inputs from development projects, and a fall in demand due to high costs arising from subsidy removals and exchange rate liberalisation. Poor infrastructure, including facilities at the ports, has contributed to the non-competitiveness of exports of agricultural produce.

The growth of the agricultural sector has been low mainly because of the above limitations, which were exacerbated by adverse macroeconomic conditions such as high rates of inflation, unstable exchange rates, and large government deficits.

7.3   POVERTY IN GHANA: A HISTORICAL ACCOUNT

Studies on income distribution in the 1960s and 1970s showed that incomes in rural Ghana were generally lower than those in the urban areas (Boateng et al., n.d.; Rourke, 1971; Dutta Roy and Mabey, 1968). An application of quality of life indices also showed rural Ghana to be worse off than urban Ghana (Awusabo, 1981/82).

Using a composite index of development as an indicator of poverty, Ewusi (1976) found that northern Ghana was the least developed, with indices less than 10 percent of that of Accra. Bequele (1980), cited in Boateng et al., also confirmed the higher poverty levels of northern Ghana relative to the south with the 1970 and 1974 agricultural census data. This difference in poverty levels has been attributed to differences in resource endowments, and capacities to respond to new economic opportunities. An analysis of data of the 1974/75 household budget survey (Ewusi, 1984) found that poverty among illiterate household heads was higher than among literate ones; larger households were also associated with higher poverty levels. Poverty among farmers was also higher than that of other occupations. A final result, which Boateng et al. did not expect, was that the incidence of poverty among males was higher than among females.

The launch of the structural adjustment programme in Ghana saw the initiative for a more regular assessment of poverty levels. The Ghana living standards surveys, the first of which was carried out in 1987, were instituted under the World Bank's Social Dimension of Adjustment to track the social and welfare implications of structural adjustment programmes and policies, especially on the poor. The 1987–88 Ghana Living Standards Survey (GLSS) was therefore to provide a baseline poverty profile for the country. That poverty profile (Boateng et al.) confirmed earlier assessments that poverty was more endemic and severe in rural Ghana than in urban areas. Also a greater proportion of the poor derived their income from agriculture than the non-poor. Their major conclusion was that a policy of raising producer prices of key agricultural commodities would be a consistent poverty-reduction strategy.

Canagarajah and Mazumdar (n.d.) have estimated changes in inequality between 1989 and 1991/92 based on the second and third rounds of the GLSS. Their analysis reveals an improvement in inequality in rural Ghana, but only in the lower end of the distribution. Also, welfare distribution among food crop farmers, export farmers and non-farm workers improved at the lower to middle levels of the distribution. They conclude that the improvements in mean expenditures and their respective distributions in rural areas and cities other than Accra accounted for the overall poverty reduction in the country.

An analysis of determinants of average per capita expenditure also showed that the poor do not benefit as much from education as do the non-poor; this is because the poor tend not to go beyond primary or middle school level, beyond which education contributes to improvements in household welfare. This result is consistent with the earlier findings from the 1974 budget data reported by Ewusi.

The poverty profiles from subsequent surveys in 1991/92 and 1998/99 show basically the same pattern of poverty in the country but with large differences in the pattern of change in both poverty and inequality. Estimation and analysis of recent changes in poverty is the subject of the next section.

7.4   MEASURING THE RESPONSIVENESS OF POVERTY TO GROWTH

The measures of poverty adopted in this analysis are the Foster–Greer–Thorbecke (FGT) indices. The interested reader can consult the technical appendix for the definition of the FGT indices and their properties.

A decomposition of poverty into poverty of different groups in the population is achieved by applying the FGT poverty measures to mutually exclusive groups in the population. The population-weighted sum of the individual population group poverty indices gives the poverty index (Grootaert and Kanbur, 1989). A group's contribution to poverty is then the population-weighted poverty index of the group expressed as a ratio of national poverty. Subgroups are defined on the basis of occupation (economic activity) of the household head, urban/rural localities, and agro-ecological zones.

The methods of Datt and Ravallion (1992) and of Ravallion and Huppi (1991) are used to decompose poverty change over time. The first method decomposes poverty into growth and inequality effects (plus a residual). For any two periods, t_0 and t_1, the growth component of a change in the poverty measure is defined as the change in poverty due to a change in mean income from μ_0 to μ_1, while holding the Lorenz curve constant at $L_0 = L(p; \pi_0)$. The redistribution component is defined as the change in poverty due to a change in the Lorenz curve from $L_0 = L(p, \pi_0)$ to $L_1 = L(p; \pi_1)$ while holding the mean income constant at μ_0. p is the poverty measure and π is the Lorenz curve parameter. The decomposition is as follows:

$$P(\mu_1/z, \pi_1) - P(\mu_0/z, \pi_0) = [P(\mu_1/z, \pi_0) - P(\mu_0/z, \pi_0)]$$
$$+ [P(\mu_0/z, \pi_1) - P(\mu_0/z, \pi_0)] + \text{Residual},$$

where

$$P(\mu_1/z, \pi_1) - P(\mu_0/z, \pi_0) \text{ is poverty change,}$$

$$[P(\mu_1/z, \pi_0) - P(\mu_0/z, \pi_0)] \text{ is the growth component, and}$$

$$[P(\mu_0/z, \pi_1) - P(\mu_0/z, \pi_0)] \text{ is the redistribution component.}$$

Positive growth reduces poverty while an increase in inequality will tend to increase poverty.

The second method, following Ravallion and Huppi (1991) decomposes intertemporal poverty change into intra-sectoral effects of the poverty change, population shift effects, and an interaction effect which gives an indication of the link between poverty changes and population shifts. A negative interaction effect means that population shifted towards sectors where poverty was declining. The computational formula for the decomposition is as follows:

$$P_\alpha^t - P_\alpha^{t0} = \sum_{i=1}^m (P_{\alpha i}^t - P_{\alpha i}^{t0})n_i^{t0} + \sum_{i=1}^m (n_{\alpha i}^t - n_i^{t0})P_{\alpha i}^{t0} + \sum_{i=1}^m (P_{\alpha i}^t - P_{\alpha i}^{t0})(n_i^t - n_i^{t0})$$

Change in sector poverty   + Change in   + Interaction between
due to sectoral changes   poverty due   sectoral changes and
in poverty   to population   population shifts
                                                     shifts

Elasticities of poverty reduction are estimated to assess the impact of welfare changes within various economic groupings on poverty levels. Following Kakwani (1993), the responsiveness of P_α indices to mean income is specified as follows:

Elasticity of head count ratio (P_0) with respect to mean income:

$$\eta_{p0} = \frac{\partial P_0}{\partial \mu}\frac{\mu}{P_0} = \frac{-zf(z)}{P_0} < 0,$$

where

P_0 is head count ratio;

z = poverty line; and
μ is mean income or welfare.

Elasticity of P_α with respect to μ:

$$\eta_{p\alpha} = \frac{\partial P_\alpha}{\partial \mu}\frac{\mu}{P_\alpha} = -\alpha\frac{[P_{\alpha-1} - P_\alpha]}{P_\alpha} \quad \text{for } \alpha = 1, 2;$$

$$\eta^*_{P_{\alpha i}} = \frac{P_{\alpha i}f_i}{P_\alpha} - \eta_{P\alpha i}$$

where

$\eta^* P_{\alpha i}$ is the elasticity of total poverty with respect to mean income of
        the ith subgroup, and

$\eta P_{\alpha i}$ is the elasticity of the ith subgroup poverty with respect to mean
        income of that subgroup and is computed as

$$\eta_{P_{\alpha i}} = \frac{\partial P_{\alpha i}}{\partial \mu_i} \frac{\mu_i}{P_{\alpha i}} = -\alpha \frac{P_{\alpha i-1} - P_{\alpha i}}{P_{\alpha i}}$$

μ_i = mean income of group i^{th} group.

7.5   DATA SOURCES

The data source for measurement of poverty in Ghana is the Ghana
Living Standards Survey (GLSS), conducted in 1987/88, 1988/89, 1991/92
and 1998/99. The GLSS is national in scope and collects information on
the many aspects of the living conditions of households. According to
the Ghana Statistical Service (GSS, 2000a), the questionnaires for the
first two rounds of the GLSS were different from those of 1991/92
and 1998/99. Therefore for ease of comparison the analysis in this study is
based on the last two surveys. The cleaned data from the 1991/92
survey include 4552 households while the 1998/99 data have 5998
households.

The GSS is the lead institution for the measurement of poverty in Ghana
and it uses a consumption-based standard of living measure. In order to
maintain consistency in the poverty analysis and to extend the analysis of
the GSS so far, we use the same standard of living measure for our analysis. The consumption welfare is estimated as an aggregation of expenditures on food (actual and imputed), housing, household utilities, education
and other non-food expenditure, and remittances. The data are adjusted for
spatial price variation using regional cost of living index to convert consumption expenditure into the constant prices of Accra in January 1999 for
the two datasets. Individual welfare estimates are then computed on an
individual basis by dividing the total household welfare by the adult
equivalent of the household.

Although the GSS defines two poverty levels, an extreme poverty level of
700,000 cedis and a normal level of 900,000 cedis, the descriptions in this
study are based on the latter. The extreme poverty line represents a
food consumption poverty line; people below this line are unable to meet
their minimum food requirements. Being restricted to food expenditure,

the extreme poverty line will tend to underestimate poverty levels in the country.

7.6 DECOMPOSING RECENT POVERTY TRENDS IN GHANA (1991/92–1998/99)

Table 7.2 presents estimates of FGT poverty measures for various population segments over the period from 1991/92 to 1998/99. Consumption poverty in 1999 was 39.5 percent. The highest poverty levels in both survey years were found in the savanna zone and among food crop farmers. The poverty level in rural Ghana was also higher than that in urban areas. Surprisingly, female-headed households had a lower level of consumption poverty than male-headed households. This is so for the national sample as well as within the agro-ecological zone (not shown in the table).

The poverty-level estimates in 1999 represent a decline from the 1992 estimates for the country as a whole and for all groups and localities. National poverty incidence declined by 23 percent. The biggest gains in poverty reduction occurred among private formal employees, export crop farmers, public sector employees and private informal employees. The forest zone, probably because of the prevalence of export crop farmers, also experienced a 37 percent reduction in the head count index. The P_1 and P_2 indices also declined, with the exception of the savanna zone, where the indices increased, suggesting a worsening condition of the poor. The most significant reductions in the depth and severity of poverty occurred in the forest zone, and among workers in the public sector, private formal sector and export crop farmers.

The substantial decline in poverty among private formal employees may be explained by the increases in the wages that occurred after 1992. Wages in the formal private sector are higher than public sector wages (Fine and Boateng, 2000), therefore a policy of wage decompression in the public sector, part of the civil service reforms in the 1990s (Wetzel, 2000), would have benefited private formal employees the most. Lack of wage statistics on the informal sector hampers the assessment of links between formal and informal sector wages.

The formal sector labour market and wage determination are controlled by institutional factors such as enterprise and sector-level collective bargaining, national-level negotiations for a minimum wage and strikes (Aryeetey and Fosu, 2002). Although the negotiated wages for formal sector workers are generally low, they are still better than wages in the informal sector. Also, within the formal sector, wages in the private sector are higher than those in the public sector. This is because many

Table 7.2 *Poverty patterns in Ghana, 1991–1999*

Group	Year	Pop. share	Average welfare	P_0	% change in P_0	P_1	% change in P_1	P_2	% change in P_2
Urban	1991/1992	33.3	1,578,452	0.277		0.074		0.029	
	1998/1999	33.3	1,955,209	0.194	−29.96	0.053	−28.38	0.021	−27.59
Rural	1991/1992	66.7	908,761	0.636		0.24		0.117	
	1998/1999	66.7	1,141,510	0.495	−22.17	0.181	−24.58	0.089	−23.93
Coastal	1991/1992	31	1,383,293	0.38		0.106		0.042	
	1998/1999	31.3	1,724,673	0.282	−25.79	0.085	−19.81	0.036	−14.29
Forest	1991/1992	40.6	1,122,128	0.519		0.183		0.083	
	1998/1999	43.3	1,489,825	0.326	−37.19	0.092	−49.73	0.037	−55.42
Savanna	1991/1992	28.4	867,589	0.664		0.273		0.144	
	1998/1999	25.4	895,807	0.649	−2.26	0.284	4.03	0.152	5.56
Male	1991/1992	73	1,073,597	0.549		0.201		0.097	
	1998/1999	72.6	1,364,955	0.41	−25.32	0.146	−27.36	0.07	−27.84
Female	1991/1992	26.9	1,285,888	0.431		0.141		0.063	
	1998/1999	27.3	1,537,658	0.352	−18.33	0.119	−15.60	0.055	−12.70
Public sector employment	1991/1992	13.5	1,470,251	0.347		0.102		0.043	
	1998/1999	10.7	1,773,604	0.227	−34.58	0.048	−52.94	0.016	−62.79
Private formal employment	1991/1992	3.9	1,523,775	0.303		0.077		0.032	
	1998/1999	4.9	2,211,525	0.113	−62.71	0.024	−68.83	0.007	−78.13
Private informal employment	1991/1992	3.1	1,376,909	0.386		0.108		0.043	
	1998/1999	2.9	1,631,575	0.252	−34.72	0.074	−31.48	0.03	−30.23
Export farmers	1991/1992	6.3	886,375	0.64		0.245		0.12	
	1998/1999	7	1,234,437	0.387	−39.53	0.103	−57.96	0.039	−67.50
Food crop farmers	1991/1992	43.6	837,862	0.681		0.268		0.134	
	1998/1999	38.6	964,027	0.594	−12.78	0.24	−10.45	0.124	−7.46

					% change				
Non-farm self-employment	1991/1992	27.6	1,348,650	0.384		0.113		0.046	
	1998/1999	33.8	1,644,407	0.286	−25.52	0.086	−23.89	0.035	−23.91
Non-working	1991/1992	2	1,829,106	0.188		0.054		0.021	
	1998/1999	2.1	2,485,164	0.204	8.51	0.074	37.04	0.035	66.67
National	1991/1992	100	1,130,674	0.517		0.185		0.088	
	1998/1999	100	1,412,142	0.395	−23.60	0.139	−24.86	0.066	−25.00

Source: Computed from GLSS data, 1991/92 and 1998/99.

private sector employers pay wages far above the statutory minimum wage.

Improvement in farm earnings is driven by increases in productivity and output prices. Crop yields did tend to rise in the 1990s although the initial increase from the 1991 levels was partly due to a change in the method of estimating yield. Real wholesale prices of cassava and rice were fairly stable during most of the 1990s. Higher cocoa producer prices, and currency depreciation contributed to the dramatic welfare gains made by export crop farmers, especially in the forest zone.

Table 7.2 suggests lower levels of poverty among females than among males and this is rather unexpected even though the result is consistent with the earlier poverty analysis. Women are generally more disadvantaged than men in terms of access to productive resources, information, and opportunities for income generation generally (Government of Ghana, 2003). The data probably reflect intra-household dynamics and other safety nets that empower female-headed households to meet their consumption needs. The poverty of women is also much more linked to access to services (water, health, education) because of their gender roles. Improvements in these services can further enhance women's quality of life.

Table 7.3 decomposes the poverty change between 1991 and 1999 into growth and inequality effects, and according to intra-sectoral and population shifts effects. In rural and urban areas, and within agro-ecological zones, growth contributed the most to poverty reduction. However, increases in inequality in all the localities, except the forest zone, limited the effect of growth on poverty reduction. For example, in rural areas, the 55 percent potential decline due to growth was eroded by an 2 percent increase in inequality to a realised poverty reduction of 22 percent. In the savanna zone the poor were affected the most by worsening inequality as reflected in positive changes in the poverty gap and severity indices. The second type of decomposition in Table 7.3 shows that growth in rural Ghana contributed between 76 and 86 percent to the poverty reduction between 1991 and 1999. Decomposition by agro-ecological zone shows that income gains in the forest zone contributed between 64 and 85 percent (depending on the index) to poverty reduction over the period.

Table 7.4 presents results of similar decompositions of poverty change but by socio-economic group. Again, growth accounted for a significant share of the poverty reduction among all the groups. However, worsening inequality among private formal employees, food crop farmers and non-farm self-employees limited the poverty-reducing effect of growth among these groups. The sector/population shifts decomposition attributes 80 to 88 percent of the poverty reduction to income gains within sectors while population shifts accounted for 11 to 18 percent of poverty reduction. The

Table 7.3 *Decomposition of poverty change (1991–1999) by locality*

Population group	Poverty measure	Change (1991–99)	Growth–inequality decomposition of poverty change 1991–99			Sectoral and population shifts decomposition of poverty change 1991–99		
			Growth effect	Inequality effect	Residual	Intra-sectoral effect	Population shift effect	Interaction effects
Rural	P_0	−0.463	−0.553	0.018	0.071	75.95	0	0
	P_1	−0.091	−0.221	0.053	−0.023	85.90	0	0
	P_2	−0.096	−0.110	0.048	−0.034	85.90	0	0
Urban	P_0	−0.233	−0.257	0.041	−0.017	24.05	0	0
	P_1	−0.063	−0.068	0.027	−0.021	14.10	0	0
	P_2	−0.025	−0.027	0.017	−0.015	14.10	0	0
Coastal	P_0	−0.098	−0.143	0.011	0.035	24.7	−0.93	0
	P_1	−0.021	−0.049	0.030	−0.001	14.15	0	0
	P_2	−0.005	−0.022	0.021	−0.005	8.45	0	0
Forest	P_0	−0.193	−0.171	−0.002	−0.020	63.70	−11.39	4.24
	P_1	−0.090	−0.085	−0.008	0.003	80.32	−10.74	5.34
	P_2	−0.046	−0.045	−0.004	0.003	84.89	−10.19	5.65
Savanna	P_0	−0.015	−0.017	0.008	−0.006	3.46	16.20	0
	P_1	0.011	−0.012	0.022	0.000	−6.79	17.80	0
	P_2	0.008	−0.008	0.017	0.000	−10.33	19.64	0

Source: Computed from GLSS data (1991/92 and 1998/99).

Total population shift and interaction effects by agro-ecological zone (%)

	P_0	P_1	P_2
Population shifts effects	3.88	7.06	9.45
Interaction effects	4.22	5.34	5.65

Table 7.4 Decomposition of poverty change (1991–1999) by occupation

Population group	Poverty measure	Change (1991–99)	Growth–inequality decomposition of poverty change 1991–99			Sectoral and population shifts decomposition of poverty change 1991–99		
			Growth effect	Inequality effect	Residual	Intra-sectoral effect (%)	Population shift effect (%)	Interaction effects (%)
Public sector workers	P_0	−0.120	−0.111	−0.018	0.010	13.28	8.03	−2.75
	P_1	−0.054	−0.039	−0.015	0.000	15.01	6.23	−3.11
	P_2	−0.026	−0.018	−0.010	0.002	14.01	5.81	−2.91
Private formal workers	P_0	−0.189	−0.204	−0.066	0.080	6.07	−2.46	1.56
	P_1	−0.053	−0.051	−0.008	0.005	5.20	−1.78	1.33
	P_2	−0.025	−0.020	−0.004	−0.001	4.05	−1.56	1.04
Private informal	P_0	−0.133	−0.122	0.031	−0.043	3.56	0.64	−0.23
	P_1	−0.034	−0.040	0.009	−0.003	2.70	0.49	−0.18
	P_2	−0.013	−0.018	0.006	−0.001	1.61	0.42	−0.10
Export crop farmers	P_0	−0.253	−0.207	−0.001	−0.046	12.91	−3.62	1.43
	P_1	−0.142	−0.117	−0.023	0.001	21.01	−3.89	2.33
	P_2	−0.081	−0.066	−0.021	0.006	26.15	−4.36	2.91
Food crop farmers	P_0	−0.086	−0.081	0.005	−0.010	32.16	27.87	3.69
	P_1	−0.028	−0.057	0.024	0.004	29.09	30.02	−3.34
	P_2	−0.010	−0.035	0.025	0.000	22.63	33.73	−2.59
Non-farm self-employed	P_0	−0.098	−0.117	0.018	0.002	20.36	−19.31	4.57
	P_1	−0.028	−0.047	0.020	0.000	12.27	15.17	2.76
	P_2	−0.011	−0.021	0.014	−0.003	14.32	−16.09	3.22
Non-working	P_0	0.016	−0.060	0.004	−0.041	−0.16	−0.16	−0.01
	P_1	0.020	−0.033	0.019	−0.016	−0.89	−0.11	−0.04
	P_2	0.021	−0.015	0.017	−0.015	−2.08	−0.10	−0.10

Source: Computed from GLSS data (1991/92 and 1998/99).

Total population shift and interaction effects by occupation (%)

	P_0	P_1	P_2
Population shifts effects	10.94	15.79	17.85
Interaction effects	0.89	−0.24	1.45

Table 7.5   Elasticities of national poverty indices to growth (1999)

Population group	P_0	P_1	P_2
National	−1.24	−1.84	−2.20
Rural	−0.01	−1.73	−0.98
Urban	−0.30	−2.65	−2.80
Coastal	−0.35	−1.42	−1.49
Forest	−0.61	−1.69	−1.66
Savanna	−0.30	−2.63	−3.97
Public sector employees	−0.23	−1.29	−0.96
Private formal employees	−0.03	−0.64	−0.52
Private informal employees	−0.05	−1.28	−1.33
Export farmers	−0.10	−2.04	−1.93
Food crop farmers	−0.51	−2.55	−3.51
Non-farm self-employees	−0.38	−1.44	−1.52

table also illustrates the potential of income gains within the food crop and export crop sectors to reduce national poverty due to the large shares of the intra-sector effects. The most favourable population shifts occurred in the food crop sector. Populations shifted away from the food crop sector to export crop farming and non-farm self-employment.

The elasticity of poverty reduction with respect to welfare improvements within groups is presented in Table 7.5. Welfare improvement in urban areas stimulates more poverty reduction than it does in rural areas. According to agro-ecological zone, the highest elasticities are associated with the savanna. Similarly, welfare improvements in the farm sector also generate high responses in national poverty reduction and this is of particular interest in assessing the role of agriculture in poverty reduction.

In summary, consumption poverty in Ghana declined between 1992 and 1999. But poverty levels are still high especially in rural areas, the savanna zone and among food crop farmers. Male-headed households had higher reductions in their poverty levels than their female counterparts. A realisation that high responsiveness of poverty reduction to growth has been among the very poor groups was limited by worsening inequality among food crop farmers, and within the coastal and savanna zones. Economic reforms that led to high producer prices for export crops and higher wages for formal sector workers had a positive impact on poverty reduction among export crop farmers and private formal employees.

7.7   THE FOOD PRICE CHANNEL

Food price and growth linkage channels are assessed in this study. A model of urban food prices on the productivity of the agricultural, industry and services sectors, and minimum wage is estimated. The sectoral productivity is measured as sectoral GDP per capita of the economically active population in the sector. Since labour data are not disaggregated for industry and services, a composite measure of the productivity of these two sectors is used, where the labour in the sectors is the estimated economically active population outside agriculture. Agricultural productivity is expected to have a dampening effect on food prices, while productivity in the other sectors will tend to exert a positive effect on food prices through the higher income of employees in those sectors. Finally, the effect of minimum wage, which is used as a proxy for wage levels (and therefore income), is also expected to be positive. The food price equation was specified as:

$$FCPIURB_t = C + b_1 AGPDTY_t + b_2 AGPDTY_{t-1} + b_3 PDTYINSE_t$$
$$+ b_4 PDTYINSE_{t-1} + b_5 MINWAGE_t + b_6 FOODIMPT + e_t,$$

where:

$FCPIURB$	=	urban food price index;
$AGPDTY$	=	agricultural labour productivity;
$PDTYINSE$	=	labour productivity of industry and services;
$MINWAGE$	=	Minimum wage; and
$FOODIMPT$	=	food imports.

The equation, presented in Table 7.6, was estimated by ordinary least squares, with data covering the 1981–2000 period. Agricultural productivity lowers urban food prices with an elasticity of –1.0 in the first year and –0.89 in the next year. Expectation that higher productivity in the non-agricultural sector and minimum wages will tend to increase earnings and in turn put an upward pressure on food prices is also borne out. However, responsiveness of price to these variables is very low with elasticities far less than 1. Also, it is the lagged effect of the non-agricultural sector productivity that is significant. Hence in spite of the high levels of food imports, domestic food production is still a crucial determinant of food prices. The value of food imports increased from US$153 million to US$330 million in 2001, a more than 100 percent increase. The coefficient of the food import variable (whether measured in value terms or quantity) was not significant and was excluded from the model.

*Table 7.6   Estimated urban food price model (dependent variable:
            FCPIURB)*

Variable	Coefficient	*t*-statistic	Prob.	Elasticity
C	95.790	4.364	0.0006	–
AGPDTY	−62.079	−2.492	0.0258	−1.02
AGPDTY$_{-1}$	−54.166	−1.987	0.0668	−0.89
PDTYINSE	−25.709	−1.194	0.2522	–
PDTYINSE$_{-1}$	32.785	1.914	0.0763	0.55
MINWAGE	0.027	9.972	0.0000	0.52
R-square	0.983			
Adjusted R-squared	0.977			
F-Statistic	162.79			
Prob (F-statistic)	0.000			
Durbin–Watson stat	1.60			

7.8   GROWTH LINKAGES

7.8.1   Methodological Approach

The growth linkages model employed in this analysis is based on the four-sector semi-input–output model of Delgado et al. (1998). The sectors include farm tradables, farm non-tradables, non-farm tradables and non-farm non-tradables. As noted by the authors, the four-sector structure makes it possible to examine the effects of supply shifters in both farm and non-farm sectors on rural growth. The key issues of model application are assumptions about the price elasticity of supply of non-tradables, the classification of commodities as tradable or non-tradable, and farm or non-farm and estimation of marginal budget shares of commodity groups for different population subgroups.

As with the original linkage models applied in Asian countries, the model assumes perfect price elasticity of supply of non-tradables. It is recognised that this assumption leads to an overestimation of growth multipliers by a margin of 30 percent. Non-tradables, by definition, either have no markets outside, or have no external sources of demand. Non-tradables are also demand constrained, therefore any increased demand through income growth must be met by new production leading to additional growth in the local economy. Identification of external reference market is the key to classifying non-tradables. This study adopts the national definition of trading space, rather than some zones within the country. By this assumption, the classification of a commodity by its tradability is based on whether the commodity is traded internationally by the country. This is different from a commodity being traded between two areas within the country. The national classification of tradability increases the number of non-traded commodities, and therefore the multiplier effect of income growth.

Following Delgado et al. (1998), goods are classified into farm and non-farm sectors, rather than food/non-food or rural/urban sectors because farmers tend to engage in both farm and non-farm activities, and farm households are also non-farm households. All raw farm produce including livestock, milk, eggs, cereals, legumes, roots and tubers and plantains, fruits and vegetables, are classified as farm commodities. Processed food items on the other hand are classified as non-farm because the value addition activities are post-harvest activities. All services and unpackaged prepared foods are classified as non-tradables. Household expenditure patterns are analysed on the basis of the average budget share (ABS), which measures the percentage of total household expenditure allocated to a commodity group, and marginal budget share (MBS), which measures the percentage of additional income that is allocated to a commodity group.[1]

The ABS is estimated as:

$$S_i = \frac{E_i}{E} = b_i + \frac{a_i}{E} + c_i \log E + \sum_{ii} (\mu_{ij} \frac{Z_j}{E} + \lambda_{ij} Z_j), \qquad (7.1)$$

where E_i is expenditure on the ith commodity (or commodity group) and E is total consumption expenditure, used as a proxy for income. Z_js are household characteristics that may affect the level and slope of the Engel functions; a_i, b_i, μ_{ij} and λ_{ij} are constants.

The MBS is estimated from the modified Working–Leser model of Hazell and Röell (1983) and Delgado et al. (1998), where the expenditure share equation is estimated with an intercept:

$$MBS_i = \frac{\partial E_i}{\partial E} = b_i + c_i(1 + \log E) + \sum_j \lambda_{ij} Z_j. \qquad (7.2)$$

The derivation of the equations for estimating growth multipliers is elaborated in Delgado et al. (1998, pp. 35–40). The model includes household consumption expenditures on farm and non-farm tradables, household savings, intermediate input demands for farm and non-farm non-tradables, total outputs of farm and non-farm non-tradables, and a household income defined in terms of value added in the four sectors. Here we reproduce only the final multiplier equations.

The multipliers for changes in the farm and non-farm tradables sectors are given by equations (7.3) and (7.4), respectively:

$$\left(\frac{1}{v_{at}}\right)\left(\frac{\partial Y}{\partial T_{at}}\right) = 1 + \left(\frac{v_{an}}{v_{at}}\right)$$

$$\times \left\{ \left(\frac{1}{D}\right)[1 - a_{mn \cdot mn} - (1-s)\beta_{mn}v_{mn}][(1-s)\beta_{an}v_{at} + a_{an \cdot at}] \right.$$

$$\left. + \left(\frac{1}{D}\right)[a_{an \cdot mn} + (1-s)\beta_{an}v_{mn}][(1-s)\beta_{mn}v_{at} + a_{mn \cdot at}] \right\}$$

$$+ \left(\frac{v_{mn}}{v_{at}}\right)\left\{ \left(\frac{1}{D}\right)[a_{mn \cdot an} + (1-s)\beta_{mn}v_{an}][(1-s)\beta_{an}v_{at} + a_{an \cdot at}] \right.$$

$$\left. + \left(\frac{1}{D}\right)[1 - a_{an \cdot an} - (1-s)\beta_{an}v_{an}][(1-s)\beta_{mn}v_{at} + a_{mn \cdot at}] \right\} \qquad (7.3)$$

$$\left(\frac{1}{v_{mt}}\right)\left(\frac{\partial Y}{\partial T_{mt}}\right) = 1 + \left(\frac{v_{an}}{v_{mt}}\right)$$

$$\times \left\{ \left(\frac{1}{D}\right)[1 - a_{mn \cdot mn} - (1-s)\beta_{mn}v_{mn}][(1-s)\beta_{an}v_{mt} + a_{an \cdot mt}] \right.$$

$$\left. + \left(\frac{1}{D}\right)[a_{an \cdot mn} + (1-s)\beta_{an}v_{mm}][(1-s)\beta_{mn}v_{mt} + a_{mn \cdot mt}] \right\}$$

$$+ \left(\frac{v_{mn}}{v_{mt}}\right)\left\{ \left(\frac{1}{D}\right)[a_{mn \cdot an} + (1-s)\beta_{mn}v_{an}][(1-s)\beta_{an}v_{mt} + a_{an \cdot mt}] \right.$$

$$\left. + \left(\frac{1}{D}\right)[1 - a_{an \cdot an} - (1-s)\beta_{an}v_{an}][(1-s)\beta_{mn}v_{mt} + a_{mn \cdot mt}] \right\} \qquad (7.4)$$

where:

β_{an} = MBS of farm non-tradables;
β_{mn} = MBS of non-farm non-tradables;
s = marginal propensity to save;
$a_{i,j}$ = intermediate deliveries from sector i to sector j (per unit of currency),
where $i = (an, mn)$ and $j = (at, mt, an, mn)$; and
v_j = the proportion of value added to gross output from sector j,
where $j = at, an, mt$ and mn.

The subscripts *a*, *m*, *t*, *n* denote farm, non-farm, tradable and non-tradables, respectively,

7.8.2   Estimation of Model Parameters

The parameters required to compute the growth multipliers are the marginal budget shares of the four commodity groups, the ratios of value added to total output of each commodity group, and transfers of intermediate inputs from the farm and non-farm non-tradable sectors to the four sectors.

Marginal budget shares and value-added shares in the farm and non-farm sectors were also estimated from the GLSS 4 data and some commodity budgets. The value-added shares for farm produce and selected processed food products were computed at the individual commodity level, as the ratio of difference between gross output and non-factor inputs and total output. The mean values used in the computation of the multiplier.

Estimates of intermediate transfers of inputs from, and into, agriculture and manufacturing sectors were derived from a SAM (Social Accounting Matrix) for Ghana (Powell and Round, 2000) and used as proxy for the transfers of inputs from and into farm and non-farm sectors. A major limitation of the SAM data is the lack of dis-aggregation between tradable and non-tradable sectors. Budget data on individual crops and cassava products from various sources were used to estimate intermediate transfer parameters. Cocoa and rice represented farm tradables, cassava (unprocessed) represented farm non-tradables, while gari represented non-farm non-tradables. The estimates of intermediate transfers are a major weakness in the quality of the multiplier estimates.

The savings rate of 13 percent used in the base model was estimated from national accounts as total private savings to GDP, and it overestimates household savings. The difference between income and expenditure, based on the 1998/99 GLSS data is negative. Powell and Round also estimated

Table 7.7   Parameter assumptions for estimation of multipliers

Sector	Value-added shares	Intermediate deliveries from non-tradables sector		Savings ratio
		Farm	Non-farm	
Farm non-tradables	0.90	0.05	0.073	0.13
Farm tradables	0.94	0.309	0.07	0.13
Non-farm non-tradables	0.43	0.325	0.014	0.13
Non-farm tradables	0.43	0.096	0.033	0.13

dis-savings of 8.7 and 0.7 percent of total income, among rural and urban households, in their SAM which was based on 1993 data. For these reasons, the savings rate is subsequently halved (assuming a 50 percent overestimation) to simulate the effect of a lower savings rate on the magnitudes of multipliers.

Multipliers are estimated for the whole sample and for subsamples of ecological zones and income levels. Assumptions about value-added shares, and intermediate transfer parameters are varied by 10 percent increments to simulate effects of productivity increases and technological improvements on the multipliers. Production multipliers are computed as multiplier values at which marginal budget shares are equal to zero. Table 7.7 presents the summary of parameter assumptions used for the estimation of growth multipliers.

7.8.3   Results

Household expenditure patterns
The expenditure patterns by commodity groups (Table 7.8) show inelastic expenditure elasticities for non-farm tradables although elasticity tends to improve with income. Elasticities of tradables also improve with income and increases from inelastic responses among the poorest and middle-third income groups to an exceptionally high level of 2.45. Consumption elasticities for farm non-tradables are elastic among the poorest third. Income increases among the poorest group will therefore stimulate the highest demand for farm non-tradables as well as some modest demand increase for non-farm non-tradables.

Growth multipliers
The multiplier estimates presented in Table 7.9 indicate the following. The multipliers for the non-farm sector are higher than those in the farm sector.

Table 7.8   Estimated average and marginal budget shares by income group

Commodity group	National			Poorest third			Middle third			Richest third		
	ABS	MBS	E	ABS	MBS	E	ABS	MBS	E	ABS	MBS	E
Farm non-tradables	0.36	0.32	0.88	0.40	0.62	1.56	0.42	0.36	0.86	0.12	0.23	1.99
Farm tradables	0.11	0.14	1.26	0.14	0.07	0.46	0.15	0.10	0.68	0.07	0.18	2.45
Non-farm non-tradables	0.34	0.37	1.07	0.31	0.31	1.00	0.25	0.48	1.95	0.49	0.37	0.75
Non-farm tradables	0.19	0.18	0.95	0.20	0.05	0.24	0.19	0.06	0.33	0.31	0.21	0.67

Table 7.9   Estimates of growth multipliers

Ghana	Lowest third		Middle third		Upper third			
	Farm	Non-farm	Farm	Non-farm	Farm	Non-farm	Farm	Non-farm
Total multiplier	2.46	3.17	4.19	5.42	2.90	3.75	2.16	2.79
Decomposed into:								
Tradables	1.00	1.00	1.00	1.00	1.00	1.00	1.00	1.00
Farm non-tradables	1.05	1.66	2.58	3.65	1.30	1.99	0.80	1.34
Non-farm non-tradables	0.41	0.51	0.61	0.77	0.60	0.76	0.36	0.45
6% savings	2.62	3.39	5.03	6.51	3.19	4.12	2.26	2.92
Change from base (%)	6.50	6.94	20.05	20.11	10.00	9.87	4.63	4.66

So a growth stimulus is more likely to generate a larger impact through the non-farm sector than through the farm sector. Second, multipliers from the farm and non-farm sectors are largest among the lowest-income groups and least for the highest-income group. Third, decomposition of each multiplier reveals the higher contribution of farm sector to overall growth multipliers than the non-farm component. The results regarding the larger size of the non-farm multipliers and the association of large multipliers with the lowest-income groups are consistent with those reported on other West African countries under a national tradability assumption (Delgado et al., 1998). The larger contribution of the additional demand in the farm sector to the total multiplier is, however, a deviation from the results of these other studies but indicates a role for the farm sector to meet the additional expenditure requirements generated from growth. Finally, production multipliers are rather low. Without any changes in expenditure allocations, a 100 cedi

Country case studies

Table 7.10   Simulation results

	Ghana		Lowest third		Middle third		Upper third	
	Farm	Non-farm	Farm	Non-farm	Farm	Non-farm	Farm	Non-farm
Base model	2.46	3.17	4.19	5.42	2.90	3.75	2.16	2.70
Value added – 10%	2.27	2.94	3.47	4.49	2.60	3.37	2.04	2.63
Change from base model (%)	−8.00	−7.00	−17.00	−17.00	−10.00	−10.00	−6.00	−3.00
Value added + 10%	2.66	3.45	5.29	6.84	3.26	4.22	2.29	2.96
Change from base model (%)	8.00	9.00	26.00	26.00	12.00	13.00	6.00	10.00
a_i−10%	2.36	2.99	3.97	5.04	2.77	3.51	2.07	2.63
Change from base model (%)	−4.00	−6.00	−5.00	−7.00	−4.00	−6.00	−4.00	−3.00
a_i+ 10%	2.56	3.11	4.43	4.80	3.03	3.58	2.24	2.78
Change from base model (%)	4.00	−2.00	6.00	−11.00	4.00	−5.00	4.00	3.00

Note: a_i = intermediate deliveries from sector i (technological parameter).

injection in the farm tradables sector stimulates only 36 cedis and 81 cedis additional income from production alone in the farm and non-farm sectors, respectively.

The estimated national multipliers have inelastic response to savings rate. The largest response of 46 to a 50 percent reduction in savings rate is from the non-farm sector multiplier. Although responses of multipliers to reduction in savings by income groups are also inelastic, the responses are larger on the low-income levels.

Simulations results on the savings rate, technological parameters and value-added shares are presented in Table 7.10. There is a positive correlation between the levels of all the parameters and multiplier estimates. So at the national level, a 10 percent decrease in all value-added shares reduces the farm multiplier by 8 percent and the non-farm multiplier by 7 percent.

The results suggest that a bigger impact from agricultural growth can be generated by increasing value-added shares than through increases in use of intermediate inputs. This result is not consistent with similar simulation results reported in Delagado et al., but it is consistent with our interpretation of changes in value-added shares. Having defined value-added shares as the difference between gross output and non-factor inputs, expressed as a ratio of gross output, higher values of the value-added shares imply either lesser use of non-factor inputs to generate the same level of output at same prices, or that costs/prices of non-factor inputs have fallen relative to output values, or that output values have risen relative to input costs. Therefore increases in value addition reflect productivity increases, or reduced marketing costs of inputs and products, all of which should contribute to higher growth multipliers.

7.9 CONCLUSIONS

Poverty levels in Ghana are high with about 40 percent of the population below a poverty line of less than two dollars. During the decade 1991–99, poverty declined but the declines were smallest in the savanna zone and among food crop farmers, among whom poverty is most severe. The poverty incidence among these groups was about 65 percent in 1999. So because of sheer numbers, growth in the agricultural sector as a whole should reduce the poverty level among these groups and in the country as a whole. That poverty among food growers did not decline could be attributed to slow growth of the agricultural sector over the period. However, the urban poor benefit from agricultural productivity improvements through lower food prices.

Although investment in the nonfarm sector generates a larger multiplier than the farm sector, there is a strong positive relation between growth in the farm sector and overall national growth. Furthermore, this growth is particularly strong among the poorest through their higher consumption responses for farm non-tradables. Expenditures on farm non-tradables generate a larger share of the consumption multiplier component of growth. The model assumption of perfectly elastic supply of non-tradables implies that income increases among the poorest groups will tend to mop up surplus or under-utilised resources for the production of farm non-tradables. However, surplus resources can only be utilised if there are no inhibitions on access to the resources. In this sense, institutional inhibitions such as land tenure, technology generation and transfer, and finance must be given priority for redress.

The present analysis demonstrates that agriculture's role in reducing poverty in Ghana will be best enhanced through targeting the poor and facilitating the production of farm non-tradables, which are the starchy staples, fruits and vegetables, and fresh meats and livestock. That agricultural productivity also lowers food prices further buttresses the need to reduce constraints that limit the production of food in general, and farm non-tradables in particular, so as to enhance this aspect of agriculture's role in poverty reduction.

The peculiar characteristic of commodities in the group of farm non-tradables is that they are highly perishable. A well-developed infrastructure, including roads and transport systems, storage and processing infrastructure, is essential to the development of these commodities. The absence of a developed infrastructure in rural Ghana has contributed to the insignificant gains in poverty reduction among food crop farmers. Public expenditure policy should do more to accelerate the pace of infrastructure provision in rural area.

Low agricultural production linkage in Ghana has been reported in previous studies (Stryker and Dumenu, 1986; Jebuni et al., 1990) and attributed to low levels of use of intermediate inputs in the agricultural sector. The larger overall growth multiplier estimated in the present study is therefore due to the effects of consumption demand, and it is the poor in Ghana who have the consumption patterns that matter in stimulating growth. Model simulation results show that modest gains in growth multipliers can be achieved from increases in the use of intermediate inputs, which is presently being constrained by a lack of access. Improved infrastructure, complemented with an effective private institutional framework for input distribution, can improve the use of intermediate inputs by farmers and food processors.

The effect of incentive prices on poverty reduction in the export crop sector suggests that direct price support in the short term can be desirable but long-term policies aimed at improving the marketing infrastructure and marketing system to ensure remunerative prices for farmers, can improve the lot of food crop farmers.

The Ministry of Food and Agriculture has recently developed a Food and Agriculture Sector Development Policy (FASDEP) (Republic of Ghana, 2002), which serves as the framework for the agriculture sector component of the Ghana Poverty Reduction Strategy. The main thrust of the sector policy is modernisation of agriculture, by supporting smallholders to shift from subsistence farming to commercial agriculture. The policy recognises the factors that have limited agricultural growth over the past decades and proposes measures to correct them.

The key measures include development of infrastructure, establishment of an Agricultural Development Fund to support long-term investment in the sector, strengthening of rural finance institutions, and facilitating efficient input and output marketing systems. Priority crops selected for development include both tradable and non-tradable commodities. All in all, the policy and strategies are consistent with the findings of the present study, and ought to give the needed boost for agricultural growth and poverty reduction. Yet Ghanaian experience has been a gap between good policies and performance. The missing link has been good implementation. Fortunately, lessons learnt[2] from the implementation of the Medium Term Agricultural Development Strategy in the 1990s will be invaluable to the implementation of FASDEP.

The present analysis does not capture the impact of availability of social services on poverty. Estimates from the Core Welfare Indicator Survey show a correlation between lack of these services and rural areas where poverty levels are high and agriculture is the main source of livelihoods. It can only be said here that the strategies for improving delivery of social services as laid out in the Poverty Reduction Strategy Paper are as important as poverty reduction measures in the productive sectors. The task is to ensure a balance in resource allocation that will enhance the complementary roles between the productive and social services.

NOTES

1. The model for estimating average and marginal budget shares and for deriving the growth multipliers is adopted from Delgado et al. (1998).
2. Some of the lessons learnt were related to institutional weaknesses such as ineffective monitoring of projects, uncoordinated donor-funded projects, ineffective enforcement of relevant laws and inadequate investment by government to support the strategy.

REFERENCES

Aryeetey, Ernest and Augustin Fosu (2002), 'Explaining African economic growth performance: the case of Ghana', Paper prepared for the African Economic Research Consortium Research Project on 'Explaining African Economic Growth Performance', Nairobi, Kenya.

Awusabo, K.A. (1981/82), 'Towards an integrated programme for rural development in Ghana', *Ghana Journal of Sociology*, **14**(2): 87–111.

Bequele, A. (1980), 'Poverty, inequality and stagnation: Ghanaian experience', World Employment Research Working Paper, Rural Employment Policy Research Programme, International Labour Organisation, Geneva.

Boateng, E. Oti, Kwadwo Ewusi, Ravi Kanbur and Andrew McKay (n.d.), 'A poverty profile for Ghana, 1987–88: social dimensions of adjustment in sub-Saharan Africa', Working Paper No. 5 Policy Analysis, World Bank, Washington, DC.

Canagarajah, Sudharshan and Dipak Mazumdar (n.d.), 'Employment, labour markets and poverty in Ghana: a study of changes during economic decline and recovery', Background paper of World Bank Economic and Sector Work on Ghana: Labour Markets and Poverty, World Bank, Washington, DC.

Datt, G. and M. Ravallion (1992), 'Growth and redistribution components of changes in poverty measures: a decomposition with applications to Brazil and India in the 1980s', *Journal of Development Economics*, **38**, 275–95.

Delgado, Christopher L., Jane Hopkins and Valerie A. Kelly (1998), 'Agricultural growth linkages in sub-Saharan Africa', Research Report 107, International Food Policy Research Institute, Washington, DC.

Delimini, L.L. (2000), 'Market for certified seeds, seedlings and planting materials in Ghana', in proceedings of a workshop on emerging agricultural production input markets in Ghana following the liberalisation in 1990 (Researcher–policy maker and civil society dialogue), Institute of Statistical, Social and Economic Research, University of Ghana, Legon.

Dutta Roy, D.K. and S.J. Mabey (1968), 'Household Budget Survey in Ghana', Technical Publication No. 2, Institute of Statistical, Social, and Economic Research, University of Ghana, Legon.

Ewusi, K. (1976), 'Disparities in levels of regional development in Ghana', *Social Indicators*, **3**(1).

Ewusi, K. (1984), 'The Dimensions and Characteristics of Rural Poverty in Ghana', ISSER Technical Publications No. 43, Institute of Statistical, Social and Economic Research, University of Ghana, Accra, Ghana.

Fine, B. and Kwabia Boateng (2000), 'Labour and employment under structural adjustment', Ernest Aryeetey, Jane Harrigan and Machiko Nissanke (eds), in *Economic Reforms in Ghana: The Miracle and the Mirage*, Oxford: James Currey and Accra: Woeli Publishing Services.

Ghana Statistical Service (GSS) (1995), 'Ghana Living Standards Survey. Report of the Third Round (GLSS 3)', September 1991 to September 1992, Ghana Statistical Service, Accra.

Ghana Statistical Service (GSS) (2000a), 'Ghana Living Standards Survey. Report of the Fourth Round (GLSS 4)', April 1998 to March 1999, Ghana Statistical Service, Accra.

Ghana Statistical Service (GSS) (2000b), 'Poverty Trends in Ghana in the 1990s', Ghana Statistical Service, Accra.

Government of Ghana (2003), *Ghana Poverty Reduction Strategy, 2003–2005. An Agenda for Growth and Prosperity. Vol. 1: Analysis and Policy Statement*, Accra: National Development Planning Commission.

Grootaert, Christian and Ravi Kanbur (1989), 'Policy-Oriented Analysis of Poverty and the Social Dimensions of Structural Adjustment. A Methodology and Proposed Application to Côte d'Ivoire, 1985–88', Social Dimensions of Adjustment, World Bank, Washington, DC.

Hazell, Peter B.R. and Ailsa Röell (1983), 'Rural growth linkages: household expenditure patterns in Malaysia and Nigeria', Research Report 41, International Food Policy Research Institute, Washington, DC.

Jebuni, C., S. Asuming-Brempong and K.Y. Fosu (1990), 'The Impact of Economic Recovery Programmes on Agriculture in Ghana', Accra, USAID (Report).

Kakwani, Nanak (1993), 'Poverty and economic growth with application to Côte d'Ivoire', *Review of Income and Wealth*, **39**(2), 121–39.

Powell, Mathew and Jeffery Round (2000), 'Structure and linkage in the economy of Ghana: a SAM approach', Ernest Aryeetey, Jane Harrigan and Machiko Nissanke (eds), in *Economic Reforms in Ghana: The Miracle and the Mirage*, Oxford: James Currey and Accra: Woeli Publishing Services, pp. 68–87.

Ravaillion, Martin and Monika Huppi (1991), 'Measuring changes in poverty: a methodological case study of Indonesia during an adjustment period', *World Bank Economic Review*, **5**(1): 57–82.

Republic of Ghana (1995), 'Ghana – Vision 2020: The first step', Presidential report to Parliament on Co-ordinated Programme of Economic and Social Development Policies, Accra.

Republic of Ghana (2002), 'Food and Agriculture Sector Development Policy', Ministry of Agriculture, Accra.

Rourke, D.E. (1971), 'Wages and Incomes of Agricultural Workers in Ghana', Technical Publication No. 13, Institute of Statistical, Social, and Economic Research, University of Ghana, Legon.

Stryker, J. and E. Dumenu (1986), 'A comparative study of the political economy of agricultural pricing policies: the case of Ghana', World Bank, Washington, DC (unpublished).

Wetzel, Deborah (2000), 'Promises and pitfalls in public expenditure', Ernest Aryeetey, Jane Harrigan and Machiko Nissanke (eds), in *Economic Reforms in Ghana: The Miracle and the Mirage*, Oxford: James Currey and Accra: Woeli Publishing Services, pp. 115–31.

8. South Africa

Johann Kirsten, Julian May, Sheryl Hendriks, Mike Lyne, Charles L. Machethe and Cecilia Punt

8.1 INTRODUCTION

A systematic investigation of the agricultural growth–poverty relationship requires identification of the main channels through which agricultural growth has an impact on poverty and an understanding of the conditions under which these channels operate effectively. The main channels through which agricultural growth potentially can contribute to poverty reduction are:

(i) a general equilibrium effect through the increase of unskilled labour wage rate and employment;
(ii) an increase in smallholders' income;
(iii) higher agricultural output leading to lower food prices; and
(iv) forward/backward linkage effects which spur non-farm income growth and investment in agro-industries and other downstream activities.

The objective of this study is to analyse the contribution of agriculture in South Africa towards poverty alleviation and food security through each of these potential channels/mechanisms. The analysis relies largely on secondary studies and some reassessment of data collected in earlier years. This study also highlights the food security contribution of agriculture and illustrates how agricultural activity in rural households influences household food security.

8.2 THE EXTENT, DISTRIBUTION AND NATURE OF POVERTY IN POST-APARTHEID SOUTH AFRICA

In 1993 almost half of South Africa's population were categorised as poor using a national poverty line, and one-fifth earned less that $1 per day

(Klasen, 1997). Over 60 percent of Africans were poor compared to just 1 percent of the white population. Woolard and Leibbrandt (2001) use a range of thresholds to provide a rigorous analysis of poverty in South Africa since the transition.[1] Using data from the 1995 Income and Expenditure Survey, they conclude that some 40–50 percent of South Africans can be categorised as poor, while 25 percent can be categorised as ultra-poor. They also find that the poverty rate is far higher in rural than in urban areas (65 percent of individuals compared to 22 percent) and 27 percent of rural dwellers are below half the poverty line, and thus are also likely to be chronically poor. In urban settlements, just 7 percent of the population fall into this group and, as a result, 78 percent of those likely to be chronically poor are located in rural areas (Woolard and Leibbrandt, 2001: 59–60). Once again, in line with other studies, a far greater proportion of Africans are poor, making up almost 80 percent of those who are poor although Africans comprised 76 percent of the population in 1996. Households headed by women are also more likely to be poor than households headed by men, while the Eastern Cape consistently emerges as one of the poorest provinces in South Africa, containing 27 percent of those likely to be chronically poor. KwaZulu-Natal and Limpopo province account for 19 and 17 percent of the chronically poor, respectively.

The World Development Report of 2000 uses the 1993 SALDRU (South African Labour and Development Research Unit) database in a table providing data on poverty in the developing world. This report shows that 11.5 percent of the South African population live on less than $1 per day, with a poverty gap of 1.8, while 35.8 percent of the population live on less than $2 per day (World Bank, 2000: 64). South Africa can thus be compared to countries such as Bolivia (11.3 percent), Colombia (11.0 percent) or Côte d'Ivoire (12.3 percent) in terms of the $1 per day measure of poverty.

However, South Africa has yet to develop its own national poverty line despite the proliferation of poverty studies during the 1990s. During the apartheid years, a number of institutions calculated alternative minimum incomes for subsistence, some of which were commissioned by the mining industry for use in wage negotiations. The most recent analysis of poverty by Statistics South Africa regarded as reliable, uses a measure that is based on a legal minimum income required to qualify for certain subsidies such as housing or services grants. The result is some disagreement as to the extent and distribution of poverty. Table 8.1 provides recent estimates of poverty using a variety of different poverty thresholds.

The data in this table show that approximately half of South Africa's population can be categorised as being poor in terms of a range of national money-metric poverty lines that are based upon the expenditure required for a minimum food basket required for subsistence. A similar result is

Table 8.1   Most recent poverty estimates

Type of poverty line	Amount/ month cut-off (rand)	% of pop below poverty line
* Population cut-off at 40th percentile of households ranked by adult equiv. exp.	R297.29	53.2
* 50 percent of national per capita exp.	R201.82	53.2
* Min. & supplemental living levels per capita (Bureau of Market Research, University of South Africa)		
• Supplemental living level (SLL)	R220.10	56.7
• Minimum living level (MLL)	R164.20	44.7
* Per adult equiv. household subsistence level (HSL) (Institute for Development Planning Research, University of Port Elizabeth)	R251.10	45.7
# Income poverty line per adult equiv. (HSL adapted for urban and rural areas)	R237.00	52.1
# Basic needs indicator (lowest rank on composite scale of housing, sanitation, water and energy)		21.9
# Nutritional poverty line (calories per adult equivalent)	1815 Cal	44.6
# Nutritional poverty line (calories per adult equivalent)	2100 Cal	56.7

Sources: * Leibbrandt and Woolard (1999); # Carter and May (1999).

found using a nutritional poverty line based upon food intake with both high and low thresholds. A basic needs indicator shows that 22 percent of households live in conditions that can be described as rudimentary or rustic. South African measures of poverty based on a minimum acceptable standard of living thus portray poverty as being more severe than the rather arbitrary international rule of thumb would imply.

The provincial distribution of poverty at the time of South Africa's transition is shown in Table 8.2, which also includes an estimate of the poverty gap (the amount required to lift all people to the poverty threshold) and the poverty gap expressed as a ratio of the provincial gross geographic product (GGP).

These data show that Limpopo was categorised as being the poorest province in South Africa in 1993 with 62 percent of households categorised as being poor, and 69 percent of individuals being categorised in the same way. It is especially noteworthy that an annual transfer of some R2.9 billion would be required to eliminate poverty in Limpopo province, equal to over

Table 8.2   Provincial distribution of poverty (1993)

Province	% H'holds living in poverty	% Indivs living in poverty	Poverty gap R million	Poverty gap as a % of GGP
Western Cape	14.1	17.9	529	1.0
North West	15.4	21.1	1551	7.3
Gauteng	29.7	41.0	917	0.6
Mpumulanga	33.8	45.1	968	3.1
KwaZulu-Natal	36.1	47.1	1159	2.0
Northern Cape	38.2	48.0	257	3.2
Eastern Cape	40.4	50.0	3303	11.4
Free State	56.8	64.0	3716	15.7
Limpopo (formerly Northern Province)	61.9	69.3	2948	21.4

Sources: DBSA (1998: 211); May (2000).

20 percent of the value of all economic output in that province. This may be compared to the situation in Gauteng or the Western Cape in which 1 percent or less of GGP would be required. The implication is that not only are a greater proportion of households poor in Limpopo province, but local economic activity is inadequate in comparison to the needs of the province.

8.3   AGRICULTURAL ACTIVITY BY RURAL HOUSEHOLDS: A SAFETY NET OR AN OPPORTUNITY OUT OF POVERTY?

Notwithstanding their usefulness, cross-sectional studies such as South Africa's October household or labour force surveys are unable to address a variety of questions, particularly those concerning dynamic processes such as the contribution of a specific activity or asset to the movement into or out of poverty. Recognising this, in 1998, a consortium of South African and international researchers revisited some 1100 households first surveyed in the KwaZulu-Natal province as a part of the well-known Project for Statistics on Living Standards and Development (PSLSD) undertaken by SALDRU in 1993. The KwaZulu-Natal Income Dynamics Study (KIDS) is a panel study that offers unique insight through the collection of survey data over a five-year period spanning South Africa's transition, the introduction of many policies intended to reduce poverty, as well as the beginning of rapid HIV/AIDS infection. Triangulating different methodologies, a subsample of households were revisited in 2001 using qualitative methodologies for research. This section[2] draws on both the quantitative and qualitative data and explores the role played by agricultural activities in alleviating poverty or facilitating mobility.

8.3.1   The KIDS Study[3]

In total, the original SALDRU survey included 1589 African, Indian, coloured and white households in KwaZulu-Natal. Of these, 160 white and coloured households were excluded from the sample frame of KIDS due to the sampling biases that seemed likely, given the small sample size and the distribution of the clusters that were sampled. A further 216 households could not be located by KIDS, of which 164 were African, while 138 mostly African households were removed from the dataset as these were suspected as having been fabricated either in 1993 or in 1998. An additional 39 households were surveyed that had split from the original households but which contained core household members. For the purposes of this analysis, these split-off households have been excluded, while five outliers with a very high monthly income compared to their monthly expenditure have also been excluded.[4] Unless otherwise specified, all tables refer to the 1031 remaining households that were successfully resurveyed. Where appropriate the data have been weighted according to the 1991 census using the 'reweight' variable provided in the original SALDRU data release. Finally, unless otherwise specified, amounts are expressed in current prices.

Despite the attrition described above, the KIDS study is considered to meet the standards thought to be acceptable for panel studies of this nature (Maluccio, 2000). In terms of the quality of the data, total monthly income and total monthly expenditure in 1993 were highly and significantly correlated with a mean expenditure of R1515.17 and mean income of R1445.03.[5] In 1998, income and expenditure diverged to a greater extent, although total monthly income and expenditure remained significantly correlated, with a mean expenditure of R2139.70 and a mean income of R2550.27.[6] This difference in the correlation between income and expenditure in 1993 and 1998 is reduced when log income and log expenditure are used. Comparing the data between the different years, while expenditure was highly and significantly correlated, incomes were far less so.[7] This is not unexpected since most analysts of poverty data agree that consumption is a more reliable and consistent indicator due to fluctuations in income over time and the tendency to under-report income (Deaton, 1997; Lipton and Ravallion, 1997). For these reasons, and in line with most international analysis, household monthly expenditure is the measure of well-being that is used in this chapter.[8]

8.3.2 Poverty Measurement

Table 8.3 presents the head count poverty measures for both years of the panel study constructed using information from the 1993 and 1998 household subsistence levels (HSLs) calculated by the Institute for Planning Research at the University of Port Elizabeth (see Potgieter, 1993a, 1993b and 1998). The HSL is built up based on fixed household subsistence costs (to cover shelter, fuel and transport), as well as food and basic clothing costs calibrated to individual resident household members' age and sex. Using the HSL cost parameters, a specific HSL was calculated for each household based on its demographic and residency structure. For 1993, separate HSL cost parameters are provided by Potgieter (1993b) for both rural and urban households. The 1998 HSL was calculated only for urban households (Potgieter, 1998), however rural cost parameters for 1998 were derived by appropriately inflating the 1993 rural cost parameters.[9] Given that about 80 percent of the poor were to be found in the rural areas in both years, the poverty threshold profile for rural areas is also provided.

The data reveal an increase in the percentage of households who have an income below the minimum threshold as calculated using the HSL approach. This is especially pronounced in the rural areas. The proportion of those earning less than half their HSL increased from 4 to 12 percent for the total sample, while those earning below the HSL increase from 28 percent of the sample to 46 percent (33 to 60 percent in rural areas).[10] The poverty gap index (PGI) and the squared poverty gap index (SPGI) confirm this increase, and also show that the increase in severity was greater in rural areas than for the sample as a whole.[11] It should be noted that this finding must not be misinterpreted to imply that poverty in KwaZulu-Natal increased during this period – these are panel data and the 1998 wave is not representative of the population as a whole since any new households that may have formed have been excluded.

Table 8.3 Poverty head counts, 1993, 1998

Poverty threshold profile	Total 1993	Total 1998	Rural 1993	Rural 1998
0–0.5 HSL	4.2	14.3	5.3	20.1
0.5–1 HSL	23.6	31.9	28.7	39.9
1–1.5 HSL	26.2	20.1	31.6	21.4
1.5–2 HSL	18.4	10.5	18.0	9.1
+ 2 HSL	27.6	23.2	16.4	9.4
PGI	0.080	0.173	0.098	0.233
SPGI	0.006	0.030	0.010	0.054

Table 8.4   Transition matrix

HSL codes 98 / HSL codes 93	0–0.5 HSL	0.5–1 HSL	1–1.5 HSL	1.5–2 HSL	+ 2 HSL
0–0.5 HSL	**30.7**	47.6	21.7	0.0	0.0
	27.2	*57.9*	*14.9*	*0.0*	*0.0*
0.5–1 HSL	25.5	**44.4**	17.2	7.2	5.7
	28.3	*45.9*	*16.5*	*5.9*	*3.5*
1–1.5 HSL	16.6	41.3	**22.1**	11.9	8.1
	19.2	*42.7*	*21.8*	*10.6*	*5.7*
,1.5–2 HSL	10.9	28.0	26.0	**12.7**	22.5
	12.3	*32.9*	*28.9*	*13.9*	*12.0*
+ 2 HSL	2.4	12.7	16.6	11.8	**56.5**
	6.7	*23.0*	*27.8*	*15.4*	*27.1*

A limitation when comparing poverty rates in different years is that it is impossible to assess whether individual households have moved into or out of poverty. Using panel data addresses this problem in part, and in most of the literature on poverty and mobility, analysis conventionally makes use of a poverty matrix in order to depict such changes in the poverty head count rate at different points of time. Using the KIDS data, this is shown in Table 8.4, which compares the status of all households in terms of the ratio of their expenditure to the poverty threshold. The figures in italics provide a transition matrix for those who had been involved in agricultural production in either of the survey years.

The matrix reveals the relatively high levels of mobility experienced by the KIDS sample between 1993 and 1998. The figures in bold on the diagonal represent households that have remained in the same position with respect to their subsistence threshold. Just 35 percent of all house-holds are to be found on this diagonal, while 45 percent moved to the left (fell behind) and 19 percent moved to the right (got ahead). Of interest is the relatively large proportion of those earning less than half of their HSL in 1993 who managed to improve their position but who were still unable to escape poverty (48 percent of those in this group). This is offset by those who were between half and the threshold amount in 1993, 25 percent of whom had fallen to below half of the threshold, and by those who were just above the poverty threshold in 1993, almost 60 percent of whom now fell below the threshold. For those households involved in agricultural production, the tendency to fall behind was more pronounced, with 58 percent of the poorest group making some progress, but failing to escape poverty and larger proportions of all groups falling behind.

In interpreting matrices such as this, it is often said that those who were poor in both periods may be thought of as being chronically poor, those who were poor in one or other of the surveys are transitory poor, while the balance are described as being never poor. This would represent 20, 34 and 46 percent, respectively, in the case of the KIDS sample. However, this approach is not theoretically grounded on any notion of what might result in such mobility (or absence thereof). If a specific activity or access to an asset is to be assessed in terms of its contribution towards mobility, an alternative approach is required and an option is explained in the following section.

8.3.3 Mapping Mobility

Carter and May (2001) attempt to deal with the problem of distinguishing transitory poverty from chronic or structural poverty. They note that if people are poor at any point in time because of the assets that they possess or the constraints that they face to the use of those assets, then time gives them an additional degree of freedom with which to eventually escape poverty. This opportunity can be used to build up the additional assets they need to move ahead or to find ways of overcoming constraints to the effective use of the assets that they own. However, time also increases the prospects of experiencing negative shocks that reduce income or erode assets and which push people further behind. The impact of time on poverty thus depends on these two interacting aspects, opportunity and shocks, as well as on people's strategic choices given preferences and their awareness of time as both opportunity and vulnerability. A household i at time t can thus be thought of as having a vector of assets, A_{it} (comprising land, human capital, financial wealth, grain stocks and so forth). Every period, the household chooses consumption (c_{it}) and investment (I_{it}) in order to maximise its discounted stream of expected well-being, making a series of inter-temporal trade-offs while doing so. An example of such trade-offs might be choosing a steady or smooth consumption stream rather than face a consumption stream with the same average value but one that fluctuates from year to year.

This typology suggests that very different kinds of households might be inappropriately grouped together if conventional chronic and transitory poverty concepts are applied. Included in the conventional transitory category will be households that were initially structurally poor and who escaped structural poverty through effective asset accumulation. Also in this category will be households that were never structurally poor but who in one period were stochastically poor, as well as households that were structurally poor in all periods but who once were stochastically non-poor. Similarly, the conventional chronically poor category could include households bound by a poverty trap as well as those twice observed to be stochastically, but not structurally, poor.

Applying this approach to the KIDS data, the mobility analysis of Carter and May (2001) shows that 48 percent of those households surveyed in 1993 and 1998 can be categorised as 'structurally never poor', 21 percent were 'structurally downward', 17 percent were 'structurally poor', and just 4 percent were 'structurally upward'. The remaining 9 percent had experienced shocks or windfalls over the reference period covered by the survey and had experienced stochastic mobility. This categorisation of households will be used for the remainder of this chapter in combination with the poverty threshold profiles used in the earlier sections.

8.3.4 The Contribution of Agriculture to Increased Mobility: Evidence from KwaZulu-Natal

The role of agriculture in South African livelihoods has been the subject of debate as is witnessed by the two-volume collection edited by Lipton et al. (1996a and b). While some argue that agriculture holds out some prospect of reducing unemployment, others are concerned that the promotion of small-scale agriculture may become unsustainable if pursued too vigorously. Although this debate remains unresolved, the KIDS data do provide a starting point from which to examine movements into and out of agriculture as well as a way of assessing the changing poverty status of those involved in such movement.

In 1993, the weighted SALDRU survey estimated that there were some 960,000 African and Indian households in KwaZulu-Natal. Of these households, about 367,000 (32 percent) had undertaken some form of agricultural activity on their own account in the preceding 12 months, whether ranching, raising small stock or chickens, field production or the cultivation of vegetable gardens. All of these households were African, suggesting some sample design problems given the presence of substantial numbers of Indian farmers in the province. Although those involved in agriculture were concentrated in rural areas (98 percent), and just under half of rural households were involved in agriculture (47.4 percent), a small number of households in the urban and metropolitan areas of KwaZulu-Natal were engaging in agricultural production in 1993 (8000 households).[12]

Between 1993 and 1998, the KIDS data show that an additional 199,000 of the households surveyed in 1993 entered agricultural production, increasing the proportion of African and Indian households involved in this work to 49 percent.[13] Thus, just over half (50.5 percent) of the households that had been involved in agricultural production in either 1993 or 1998 had performed this activity in both years, 11 percent had been involved in 1993 only, and 38 percent were involved in 1998 only. Following the language used in the poverty profile presented earlier, these last two groups may be described as transitory agricultural producers. This result suggests a comparatively high level of stability over the five-year period, with 81 percent of households producing in 1993 still involved in agricultural production in 1998. This stands in dramatic contrast to those working in the informal sector. In this case, although the total proportion of households in the informal sector was similar for both years, just 17 percent of those in the informal sector in 1993 were still working in this sector in 1998, while 18 percent involved in informal sector activities in 1998 were also involved in such activities in 1993. Indeed, agricultural production emerges as the destination of almost half of these 'dissatisfied' informal sector producers in 1998. Of those who made the move from informal production to agricultural production, 34 percent were categorised as 'structurally downward' and 24 percent as 'structurally poor' in terms of the Carter/May typology, suggesting that this group came to view agricultural production as a more viable option for poverty reduction.[14]

Table 8.5 compares the 1998 poverty threshold profiles of households in rural areas that had never been involved in agriculture, with those that were transitorily involved in agriculture in either 1993 or 1998 and with those that had been involved in both years. The table also shows the mean annual income earned by producing households from agriculture in the two years for which data were gathered.[15]

The data suggest that households involved in agriculture in one or both periods are less likely to be in the poorest categories. While 24 percent of rural households that had never engaged in agriculture received incomes

Table 8.5 Poverty head count and agriculture

1998 Poverty threshold profile	Never	Transitory	Both
0–0.5 HSL	23.9	20.8	17.7
0.5–1 HSL	42.2	38.9	39.7
1–1.5 HSL	19.2	19.5	24.3
1.5–2 HSL	5.1	11.9	8.7
+ 2 HSL	9.7	8.9	9.7
PGI	0.259	0.238	0.214
SPGI	0.067	0.057	0.046
Ag income 93 + 98	0.0	25.05	143.00
(1993 prices)		(67.64)	(379.70)

that were less than half their threshold, this proportion declines to 21 percent of those that were transitory agricultural producers, and 18 percent of those who produced in both periods. In fact, 33 percent of those who never produced fell above the threshold income, while 40 and 43 percent of those transitorily or permanently involved in agriculture were above the threshold.[16] The poverty gap shows that the average depth of poverty among the permanent agricultural producers is lower than that for those who never engaged in agriculture while the squared poverty gap shows that the severity of poverty is also lower for this group.

In an attempt to depict this relationship between income and involvement in agriculture, the data show that regardless of whether the income distribution for 1993 or 1998 is used, a greater proportion of households in the higher-income groups have attempted production, rising from around 60 percent of the poorest groups to 90 percent of the richest.

Turning to the income that was earned by farming households, mean monthly income fell from R97 in 1993 to R72 in 1998.[17] Although small, if this contribution is removed from total income of households, the proportion of households involved in agricultural production that were below the poverty threshold increases from 31 to 38 percent in 1993 and from 42 to 50 percent in 1998. This suggests that although the amounts are comparatively modest, agriculture production did enable a significant proportion of households to remain above their threshold. It is also clear that the amount of agricultural income thus increases as household income increases, implying that agricultural production remains an attractive option even for wealthier households who are deriving larger proportions of income from other sources.

Using the mobility analysis described earlier in preference to the static approach based on the head count below a poverty threshold, or the matrix approach, confirms this contention that agriculture plays an important but dual role in household mobility. The majority of those involved in agriculture in 1993 and 1998 had followed a trajectory that resulted in them never having been poor (37 and 38 percent, respectively). However, 36 percent of those involved in agriculture in 1993 followed a trajectory in which they were structurally downward, while 18 percent were categorised as remaining structurally poor. Compared to the total population, a smaller proportion of those involved in agriculture were 'never poor', and larger proportions were structurally poor, or structurally downward. A small, but almost equal proportion of agricultural producers and all rural households were accumulating resources and can be described as 'structurally upward' (5.5 percent of those in agriculture compared to 4.1 percent of the total population. By 1998, a smaller proportion of the sample involved in agriculture was structurally downward, and a larger proportion was structurally poor.

Table 8.6 Mobility and agriculture

Mobility categories	Never agriculture	Transitory agriculture	Permanent agriculture
Dual failures	0.9	0.0	0.0
Structurally poor	29.7	17.3	28.2
Stochastically upward	3.5	5.5	2.9
Structurally upward	8.4	5.2	5.2
Stochastically downward	1.9	0.0	0.0
Structurally downward	30.1	34.8	27.3
Never poor	25.6	37.1	36.4

This picture of the role of agriculture becomes clearer when distinguishing those that were never involved from those who were transitorily involved and those that participated in both 1993 and 1998. This is shown in Table 8.6.

The proportion of households who experienced dual failures, that is to say, households which had experienced shocks in both years, is insignificant, and no households were observed to fall into this group among those who were involved in agriculture. Those that had never been involved in agriculture were concentrated in the 'structurally poor' and 'structurally downward' groups in comparison to those who had participated in agriculture in which about 37 percent fell into the 'never poor' group. Compared to the other groups, those permanently involved in agriculture were less likely to be 'structurally downward', although a substantial proportion were to be found among the 'structurally poor'. From this table, participation in agriculture appears to play a dual role, and confusingly, causality may operate in both directions. For those at the lowest end of the income distribution, equally split between the 'structurally poor' and the 'structurally downward', agriculture appears to serve as a buffer against indigence. For those that are 'structurally never poor', despite the preponderance of income earned from other activities, agriculture continues to serve as a means to generate additional wealth.

8.3.5 Conclusions

This section used panel data collected in two waves in 1993 and again in 1998 to investigate the relationship between participation in agricultural production, poverty and mobility. Noting that both the incidence and severity of poverty increased for the households that were sampled over this five-year period, the chapter has shown that there was a net increase in participation in small-scale agricultural activities. This is not simply due to rising unemployment during the study period, since many of those households that entered production had previously been involved in informal sector work. The data show that a large percentage of rural households participate at least in transitory agriculture, and that compared to informal work, a comparatively large proportion of households remain permanently involved in agriculture. Looking at the relationship between poverty and agricultural production, it seems that agriculture forms a small but important buffer against poverty for some households, acts as a cushion for the most poor, while also acting as a strategy for wealth creation for wealthier households. The data suggest that modelling this result using standard multivariate procedures may prove complex, in that at lower incomes, the direction of causality may be ambiguous. Low incomes from other sources may compel poor households to involve themselves in production, while also affording them the opportunity to boost their income, albeit insufficient to escape poverty. The mobility analysis adopted in earlier work appears to confirm this, whereby a substantial proportion of those who are structurally poor, and those who are structurally not poor, continue to participate in agricultural production.

Most studies of rural households in the former homeland areas of South Africa, including the above analysis, have highlighted the large-scale participation of these households, albeit largely at subsistence level. This does, however, point to the large potential of agriculture-led growth in these impoverished areas – an aspect that is discussed in the next section.

8.4   THE ECONOMY-WIDE EFFECTS OF AGRICULTURAL GROWTH: AN APPLICATION OF AGRICULTURAL GROWTH MULTIPLIERS

Given the widespread practice of agriculture in the former homelands (albeit predominantly subsistence agriculture), it would seem reasonable to assume that encouraging agriculture-led growth would have widespread benefits for both farm and non-farm households and may spill over to urban populations, for example through lower food prices. The benefits of growth linkages, namely raised rural incomes, increased non-farm activity and improved employment rates (Hazell and Röell, 1984; Hazell and Haggblade, 1993) are urgently needed to provide livelihood opportunities for millions of poor households – most of whom live in rural areas (May, 1998).

Widespread increments to rural incomes may mobilise underused resources through creating enterprise and employment opportunities in non-tradable[18] farm and non-farm sectors. Appropriate policy choice rests on knowing how much increased employment can be supported by food supplies; employment opportunities from alternative production technologies, and the efficiency of various policies, strategies, investments and other support measures that stimulate production of tradable commodities and increase the price elasticity of non-tradable output supply (Mellor, 1976, p. 171; de Janvry, 1994).

Hazell's (1984) growth linkage methodology was applied to two rural villages in KwaZulu-Natal province (Swayimana and Umzumbe). The estimated growth multipliers show the resultant additions (from consumption and production of farm and non-farm non-tradables) to gross income of local households following an initial income shock of one South African rand. This shock could come from any positive outside effect such as improved technology, better infrastructure or institutional support that increases profit in the production and marketing of rural tradables. The case study results show that a R1.00 increase in the income of the sample households could lead to R0.09 and R0.19 of additional income from spending on farm and non-farm non-tradables, respectively. The multiplier (1.00 + 0.09 + 0.19 = 1.28) implies total value added from spending on these demand-constrained items of R0.28 (Hendriks and Lyne, 2003b).

The total value added by a R1.00 income shock in Swayimana households is R1.32 for farm and non-farm tradables, slightly higher than the R1.24 estimated for the less remote Umzumbe households. The multiplier for the wealthier income group is only four cents higher than the multiplier for the poorer households, implying negligible difference between income groups with regard to the way in which they would spend additions to income. Distance from urban centres appears to have more influence on consumption than does relative wealth in these rural areas.

The multipliers estimated in this study are slightly lower than Belete et al.'s (1999) estimate of 1.35 for a sample of food plot farmers in the Eastern Cape province, 35 percent lower than Ngqangweni's (2000) estimate of 1.98 for the local economy of Middledrift in the Eastern Cape, and lower than all but one multiplier estimated for other African and Asian countries. These results suggest that agriculture does have potential to drive growth in rural KwaZulu-Natal, but that growth linkages are weaker than for most other African economies. South African households are generally less remote and less isolated than are rural households in other parts of Africa.

Overall, the results suggest that rural incomes could grow by an additional 28 cents in KwaZulu-Natal following an initial income shock of R1.00, with most of this growth coming from the non-farm sector. Although this does not represent a particularly strong growth linkage, it is clear that increased incomes could generate additional growth through consumption linkages. The results raise two important policy issues. First,

Table 8.7   Growth multipliers for Swayimana and Umzumbe, 1997 (n = 93)

Commodity	Whole sample	Swayimana	Umzumbe	Wealthier households	Poorer households
Tradables	1.00	1.00	1.00	1.00	1.00
Value added from farm non-tradables	0.09	0.12	0.06	0.10	0.09
Value added from non-farm non-tradables	0.19	0.20	0.18	0.21	0.18
Multiplier	1.28	1.32	1.24	1.31	1.27

Source: Hendriks and Lyne (2003b).

the multiplier indicates only *potential* growth linkages because the supply of non-tradables may not be perfectly elastic. Second, while potential growth linkages are driven by non-tradables, these are unlikely to generate the initial income shock, as they are demand constrained.

The results suggest that an increase in farm income has the potential to stimulate economic growth in the communal areas of KwaZulu-Natal, but that this growth may be considerably lower than what government expects from the small-scale agricultural sector.

8.5   IMPACT OF AGRICULTURAL EXPORT GROWTH ON HOUSEHOLD INCOME AND EMPLOYMENT THROUGH INCOME MULTIPLIERS: A CASE STUDY IN THE WESTERN CAPE

The impact of an increase in agricultural and processed food exports on the Western Cape economy was analysed with income multipliers. The study attempts to quantify the anticipated stimulation of economic activity and benefits to households as a result of export growth. In the first scenario, a 5 percent increase in agricultural exports is assumed. The agricultural exports refer only to unprocessed produce. Approximately 30 percent of all agricultural supply is further processed by the food manufacturing industry. The agricultural products comprise 26 percent of total intermediates used by the food manufacturing industry. In an attempt to capture the importance of the agricultural sector's role due to its linkages with the manufacturing sector the second scenario assumes a 5 percent increase in exports of manufactured food products.

The direct effect (the 5 percent increase in exports) is excluded from the results on the increase in commodity demand, therefore only the indirect effects are reported. Results are sorted separately for each of the scenarios. In the Western Cape the value of agricultural exports is approximately 60 percent that of exports of manufactured food products. This implies that a 5 percent increase in manufactured food products is a relatively greater increase in exports than a 5 percent increase in agricultural exports. The results therefore cannot be used to compare the impact of exports from two different industries. The focus is rather on the fact that there is a positive economic impact when production is stimulated in the agricultural industry through an increase in demand for exports, regardless of whether this is achieved directly via demand for agricultural exports or indirectly via demand for processed food exports.

Results show that gross output of the agricultural sector increases by 1.84 percent if agricultural exports increase by 5 percent (scenario 1), while the gross output of manufactured food industries increase by 0.18 percent. In the second scenario the gross output of the agricultural sector increases by 0.5 percent, while that of manufactured food industries increases by 1.46 percent. Production increases in response to a demand for products, hence the relative magnitude of increases in gross output follows similar patterns as in the first scenario.

Income multipliers were used to estimate the economic impact of an increase in exports of agricultural products. The impact of increased demand for processed food products was also explored. Export growth stimulates economic activity, especially in the chemical industry, the trade, transport and communications industry and the wood and paper industry. Skilled agricultural workers followed by labourers in elementary occupations experienced the greatest increase in labour income. Technicians and professionals benefit least. There is no notable income redistribution from high- to low-income households or from one population group to another. Results showed that the income of rural households increase relatively more than that of urban households. The redistribution therefore takes place from urban to rural households. Poverty is regarded as being more prevalent in the rural areas in the Western Cape than in the urban areas, therefore it can be expected that the increases in household income as a result of export growth will contribute towards poverty alleviation, especially in the rural areas.

8.6   AGRICULTURAL GROWTH AND FOOD PRICES

Agriculture's role in poverty alleviation and food security can also be achieved through lower food prices. By making food more affordable to the average poor household, real income of these households will increase. Economic theory shows that an increase in agricultural supply through technological improvements, investment in irrigation and expansion of areas planted and herd sizes should lead to lower prices of food *ceteris paribus*. However, inefficiencies in supply and distribution chains, monopolistic structures and concentration in the food-manufacturing sector could undo gains at producer level without any benefit flowing to the consumer.

In order to estimate the main long-run determinants of the CPI of food, an error correction model (ECM) was estimated. Data on the CPI for food, volume of agricultural production and a number of other independent variables for the period 1976–2001 were used. The ECM was used because all the data series were non-stationary thus using OLS would have resulted in spurious regression. With spurious regression, statistically significant relationships are indicated where in fact there are none due to the fact that the variables trend together over time.

The coefficients of the ECM were statistically significant at the 5 percent level and all coefficients displayed the expected signs. The R^2 of the ECM was 82 percent thus indicating a good fit. The variables used in the long run cointegration equation were: volume of food production (by the agricultural sector); average interest rates; average R/US$ exchange rate; and fuel price index. All the variables, except the exchange rate, were indexed with base year 1995. Table 8.8 reports the long run elasticities estimated. The results confirm the hypothesis that a growth in volume of agricultural production should lead to lower food prices – suggesting the positive contribution of agricultural growth to food inflation.

However, despite stable growth in agricultural production and agricultural exports, South Africa recently (2001/2002) experienced a severe 'food price crisis'. Retail prices of staple foods increased rapidly during the

Table 8.8   Error correction model for impact of growth in agricultural output on food inflation (CPI-food): 1976–2001

Variable	Long-run elasticity
Volume of food production	−0.539
Average interest rates	+0.802
R/US$ exchange rate	+0.834
Fuel price index	+0.318

period from November 2001 to December 2002, to the extent that they adversely affected the state's ability to reach its inflation targets. These increases have caused concerns for the plight of the rural and urban poor in the country, for sound macroeconomic management, and for those concerned with the possibility of market manipulation and even corruption in the price-setting process.

Vink and Kirsten (2002) came to the conclusion that the increase in the farm gate price of basic food commodities during 2002 came about as a result of a unique combination of five factors. These are (a) increasing world prices for these commodities; (b) a lack of competition in the supply chain beyond the farm gate, especially at the retail level; (c) a fast and severe depreciation in the value of the currency; (d) a shortage of maize in the SADC region; and (e) a climate of uncertainty, created specifically by the unfortunate circumstances surrounding the land reform programme and elections in Zimbabwe, and more generally by instability in parts of Central and Southern Africa.

Vink and Kirsten's analysis also shows that the South African circumstances differ from many other developing countries. *First*, the evidence is that the world price of maize and many other basic commodities reached high levels during 2001/02. The analysis has also shown that in a liberalised market, these higher international prices are transferred into the domestic market almost immediately. *Second*, however, the lack of competition further down the supply chain has had a bigger effect on the prices that poor people pay for their basic needs than has the supply of farm commodities. *Third*, we live in a world characterised by market-determined exchange rates, and the exchange rate has had a bigger and more immediate impact on the South African domestic price of farm commodities than has the world price.

The poor in South Africa have been adversely affected by higher retail food prices, and it seems that the trends in these prices are largely divorced from prices at the farm gate, especially in the case of maize and wheat. There is little evidence that small farmers have benefited from the new trading environment in agriculture, while there is strong evidence that the efficiency and the fairness of the agricultural sector would be enhanced by a successful land reform and small-farmer support programme. As a result, most small farmers in South Africa are still poor, are net food buyers, and are as adversely affected by higher consumer prices for food, as are the landless rural and urban poor.

For this reason, Vink and Kirsten (2002) recommended that greater consideration be given to successful land reform and farmer support programmes that result in the creation of successful livelihoods for the millions of current (and potential) farmers from disadvantaged communities who deserve these opportunities. While the plight of the rural poor in South Africa is better now than a decade ago, the agricultural sector has not been allowed to play the important role that it should in the fight against rural poverty. Government needs to reverse the decay in agricultural infrastructure, and refocus efforts in support of poor and disadvantaged farmers.

It is clear that poor people living in the rural, urban and peri-urban areas have been most affected by the increase in the farm gate prices of staple foods. Vink and Kirsten have indicated that there is a strong argument for measures to alleviate the plight of the poor.

While there is a need for remedial action, South Africa already has mechanisms in place to combat poverty and food insecurity. These include the Public Works Programme, the Primary School Nutrition Programme, the Draft Integrated Food Security Strategy and the proposed Comprehensive System of Social Security. Further, experience has shown that specific food subsidies have unintended consequences and, like all subsidy programmes, are difficult to terminate once initiated.

Despite relatively low and stable food price inflation following agricultural market liberalisation in South Africa, the recent sharp increase in food prices has put a limit to the extent which those in South Africa can argue for, and show, the positive externalities of cheaper food prices through agricultural production. However, as part of their suggested interventions to government, Vink and Kirsten (2002) used the 'food price externality' as a way of motivating the government to take food and agricultural policy seriously and invest more of the fiscus in agriculture and food production. In recent (2003) speeches by the minister of finance it was clearly indicated that a greater proportion of the government budget would in the next few financial years be spent on agricultural research, farmer support and land reform. The results from the econometric model reported earlier confirms that over the long-term agricultural growth will have a positive effect on food prices and thus provide sufficient support for this type of policy direction.

8.7   AGRICULTURE'S CONTRIBUTION TO HOUSEHOLD FOOD SECURITY

Household food security is commonly accepted as meaning household access to enough food of appropriate quality and quantity for an active, healthy life. As the previous chapters have illustrated, agricultural growth has obvious, direct benefits for increasing food supply and increasing incomes from farm and non-farm sources. However, widespread increased agricultural production also has numerous indirect benefits for improving food security. One such benefit of agriculture-led rural economic development is the potential for nutritional benefits. Knowing the likely impact of increased income on household consumption patterns is key to estimating the likely benefits of increased income on consumption of a range of food and non-food products. Moreover, knowing how expenditure will influence the demand for agricultural production with direct benefits for the wider population is vital for anticipating the nutritional impact of increased agricultural production and/or agricultural-led growth in South Africa.

This section (largely based on Hendriks and Lyne, 2003a and Hendriks, 2003) focuses on how agriculture-led rural economic growth may have positive externalities with regard to the quality and quantity of food consumed by rural households. Hendriks and Lyne (2003a) predict that increased incomes for rural households in two communal areas of KwaZulu-Natal are likely to lead to increased demand for meat and meat products, poultry and exceptionally high demand increase for horticultural products. In addition, the possibilities of increased incomes for small-scale farmers who respond to this demand, increased consumption of these foods could considerably improve the nutritional status of rural populations.

Schmidt and Vorster (1995) report that parents of a small sample of parents who participated in a communal garden in Bophuthatswana (a former South African homeland) claimed that the main advantage of the garden was that the garden saved them money and led to a greater variety of food. However, households only produced 20 percent of their minimum vegetables requirements on the 13 square metre plots they cultivated in the communal garden, while gardens of 64 square metres were required to cultivate sufficient vegetables to meet dietary requirements. Schmidt and Vorster (1995) report that children's diets lacked diversity and varied little between households. Diets were very low in energy and protein. The children seldom ate meat or tinned fish, and ate chicken once a month or less often. None of the participating households ate vegetables every day, while most households reported that they rarely ate fruit. Schmidt and Vorster were not able to differentiate between children's anthropometrics, and the macro and micro nutrient status of children from households participating in the garden and those from non-gardening households. While Kirsten et al.'s (1998) study for 173 rural households with children 0–60 months in two tribal wards of KwaZulu-Natal shows that 'households which participate seriously in agricultural activities have better nutritional status' (Kirsten et al., 1998, p. 584). Kirsten et al.'s (1998) study found that households that purchased seed and used improved cultivation techniques had a lower probability of stunted children. Such household are likely to participate in production beyond the level of subsistence.

Seemingly, vegetable gardens are not able to address the need for increased energy consumption desperately needed to overcome stunting among South African children. Stunting is the most prevalent nutrition related problem in South Africa, with 25 percent of a national sample of children between 1 and 9 years old showing impaired growth (Labararios, 1999, cited by VIC, 2001). Only 5 percent of the same sample showed signs of wasting (Labadarios, 1999 cited by VIC, 2001), while Steyn et al. (2001) report that 9 percent of South African preschoolers show signs of wasting. Schmidt and Vorster (1995) found that households who grew vegetables did not purchase additional vegetables, but used the savings to purchase other foods, such as oil and fat (which did affect Schmidt and Vorster's (1995) bio-chemical findings). Therefore, vegetable gardens may have a more import-ant indirect nutritional benefit through household income replacement.

However, Hendriks and Lyne's (2003a) study shows that although rural South African consumers are likely to spend more of any increment on imported goods, local demand for horticultural products (fruit and veg-etables), meat and poultry products will increase. Increasing dietary diver-sity lack of availability of foods, types of foods available (for example, typically low fat), and the monotony of most rural diets contribute to a vicious cycle of low energy intakes, exacerbated by reduced micro-nutrient intakes (Maunder et al., 2001). Therefore an increase in the variety of foods in rural diets would likely lead to improved micronutrient and energy intakes (Hendriks, 2003), for example:

- Increased dietary diversity,
- Increased consumption of animal products and would improve protein and fats intakes, offering potentially significant increases in the energy intake of household members,
- An increased consumption of meat and poultry would also increase the intake of calcium, iron, zinc, and B vitamins (Scholtz et al., 2001). Animal fat also provides rich sources of vitamin A.
- Consumption of additional green leafy vegetables would increase the intake of vitamin B6 and iron (ACC/SCN, 1991),
- Citrus fruits and fruit such as guavas could make available much-needed vitamin C (Love and Sayed, 2001),
- While green leafy vegetables, and yellow and orange fruit and vege-tables could address prevalent vitamin A deficiencies in rural popu-lations (ACC/SCN, 2000). Fresh and preserved fruit is also a source of additional energy, especially palatable for children.

Agriculture could ensure a more stable food supply and improve nutrition at household level, both directly through improved dietary diversity and increased macronutrient intake, and indirectly through income replace-ment behaviour that seems to have greater impact on improving energy intakes among South Africa's rural populations. Wide-scale increased agricultural production could increase local food supply, decrease local food prices, and make food more affordable for rural households (Hendriks, 2003). Moreover, greater dietary diversity could be promoted by increased availability of foods as production is diversified to exploit untapped, niche and under-supplied markets in search of maxim profit, smoothing household income and food supply simultaneously.

The net social benefits of improved nutrition are undisputed as nutrition is both an effect and a cause of income-opportunities (Gillespie, 1997). Improved nutrition is clearly a positive externality for increased agricultural production in South Africa's rural areas. However, the scale of agricultural production strongly determines the magnitude of these nutritional benefits. To have significant impact on nutritional status of rural populations, agricultural production must develop beyond subsistence level (Hendriks, 2003). While production for home consumption increases the availability of vegetables and increases micronutrient intake, the income 'savings' derived from home production seems to have more positive influences on the nutritional status of rural populations than increased production alone. Income replacement leads to increased purchases of energy-dense foods such as fats, oils and meat. While increased micronutrients have undisputed benefits for nutrition, increased protein and energy from fats and meat would contribute more significantly to reducing South Africa's unacceptably high rate of stunting among children, while simultaneously benefiting micronutrient deficiencies. Increased incomes from agricultural sales are also likely to lead to increased dietary diversity, increasing the nutritional adequacy of rural diets. Improved nutrition would lead to a number of additional positive benefits related to improved health, resistance to disease, improved human capacity, improved ability to benefit from education that increases access to information (agricultural and nutritional), and overall increased productivity.

8.8   SYNTHESIS

In addressing the poverty alleviation and food security role of agriculture in South Africa this chapter focused mainly on the role of agriculture in the context of the former homeland areas where the majority of poor and rural poor reside. Most of the case studies used to test our hypothesis were thus set in that particular institutional and historic context. Only one case focused on commercial agriculture, namely the export sector in the Western Cape Province which illustrated the wage and employment benefits of agricultural growth.

The chapter shows that a large percentage of rural households participate at least in transitory agriculture, and that compared to informal work,
a comparatively large proportion of households remains permanently
involved in this type of work. Looking at the relationship between poverty
and agricultural production, it seems that agriculture forms a small but
important buffer against poverty for some households, and acts as a
cushion for the most poor, while also acting as a strategy for wealth creation for wealthier households.

In a recent report on the impact of deregulation on household food
security completed for the National Agricultural Marketing Council
(2002), it was concluded that the single most important determinant of
food security in South Africa is cash in hand. This implies that the more
serious issues to be addressed are the sources and levels of income for
households to be able to purchase food. This is an important conclusion,
showing that South Africa is in some way different from other African (or
developing) nations. This also strengthens the case that unless agricultural
production moves out of subsistence to some scale of commercialisation,
little impact is possible on food insecurity and poverty.

This argument links up with the results from the growth multiplier
analysis which suggest that an increase in farm income has the potential
to stimulate economic growth in the communal areas but that this growth
may be considerably lower than what government expects from the small-
scale agricultural sector. This was further confirmed by the SAM analysis of export growth in Western Cape agriculture. Here it was shown that
export growth stimulates economic activity, especially in the chemical
industry, the trade, transport and communications industry, and the
wood and paper industry. Skilled agricultural workers followed by the
labourers in elementary occupations experience the greatest increase in
labour income. Technicians and professionals benefit least. There is
no notable income redistribution from high- to low-income households
or from one population group to another. The results also showed that
the household income of rural households increases relatively more than
that of urban households, which suggest a positive impact on rural
poverty.

Agriculture's contribution to household food security has been analysed
by previous nutritional studies showing that, 'households which participate
seriously in agricultural activities have better nutritional status'. The participating households grew and sold a variety of crops and many kept
livestock. Such households are likely to participate in production beyond
the level of subsistence. Thus the improvement of agricultural productivity
in less-developed areas of South Africa has the potential to improve household and child nutritional status.

Results from studies in South Africa, provide sufficient evidence that agriculture ensures a more stable food supply and improves nutrition at household level. This takes place directly through improved dietary diversity and increased macronutrient intake and indirectly through income replacement behaviour that seems to have a greater impact on improving energy intakes among South Africa's rural populations. The magnitude of the nutritional benefits seems primarily based on whether the scale of production is beyond subsistence level.

The poverty/food security role of agriculture depends to a large extent on the policy and institutional framework within both sectors of our dualistic economy. In the commercial agricultural sector of South Africa, various past and current policies have influenced the structure of agriculture as well as the input intensity of the sector. Capital subsidies, guaranteed prices and import protection contributed to larger farms and thus a decline in the number of farm families. The policies of cheap credit and tax write-offs favoured the use of more capital equipment in agriculture, leading to huge losses in agricultural jobs during the 1970s and 1980s. Later on, and very recently, various labour policies such as minimum work conditions and minimum wage legislation all contributed to further shedding of jobs in commercial agriculture. This illustrates that despite the potential poverty and food security benefits of agriculture, various other policies could eliminate those potential multiplier benefits of agriculture fairly quickly.

Another example of past policy changes that has affected employment levels in rural areas has been the withdrawal of labour-intensive public works programmes in rural areas. This not only reduced employment but also put a halt to efforts to improve much-needed rural infrastructure. It is interesting to note that the South African government announced in July 2003 that it would embark on a renewed labour-intensive public works programme.

The collection of studies presented here has illustrated that agricultural growth can provide the necessary stimulus for widespread job creation and increased household income if the appropriate policy and support framework is in place. By investing in these aspects, agricultural growth could not only ensure the direct benefit of increased household income and imported food security and nutrition but could also generate a range of indirect benefits. Understanding and highlighting the mechanisms through which agriculture could more effectively play its poverty alleviation and food security role now brings us to a point where policy proposals can be made to enhance this specific role of agriculture.

In the former homeland areas, with largely subsistence and small-scale agriculture and characterised by households with diverse livelihoods, the policy focus should be to enhance agricultural production (more so for areas of high agricultural potential). For this purpose a comprehensive farmer support programme[19] needs to be in place which will ensure access to land, financial, output and input markets. Previous experience with such comprehensive programmes in Limpopo and KwaZulu-Natal has shown the positive income and food security effects that agriculture could have under such conducive circumstances. There exists the perception in certain provinces that government support and the enabling environment that is necessary to encourage agricultural production beyond the subsistence level has deteriorated and/or disappeared.[20] This could put a limit on the potential role of agriculture in providing household food security and nutrition and alleviating poverty. If this is a true trend then government has to take drastic action to reverse the disappearance of government programmes in order to encourage agricultural production. The proposed integrated food security strategy (National Department of Agriculture, 2002) goes a long way to address some of these issues through integration of various departments related to food security (more about this in the policy matrix; see Table 8.9).

A common theme that emerged is the importance of increasing the supply of tradable commodities or to convert non-tradables into tradables. Aspects discussed above are necessary but then it will also be necessary to focus on those investments and activities that could lower transaction costs for small-scale and emerging farmers. Lowering transaction costs would be the key to unlock opportunities to trade. Examples could include:

- Support for collective action in marketing. Investigation and exploration of various forms of collective marketing arrangements such as stokvel based cooperatives, producer–marketer cooperatives, contract farming, indigenous franchises, trader associations, partnerships, and formation of village-level cooperatives could be important institutional innovations to increase market access and lower transaction costs for small and emerging farmers.
- Establishing government depots (including pack-houses and refrigerated storage and transport) that act as buying points or sourcing agents for government institutions such as jails, hospitals and so on or market intermediaries.
- Large-scale public investment in rural physical infrastructure such as all-weather roads, postal services, education, electricity, treated water and telecommunication.
- Creating legal certainty in contracts in communal areas – especially related to land tenure and rental contracts. This could lower transaction costs, motivate intensification and expansion of agriculture,

Table 8.9   Policy matrix

Policies impacting on food security and poverty[21]	Impact on food security[22]	Impact on poverty[22]
Constitution of 1994	South Africa is among just over 20 countries where the right to food is enshrined in the constitution. Section 27 of the constitution states that every citizen has the right to have access to sufficient food and water and that 'the state must by legislation and other measures, within its available resources, avail to progressive realisation of the right to sufficient food'.	Seemingly none as no evidence of improvement for the poor. Lack of definitive poverty line makes it impossible to determine and monitor the impact of transition over time.
RDP	Social schemes such as feeding schemes; free health for children under 6, pregnant and lactating women; child support grants; pensions; food for work programmes; provincial community food garden projects; land reform; farmer settlement; production loan schemes for small farmers; infrastructure grants or small farmer; and the Presidential tractor mechanisation scheme. Little has changed in rural areas where inadequate infrastructure increases transaction costs for farmers and constrains further development. Food production and access has not improved for these populations.	Although access to basic services such as health, welfare, water and electricity have been broadened and intensified, little evidence that poverty has decreased and that households are better off than before.
Integrated food security strategy (NDA, 2002) **Goal is to eradicate hunger**	Prior to 2002, there was a lack of agreement among government departments as to how to address food security. Combined with no clear definition of what	The poor are most vulnerable to economic, health and environmental shocks. South Africa lacks effective safety nets to protect

213

Table 8.9 (continued)

Policies impacting on food security and poverty[21]	Impact on food security[22]	Impact on poverty
and food insecurity by 2015 (in line with FAO World food Summit Goals)	food security means in South Africa, household subsistence was commonly labelled food security and denied importance by government who did want to be seen to support subsistence agriculture and petty informal activities associated with poverty. Prior to 2002, community garden projects were the focus of provincial food security programmes initiated by Departments of Agriculture and Health (Nutrition). The National Agricultural Marketing Council study of the impact of market deregulation (2002) identified cash in hand as a key component to improving food security in South Africa, and driven by preparation for the World Food Summit and World Summit on Sustainable Development, government has been able to link their strategic initiatives to improve incomes and generate employment to the need to move farm households out of subsistence agriculture towards commercialisation of production while underpinning the most vulnerable segments of the population. South Africa lacks a food security monitoring and evaluation system as well as early warning systems and food aid strategies to cope with disaster. This	and underpin the poor in times of rising prices, natural disasters and health shocks such as HIV/AIDS.

214

makes the vulnerable more vulnerable in the wake of shocks.

Deregulation of markets through the Marketing of Agricultural Products Act, no 47 of 1996	NAMC report (2002) shows that market deregulation has had little or no impact on household food insecurity and poverty for those who most need assistance. Small and emerging farmers have not benefited from deregulation of markets nor export opportunities. Fluctuating currency, initial weak Rand led to food price rise, strengthening of the Rand has not translated into reduced market prices for consumers.	
Land reform	Farmer settlement programme settled a large number of households on agricultural land but as most did not farm, productive land was lost and the food security status of land reform participants worsened. While some have been given land, land reform has often shifted households into geographical positions where they have fewer opportunities for income generation and lack the skills to generate agricultural incomes. Whether households have moved to urban, peri-urban or rural and reform settlements, the environments lack infrastructural support conducive to access to gainful employment or agricultural production. In fact, urban housing schemes provide plots far too small for even household food production.

Land tenure insecurity stifles introduction of new technologies and/or investment in high value crops and constrains the land rental market crucial for expansion of production activities.

Insecure tenure also constrains development and investment in the non-farm sector, | Land reform has not a visible positive influence on poverty. Without securing land tenure, there is little possibility of improving rural livelihoods. |

215

Table 8.9 (continued)

Policies impacting on food security and poverty[21]	Impact on food security[22]	Impact on poverty
	which is crucial to fuelling wide-spread agricultural development.	
Water rights and Water Act, no 36 of 1998	Although this act favours small-scale producers and provision of 600 k P of free water per household, little impact as yet. The intensified provision of on-site water to previously disadvantaged households and the basic free delivery has the potential to impact positively on household food security due to possible improved sanitation and food safety.	
Labour **Labour Relations Act (1995)** **Basic Conditions of Employment Act (1997)** **Skills Development Act (1998)** **Employment Equity Act (1998)**	Introduction of new labour laws and minimum wage rates has seen the reduction of employment in the agricultural sector and increased mechanisation of commercial agriculture. This spells food insecurity for agricultural labourers and their families.	Increased poverty and unemployment rather than a positive effect although for some households, fixing a minimum wage may increase incomes, but for many households, enforcement of minimum wages will lead to loss of employment.
Extension services and support	Decreased public support for services and research has a negative impact on agricultural households. Integration of former homeland and provincial extension services and the segregated training of extension officers along racial lines to serve farmers	Little measurable and direct positive impact reported.

in various sectors of the population prior to 1994, has led to changes in the extension service, but most extension staff are ill equipped to cope with mixed cropping, low input production among small and emerging farmers and very few field staff are able to assist with marketing. Provincial funded programmes have tended to focus on group projects with little success such as community gardens, poultry projects and agricultural co-operatives.

Extension services need to offer services beyond only agricultural production, including training and support in enterprise development, management, and marketing of farm and non-farm products and services.

Agricultural credit

Although government has made some advances in broadening the access to credit, most small and emerging farmers do not have access to affordable credit for investment in the technology imperative for expanding and intensifying agricultural production or diversification of production into high value crops.

HIV/AIDS

Lack of government recognition of AIDS will have a severe impact on food security as households carry, cope with and shoulder the burdens of inadequate healthcare, meagre incomes and little support.

The impact of HIV will affect food production as the agricultural labour forces and rural subsistence agriculture households will carry a large share of the consequences of the epidemic.

Poverty will deepen.

improve allocative efficiency, encourage investment in improved technology (in terms of equipment, crop types and diversity and farming
practice), and increase farm income and employment.

- Conversion of open access grazing to non-user common property
  resources.
- Investigation of which public investments would have the greatest
  returns with regard to lifting the vulnerable out of poverty and food
  insecurity.

The research on which this study is based illustrated with some success
the important role that the agricultural sector can play in addressing two
areas of major concern to the South African government, that is, poverty
and household food security. The synthesis highlights a number of institutional and policy changes that could unlock the potential of agriculture to
fulfil this important role on behalf of society.

In the discussion so far it has been argued that agriculture-led growth
warrants a conducive regulatory environment and informed policy measures to transform non-tradables into tradable commodities, increase
income from farm tradables, and improve the price elasticity of supply for
non-tradables. This would lead to increased incomes for farm households
and have spillover effects through downstream benefits for non-farm
households and increased demand for labour.

The policy matrix presented in Table 8.9 provides an indication of how
different policies impact on the poverty and food security role of agriculture. The matrix goes beyond the agricultural policies discussed above and
also considers the constitution and other macro policies in influencing the
role of agriculture. Since in this study, the national food security dimension
is not considered and only focuses on household food security, it is rather
difficult to separate out the food security and poverty impact of the agricultural sector as different policy frameworks determine it.

NOTES

1. For most of their analysis, Woolard and Leibbrandt (2001: 56) settle on the household subsistence level and $1 a day 'International' line (respectively, R3509 and R2200 per annum
   per adult equivalent in 1995 rand). The latter may be thought of as the ultra-poverty line.
2. Based on the input from Julian May (2000).
3. May et al. (2000) provide a fuller account of the KIDS methodology and the limitations
   of the study, while May and Roberts (2001) review the design and use of panel data with
   respect to the South African context.
4. In three of these cases, the household had received a retrenchment package or inher-
   itance; in the remaining two cases, members of the household were running shops, and
   drawings from the business appear to have been confused with the turnover.

5. Pearsons = 0.8, sig 0.000, standard errors of the means are 39.59 and 94.8, respectively. On average, household income was reported to be 0.9 of expenditure.
6. Pearsons = 0.58, sig 0.000, standard errors of the means are 68.32 and 93.50, respectively. On average, household income was reported to be 1.32 of expenditure.
7. Pearsons = 0.736 and 0.376, respectively, sig 0.000. Using log income and log expenditure returns the relationship to the levels reported above.
8. The deficiencies of this approach are acknowledged; they include problems associated with a money-metric conceptualisation of poverty, and issues of intra-household distribution.
9. The HSL calculated for this chapter differs slightly from earlier work (Carter and May, 2001) in that a portion of the living costs of migrants who spend less than 15 days per month at home has been included. If anything, this may slightly inflate the expenditure required to achieve the household specific threshold. Following these procedures, the average poverty threshold was R895.75 (standard error = 0.358) in 1993 and R1391.14 (standard error = 0.578) in 1998, both figures expressed in current prices.
10. In all cases, chi square tests indicate that the groups are statistically different.
11. These measures have been calculated using the well-known Foster–Greer–Thorbecke (FGT) approach, and give an indication of the depth and severity of poverty.
12. It must be emphasised that the analysis of agricultural production does not refer to employment as farm workers, but in most cases, refers to small-scale and subsistence farming.
13. Given the nature of the panel study, the 1998 data cannot be generalised to the whole population since any new households that might have formed between the surveys are excluded. However, this analysis gives an indication of the scale of involvement in agriculture.
14. Given the low barriers of entry that are said to categorise informal work, it seems unlikely that these households were forced to abandon this work due to their being unable to meet input costs.
15. Income from agricultural production in 1993 and 1998 had been summed and divided by two after deflating to 1993 prices. The standard deviation is shown in italics.
16. In all cases chi square tests indicate that the groups are statistically different.
17. It should be noted that this figure may be misleading since the data were gathered at different seasons, and estimates of production may have been affected as a result. These figures are in 1993 prices.
18. Non-tradable commodities were defined as those goods that were neither imported nor exported from the districts, where the prices of these goods are largely determined by local supply and demand and for which these were no close consumption substitutes.
19. The provision of extension services is a critical part of such comprehensive support programmes. It is important to argue that extension services need to go beyond traditional service delivery to include production of crops with comparative advantages and niche market products in both farm and non-farm goods and services sectors. Moreover, extension agents need to provide training and support in enterprise development and marketing skills for farm and non-farm goods and services. To do so, most will have to be retrained.
20. However, in provinces such as KwaZulu-Natal, the Department of Agriculture has focused on 'unlocking the potential of agriculture', determined to move small farmers into productive and competitive markets and increase the agricultural output of the province by 350 percent by 2020.
21. Although agricultural policy is not the only policy factor that impacts on food security and poverty, only agriculture-related policies are discussed here apart from mention of Constitutional change and over-riding national policy frameworks such as the ANC's Reconstruction and Development Policy that formed the framework for societal transformation in South Africa post 1994.
22. Separation of the impacts of policies on food security and poverty are artificial for South Africa as national food security has not been and is not a concern for South Africa, while household food security and poverty cannot be separated as the two are mutually causative and interdependent.

REFERENCES

ACC/SCN (1991), 'Controlling Iron Deficiency: A report based on an ACC/SCN Workshop', ACC/SCN State-of-the-art Series, Nutrition Policy Discussion Paper No. 9. United Nations Administrative Committee on Coordination – Subcommittee on Nutrition, Geneva.

ACC/SCN (2000), 'Nutrition Through the Life Cycle: 4th Report on the World Nutrition Situation', United Nations Administrative Committee on Coordination – Subcommittee on Nutrition in collaboration with the International Food and Policy Research Institute, Geneva.

Belete, A., C.O. Igodan, C. M'Marete and W. van Averbeke (1999), 'Analysis of rural household consumption expenditure in South Africa: the case of food plot holders in the Tyefu irrigation scheme in the Eastern Cape Province', *Agrekon*, **38**(2): 194–201.

Carter, M.R. and J. May (1999), 'Poverty, livelihood and class in rural South Africa', *World Development*, **27**(1): 1–20.

Carter, M.R. and J. May (2001), 'One kind of freedom: poverty dynamics in post-Apartheid South Africa', *World Development*, **29**(12): 198–2006.

DBSA (1998), *Development Report 1998*, Midrand: a Development Bank of South Africa.

De Janvry, A. (1994), 'Farm–non-farm synergies in Africa: discussion', *American Journal of Agricultural Economics*, **76**: 1183–5.

Deaton, A. (1997), *The Analysis of Household Surveys*, Baltimore, MD and London: Johns Hopkins University Press.

Gibney, M. and H. Vorster (2001), 'Editorial: South African food based dietary guidelines', *South African Journal of Clinical Nutrition*, **14**(3): S2.

Gillespie, S. (1997), 'Chapter one: An overview', in ACC/SCN (eds), *Nutrition and Poverty: Papers from the ACC/SCN 24th Session Symposium*, March, Kathmandu.

Hazell, P.B.R. and S. Haggblade (1993), 'Farm–non-farm growth linkages and the welfare of the poor', in M. Lipton and J. van der Gaag (eds), *Including the Poor: Proceedings of a Symposium Organized by the World Bank and the International Food Policy Research Institute*, Washington, DC: World Bank, pp. 190–204.

Hazell, P.B.R. and A. Röell (1984), 'Rural growth linkages: household expenditure patterns in Malaysia and Nigeria', Research Report 41, International Food Policy Institute, Washington, DC.

Hendriks, S.L. (2003), 'The potential for nutritional benefits from increased agricultural production in KwaZulu-Natal', *South African Journal of Agricultural Extension*, **32**: 28–44.

Hendriks, S.L. and M.C. Lyne (2003a), 'Expenditure elasticities and consumption patterns for households in two communal areas of KwaZulu-Natal', *Development Southern Africa*, **20**(1): 105–27.

Hendriks, S.L. and M.C. Lyne (2003b), 'Agricultural growth multipliers for two communal areas of KwaZulu-Natal', *Development Southern Africa*, **20**(3): 423–44.

Kirsten, J., R. Townsend and C. Gibson (1998), 'Determination of agricultural production to household nutritional status in KwaZulu-Natal, South Africa', *Development Southern Africa*, **15**(4): 573–87.

Klasen, S. (1997), 'Poverty and inequality in South Africa: an analysis of the 1993 SALDRU Survey', *Social Indicators Research*, **41**: 51–94.

Leibbrandt, M. and I. Woolard (1999), 'A comparison of poverty in South Africa's nine provinces', *Development Southern Africa*, **16**(1): 37–54.

Lipton, M., M. De Klerk and M. Lipton (eds) (1996a), *Land, Labour and Livelihoods in Rural South Africa. Volume One: Western Cape*, Durban: Indicator Press.

Lipton, M., M. De Klerk and M. Lipton (eds) (1996b), *Land, Labour and Livelihoods in Rural South Africa. Volume Two: KwaZulu-Natal and Northern Province*, Durban: Indicator Press.

Lipton, M. and M. Ravallion (1997), 'Poverty and policy', Chapter 41, in Behrman J. and T.N. Srinivasan (eds), *Handbook of Development Economics*, Vol. 3, Amsterdam; North-Holland, pp. 2553–658.

Love, P. and N. Sayed (2001), 'Eat plenty of vegetables and fruits everyday', *South African Journal of Clinical Nutrition*, **14**(3): S24–32.

Maluccio, J.A. (2000), 'Attrition in the KwaZulu-Natal income dynamics study 1993–1998', Food Consumption and Nutrition Division Discussion Paper, International Food Policy Research Institute, Washington, DC.

Maunder, E.M.W., J. Matji and T. Hlatshwayo-Molea (2001), 'Enjoy a variety of foods: difficult but necessary in developing countries', *South African Journal of Clinical Nutrition*, **14**(3): S3–11.

May, J. (1998), 'Poverty and In equality in South Africa', Report prepared for the Office of the Executive Deputy President and the Inter-Ministerial Committee for Poverty and Inequality, Summary Report, URL: www.gov.za/reports/1998/pirsum.htm, October 1999.

May, J. (2000), 'The structure and composition of rural poverty and livelihoods in South Africa', in B. Cousins, *At the Crossroads: Land and Agrarian Reform in South Africa into the 21st Century*, Cape Town Programme for Land and Agrarian Studies, University of the Western Cape.

May, J., M.R. Carter, L. Haddad and J. Maluccio (2000), 'KwaZulu-Natal Income Dynamics Study (KIDS) 1993–1998: a longitudinal household data set for South African policy analysis', *Development Southern Africa*, **17**(4): 567–81.

May, J. and A. Norton (1997), 'A difficult life: the experience and perceptions of poverty in South Africa', *Social Indicators Research*, **41**(1–3): 9239–4625–118.

May, J. and B. Roberts (2001), 'Panel data and policy analysis in South Africa: taking a long view', *Social Dynamics*, **27**(1).

Mellor, J. (1976), *The New Economics of Growth: A Strategy for India and the Developing World*, Ithaca, NY: Cornell University Press.

National Agricultural Marketing Council (2002), 'The food security effects of deregulation of agricultural marketing in South Africa', Report by Ebony Consultancy International, Pretoria.

National Department of Agriculture (NDA) (2002), *The Integrated Food Security Strategy for South Africa*, Pretoria: National Department of Agriculture.

Ngqangweni, S.S. (2000), 'Promoting income and employment growth in the rural economy of the Eastern Cape through smallholder agriculture', Unpublished PhD Thesis, Department of Agricultural Economics, Extension and Rural Development, University of Pretoria.

Potgieter, J. (1993a), 'The household subsistence level in the major urban centres of the Republic of South Africa', Institute for Planning Research, University of Port Elizabeth, Port Elizabeth, September.

Potgieter, J. (1993b), 'The household subsistence level in selected rural centres of the Republic of South Africa', Institute for Planning Research, University of Port Elizabeth, Port Elizabeth.

Potgieter, J. (1998), 'The household subsistence level in the major urban centres of the Republic of South Africa', University of Port Elizabeth, Port Elizabeth.

Schmidt, M.I. and H.H. Vorster (1995), 'The effect of communal vegetable gardens on nutritional status', *Development Southern Africa*, **12**(5): 713–24.

Scholtz, S.C., H.H. Vorster, (Jr), L. Matshego and H.H. Vorster (2001), 'Foods from animals can be eaten every day: not a conundrum!', *South African Journal of Clinical Nutrition*, **14**(3): S39–47.

Singh, N. (2002), Address by Mr Narend Singh, KwaZulu-Natal Minister of Agriculture and Environmental Affairs and Patron of the KwaZulu-Natal Development Trust, at the launch of the KwaZulu-Natal Agricultural Development Forum, 15 February, Cedara Research Station.

Steyn, N.P., R. Abercrombie and D. Labadarios (2001), 'Food security: an update for health professionals', *South African Journal of Clinical Nutrition*, **14**(3): 98–102.

Vink, N. and J. Kirsten (2002), 'Pricing behaviour in the South Africa food and agricultural sector', Report to the National Treasury, Pretoria, June.

Vitamin Information Centre (VIC) (2001), 'National food consumption survey in children aged 1–9 years: South Africa 1999', *Medical Update*, **37**, April.

Woolard, I. and M. Leibbrandt (2001), 'Measuring poverty in South Africa', in H. Bhorat, M. Leibbrandt, M. Maziya, S. van der Berg and I. Woolard, *Fighting Poverty: Labour Markets and Inequality in South Africa*, Cape Town: University of Cape Town Press.

World Bank (2000), *World Development Report 2000/2001: Attacking Poverty*, Washington, DC: World Bank.

Technical appendix   Poverty lines and poverty measures[1]

Poverty is commonly measured with reference to a poverty line (PL) defined in terms of an absolute income or consumption level used as a benchmark to distinguish the poor and the non-poor. Poverty lines are intended to reflect the minimum level of income necessary to meet a level of consumption of a set of goods that are either socially deemed as necessary or required or that reflect the consumption behavior of a reference population group. The reader is directed to the excellent discussion by Ravallion (1998) on how poverty lines are defined and computed.

To measure magnitude of poverty, alternative indices are used based on income or consumption size distribution data and the poverty line. A popular index of poverty is what is known as the head count ratio (HCR) which expresses the number of poor in a community as a percentage of the total population. It fails to take into account the intensity of poverty of a person or household. Sen (1976) pointed out some conceptual difficulties with HCR in so far as it violates two desirable axioms, the monotonicity axiom and the transfer axiom. The first axiom states that, given other things, a reduction in the income of a poor person should increase poverty. The second axiom states that a transfer of income from a poor person to someone less poor should increase poverty. Even though HCR violates these two axioms, the proportion of people below the PL reflects an important dimension of poverty in a society in a simple manner.

Another index of poverty called the poverty gap (PG) is based on the proportionate income shortfalls of all the poor from the PL. It takes into account intensity of poverty and satisfies the monotonicity axiom, but violates the transfer axiom. In order to solve the conceptual problems in measurement of poverty, Sen (1976) derived an index based on the weighted sum of the poverty gaps with a weighting pattern such that the poorest among the poor get the highest weight and the richest poor the lowest weight.

Foster, Greer and Thorbecke (1984) followed this approach further and derived a class of decomposable poverty measures using a function of the income shortfall itself as the weight attached to the poverty gap. Many investigators have used the Foster–Greer–Thorbecke (FGT) index in recent years. It takes the following form:

$$FGT = \left(\frac{1}{n}\right) \sum_{i=1}^{m} \left(\frac{z - y_i}{z}\right)^{\varepsilon}$$

where:

y_i = income of ith poor;
z = poverty line;
n = total population; and
m = number of poor.

This index in fact is a general form of the poverty indices discussed above. For $\varepsilon = 0$, it reduces to the proportion of people living below the poverty line:

$$HCR = \frac{m}{n}.$$

For $\varepsilon = 1$, it turns out to be the poverty gap measure:

$$PG = \left(\frac{1}{n}\right) \sum_{i=1}^{m} \frac{z - y_i}{z}$$

If we define the poverty gap as zero for the non-poor, PG could be interpreted as the average income gap expressed as a proportion of the poverty line, the average being taken over the entire population.

Another form of FGT used often is when $\varepsilon = 2$ and is referred to as the squared poverty gap (SPG) index:

$$SPG = \left(\frac{1}{n}\right) \sum_{i=1}^{m} \left(\frac{z - y_i}{z}\right)^{2}.$$

An in-depth analysis of the mathematical properties of the FGT poverty measures can be found in Ravallion (1998) and of course in Foster, Greer and Thorbecke (1984).

NOTE

1. This appendix is intended to provide the reader with a very brief introduction to the measures of poverty used in most of the case studies of the book. The text draws heavily from the original RoA study on poverty in India.

REFERENCES

Foster, J., J. Greer and E. Thorbecke (1984), 'A class of decomposable poverty measures', *Econometrica*, **52**(3), May, 761–6.
Ravallion, M. (1998), 'Poverty lines in theory and measurement', Living Standards Measurement Study Working Paper No. 133, World Bank, Washington, DC.
Sen, A. (1976), 'Poverty: an ordinal approach to measurement', *Econometrica*, **44**(2), 219–31.

Index